We're Not Keeping You Up, Are We?

We're Not Keeping You Up, Are We?

The story of Read's restaurant

by David Pitchford

Live Wire Books

Published in 2018 by
Live Wire Books,
The Orchard, School Lane,
Warmington, Banbury,
Oxfordshire OX17 1DE
www.livewirebooks.com

Front cover photograph by Brian Aris
Photograph facing page 193 by Anna Zeville

ISBN: 978-0-9933464-0-8

Printed and bound in England by Short Run Press Ltd

Contents

Dedication

For Bert and Eva North, without whose love, encouragement and support Read's might never have come to exist.

Foreword

I have always believed that in order to run a successful restaurant out in the country, especially one with rooms, one has fully to understand the true meaning of the word hospitality, which the dictionary defines as the friendly and liberal reception of guests and strangers. Over the years, the great French restaurants have, in my experience, underlined the importance of this principle and ambitious chefs everywhere have aspired to follow the example of the Michelin-starred restaurants in offering superb hospitality as well as great gastronomic experiences.

In this respect, David and Rona and the team at Read's have excelled, successfully establishing and running a restaurant of such consistently high quality that it retained a Michelin star for more than twenty years, while also winning numerous other awards and accolades along with recognition in all the most prestigious food guides. And from its earliest days back in 1977 it has attracted discerning diners from all over the UK and even further afield to what was, originally, a rather out-of-the-way location in a backwater of rural Kent.

I consider myself very fortunate to have known David for many years and I have always been impressed with his love of good food, his determination to encourage young people into our industry and his desire to teach and train them in the very best of the culinary arts. David's team, both front and back of house, are all part of his extended family and are treated as such, as are his legion of regular customers. Read's has for many years been an iconic example of a well-loved, well-run restaurant, having a perfect relationship with its suppliers and also being largely self-sufficient in terms of the vegetables and herbs produced in its own extensive kitchen garden.

David and Rona's achievement in having actively run a restaurant of such high quality together as a husband-and-wife team for forty-one years, and still counting, must probably be unique in our industry. Both having been involved in high-end catering and cookery since leaving school, they complement each other perfectly businesswise, Rona's welcoming front-of-house presence, which is founded on her own deep knowledge of food and wine and her all-round administrative expertise, matching David's skills in the kitchen. This was formally recognised in 2015 with her induction into the UK Restaurateurs Hall of Fame by the Academy of Food and Wine Service. David, a former Chef of the Year, has been a very active member of the Royal Academy of Culinary Arts for over thirty years where, amongst other initiatives, he has led the team running the Master of Culinary Arts Award for the past twenty years.

In this entertaining and often highly amusing autobiography, David traces his unusual and inspiring lifetime success story, from humble beginnings to the peak of his profession as an award-winning chef and as the proprietor, in partnership with Rona, of Read's, providing a fascinating insight along the way into how the restaurant and hotel business operates at the highest level, and the dedication needed to become an everyday masterchef.

Long may Read's, and all it stands for, continue to flourish!

Brian J. Turner CBE
October 2018

Introduction

Had you told me back in my younger days that as I approached the age of seventy I would be totally consumed by my extended family, and that they would be the main reason why I got up and went to work every day, I would have found it hard to believe – just as I would have scoffed at the idea of it actually being great to be a granddad. And yet that's exactly the way it is. I know there is no such thing as the perfect family, but I genuinely believe that what my wife, Rona, and I are fortunate enough to have is just about as close as it is possible to get to that ideal. And for that I mostly have to thank Rona.

She is the hardest working, most dedicated and all-round most wonderful individual that I have ever met – a loving and endlessly supportive wife, mother and grandmother, to whom I owe almost everything. But for her, I might well have ended up down on the Thames Embankment, sleeping rough in a cardboard box, with my bottle of VP sherry close at hand, just as my father, sadly, had done for a period of his life.

I also have the two most brilliant sons that a father could ever wish for. They have never been in the least bit difficult and have never let me down in any way. I love them so much and I am so very proud of each of them. There were a couple of girlfriends they brought home when they were first dating that gave us cause for concern, but the ones that they eventually chose to spend the rest of their lives with are both fantastic girls and I love and admire them just as much as if they were my own daughters.

There are then the five amazing grandchildren, with whom I never tire of playing the role of a doting grandpa. In descending order of age, we have Lola and Evie, the daughters of our eldest son Sam and his partner, Mel, plus Wilfred, Millie and Margot, the children of younger son Alex and his wife, Sarah.

The idea of writing this book was born one day as I was walking home with the two eldest girls after collecting them from school. Evie, who was six at the time, was busy smashing blackberries off the hedgerow brambles with a big stick, while Lola, who was nine, was plying me with a whole lot of questions, mostly about the family-owned restaurant that Rona and I have now been running together for four decades. The queries came thick and fast:

"Granddad, why is it called Read's when our name is Pitchford?"

"Has it always been at Macknade, Granddad?"

"How old were you and Nanny when you first started it?"

"Granddad, where did you learn to cook – did Great Nanny teach you?"

By the time Mel called in to collect the girls on her way back from work Lola's endless curiosity and insatiable thirst for knowledge had still not been satisfied and I was still being grilled as she was loaded into the car. As I waved them off I shouted after her: "If there's anything else you want to know, just ask your dad."

However, the next time I saw her she complained: "Daddy didn't know the answers to some of my questions". It dawned on me then that there was a whole lot that had happened even before our children were born, let alone our grandchildren, and even if only for Lola's sake, it ought to be recorded in some way.

What I had in mind as I started putting pen to paper – or, more accurately, finger to computer keyboard – was a book that would be part autobiography, but mostly the history of Read's, tracing the restaurant's development from mere pipe dream to Michelin-starred reality, all of it interspersed with some of the countless anecdotes that have amused, entertained or crucified us along the way. The seeds of Read's were sown back in 1967 when, as a spotty eighteen-year-old but nevertheless proud young Salopian, I had successfully completed a two-year City & Guilds professional cookery course and, armed with my diploma, was plotting my assault on the culinary world – a project that was to consume me for the next fifty years. To be perfectly honest, looking back, I may not have been the sharpest knife in the drawer (I do like a pun!), but at least I was intelligent enough to realise that remaining in Shrewsbury would not allow me to reach the pinnacles of achievement as a celebrated chef that I had in mind for myself. So, my plans temporarily delayed by a serious road accident, I set about moving to London where, quite by chance as it turned out, things were all just beginning to happen.

I wandered, wide-eyed, around the capital in search of the best places in which to work at the time, places where I could steal the ideas of the top chefs in the land. In those days they were mostly Swiss, French, German or Italian, with not a single Brit in sight, except at the very lower end of the kitchen hierarchy. I dreamed of one day owning my own restaurant, though secretly admitting to myself that, really, such high ambition was unlikely ever to be fulfilled.

I nailed myself to the culinary cross for the next seven years and worked to the exclusion of virtually everything else, dedicated to the task of learning my trade in the dungeons that were the London restaurant and hotel kitchens of the time. It was dark when I went in to work and it was dark when I came out and went home. During that time, when I was learning the basic principles of good cooking, I often used to dream of the dishes that I would like to prepare if ever I was lucky enough, one day, to be able to compile my own menus. Of course, those dishes would change from time to time as my expertise developed and my repertoire expanded. But not once in any of my dreams did I imagine having to include six vegetarian options, which is what we offer at Read's (and which is nowadays, apparently, still not enough); not once did the needs of the lacto-intolerant figure, or the requirements of the gluten-free brigade; and I can't remember ever lying awake at night formulating a vegetarian, vegan, dairy-free, sugar-free, fat-free, salt-free and yeast-free section, along with a selection of special dishes free from any listed allergens.

As Rona and I now start to contemplate the end of our careers as restaurateurs, I often think how nice it would be if I could just plan a menu at Read's that was at least vaguely similar to the ones in my dreams. I sometimes long for the return of the days when most customers would order dishes from our menu without wanting to customise them, changing the component parts or adapting them to their own individual dietary requirements in some way, shape or form. Maybe for the last year before we do finally retire we will dig our heels in and offer a selection of all our favourite dishes, cooked and served exactly as they should be, and if people don't like it – well, never mind!

During the four decades that Read's has been in existence, we've been through three major recessions, with Brexit threatening to result in a fourth at the time of writing. At home we have suffered our fair share of family crises and sad bereavements and at work – downstairs on the same premises for the first twenty-three years after first opening for business in Painters Forstal – we have had to deal with almost every imaginable drama from kitchen staff attacking each other with fists, knives and rolling pins to all manner of outrageous behaviour by customers, including, on one occasion, an angry fight between two men armed with snooker cues and also a violent domestic argument during which the husband laid his wife out cold with a solid left hook. At the opposite end of the relationship scale there was the couple who ended up getting over-amorous behind the dustbins out at the back of the restaurant, while another pair were caught on CCTV committing full-on adultery in the lounge bar in the early hours following a wedding reception, while their respective spouses were asleep upstairs in their separate guest rooms, blissfully unaware of what was going on. And then there was the local aristocrat who, having taken over the restaurant one night to host a private dinner party, ended up exposing himself to his guests while encouraging the other men around the table to do the same in order to prove a point; more of that and other escapades later in the book.

Over the years we have also been amused, entertained and often befriended by a colourful cast of occasionally eccentric characters among our regular customers, while frequently being driven to distraction by the awkward and almost invariably humourless sort who are endlessly demanding and never happy unless they have something to complain about, or a fault to pick. We have had to put up with dodgy restaurant reviews by the odd poison pen journo and vindictive online Trip Advisor comments that have reduced us to tears. And in a business where reliable kitchen staff are notoriously hard to find and the turnover is high, we have at various times unwittingly employed a murderer, a paedophile, various kleptomaniacs, numerous druggies and drunks and, perhaps most surprisingly, a Parisian waiter who actually turned out to be the worst of the lot!

So, one way and another, life has certainly never been dull. I am not in the least bit religious, but as I get older I am constantly reminded of Reinhold Niebuhr's serenity prayer: "God grant me the serenity to accept the things I cannot change, the courage to change things I can, and the wisdom to know the difference". Nice one Reinhold! Now there's a chap who's thought things out.

On the very rare occasions that Rona and I are able to find the time and energy to enjoy a busman's holiday and have some friends around for dinner on our day off I sometimes get drawn in to telling stories about what it's really like to run a restaurant, and about some of the extraordinary things that have happened to us over the years, at the end of which people invariably tell me: "You should write a book".

I never really seriously considered doing so until Lola starting quizzing me, at which point I began to think – why not? I've never really come near to being a headline-hitting celebrity chef like Gordon Ramsay, Jamie Oliver or Marco Pierre White, but I have been privileged to know and to work closely alongside some of the greatest names in the business and I do have quite a story to tell that I hope may be of interest to people other than just family and friends.

Having decided to write the book, I had to choose a title. An early contender was *Read's – All About It*, a play on the old newsvendors' cry, but I then discovered that the late hell-raising film star Oliver Reed had got there first with something very similar for his autobiography. Looking for something that would grab attention, I then toyed briefly with *What Would YOU Do If Hitler Raped YOUR Daughter?* ! This was the punchline – almost literally! – delivered at the climax of a rather inebriated late night argument between two customers in the restaurant. Everybody else had gone home apart from this one table of four, made up of two couples, and I emerged from the kitchen just as one of the men rose to his feet, leaned across the table and with his face inches from that of the chap opposite, jabbed his finger into the other man's shoulder and spat out his somewhat less than polite inquiry. It seemed there was no answer and things then thankfully quietened down a bit, but I have found myself wondering ever since what it was they had been arguing about that could have led up to such a question? Now I'll never know.

I eventually settled on *We're Not Keeping You Up, Are We?* – a question I've all too often been asked in the early hours of the morning by customers who have long outstayed their welcome, but who are nevertheless intent on having yet one more for the road. Of course, I've always been far too polite and too wary of losing return business to tell them the truth, to say bluntly: "Yes, actually, I'm afraid you are – time for you to go home. I've been up since 6.30 am, it's now 2.00am and I'm going to be up again in four or five hours time to start all over again." Instead, I usually end up muttering something like: "Oh no, I'm sure there's something I could be getting on with", while fiddling around behind the bar trying desperately to stay awake. *A Hard Day's Night* would be another rather appropriate way of summing up the daily routine of a chef/proprietor running a busy high-end restaurant, especially one with rooms attached. Lack of sleep has always been something of an occupational hazard.

However, for anyone reading it, this book will hopefully turn out to be the opposite of a cure for insomnia! And for those of you who make it to the final page, there's a rather nice little twist in the tale. No peeking!

David Pitchford
October 2018

1 : A Shropshire Lad

I was born in Shrewsbury – or *Shrowsbury*, depending, it seems, on whether you watch the BBC or ITV. Personally, I think that Shakespeare got the pronunciation correct; The Taming of The *Shrow*? – I don't think so!

My parents, Daphne and Joe, split up when I was two years old, Joe walking out on his family and leaving my mother to raise me and my younger brother, Joe Jnr, single-handedly, which she did with unwavering love, self-sacrifice and devotion.

Daphne Bond had been born in Guernsey on Valentine's Day 1922. Her father, Willy – christened Willy, not William, although William is the name on his gravestone – was listed on her birth certificate as a tram conductor, but went on to set up a successful business as a gentlemen's hairdresser.

Daphne's mother, Gladys, died of tuberculosis at the age of twenty-seven, when Daphne was just six years old. At the time the family were living on the neighbouring Channel Island of Alderney, running a public house called The Divers Inn. The Divers still exists on the same site to this day and is usually full of local fishermen, as well as holidaymakers. After her mother's death, Daphne returned with her father to Guernsey, where she was mostly brought up by two of his sisters, Elsie and Lily Bond. Elsie and Lily, especially, made great sacrifices both in their Salvation Army careers and their personal lives in order to take care of their young niece.

Daphne was educated at a convent, Les Cotils, and after leaving school she went to work as a telephone operator at the exchange in St. Peter Port, the island capital, where she remained until the outbreak of war and the German invasion of the Channel Islands in 1940. At the age of eighteen, she was understandably terrified by the thought of what the German invaders might do to the islanders during their occupation, but her general recollection of that period was that the majority of the soldiers were actually ordinary young men who just wanted to go home.

The first priority of the invading force was, of course, to cut all lines of communication and Daphne vividly remembered being at work on the morning of the invasion, talking to the English operators at the mainland telephone exchange in London and then suddenly having to tell them that German officers were coming up the stairs and into the exchange. One of the officers took command of the switchboard and the last words from London that were spoken to Daphne were: "We are so sorry, Guernsey. Good luck".

Prior to the invasion Daphne had applied to join the Women's Auxiliary Air Force and in order to be accepted she lied about her age. However, the Germans then arrived just before she was due to leave for London to join up, so she was unable to go. Her father apparently told her: "That's what you get for telling lies!"

In her later years, Mum and I talked a lot about her early life in Guernsey and what it was like living under the German occupation, and the stories she told me of the hardships suffered by the islanders during that wartime period really brought it home to me how difficult things had been for them. At times they were genuinely close to starvation, struggling to find enough food on a small island that was nowhere near to being self-sufficient. Farm produce of any sort was in short supply and although there were plenty of fish in the surrounding sea, the Germans imposed tight restrictions on fishing after several fishermen used their boats to escape to England; they also reserved a hefty proportion of all catches for themselves, while rationing the islanders to 1lb per household per week. On very rare occasions fish could be had on the black market, but if the fishermen were caught they were severely punished. As highlighted in the best-selling book and film *The Guernsey Literary and Potato Peel Pie Society*, meat was in desperately short supply, with the rearing of pigs on local farms and smallholdings being strictly controlled by the Germans. People resorted to baking acorns and grating them to make a sort of coffee, while crushed dried blackberry bramble leaves made a passable cup of tea. The only things that were in comparatively plentiful supply, at least as far as my mother was concerned, were potatoes, parsnips and cauliflowers, with every bit of available garden space given over to home-grown fruit and veg.

Money became all but obsolete and a bartering system developed. A haircut from Daphne's father was worth a large potato, or an ounce of rice. Her father had a friend who was a cobbler and who used to make shoes from old leather car seats that could be swapped for regular haircuts. Daphne's shoes, she once told me, were the envy of all her girlfriends.

Towards the end of the war each person on the island received a food parcel once a month from a neutral country – Daphne thought the Swiss ones were the best. Among other things, the Red Cross parcels that were also sent over contained biscuits so hard that they had to be soaked in water overnight before being mixed with powdered milk the next morning to make a passable sort of porridge. On one occasion someone broke into the house during the night and stole only the soaking biscuits, nothing else. Daphne actually suspected that the thief might have been a German soldier as they, too, were close to starving.

For a while, Daphne lived in New Street, St. Peter Port with her father and stepmother, Willy having remarried by then. Another fact of life on the island during the occupation was that German soldiers were forcibly billeted with Guernsey families, so as to provide a human shield that would deter bombing by the RAF. Although Daphne's recollections of the German soldiers were not all bad, she remembered that her family was particularly unlucky with the one allotted to them, as he turned out to be an extremely arrogant and unpleasant specimen who, on more than one occasion, took to discharging his pistol inside the house, whilst ranting and raving in an apparently uncontrollable rage.

Willy Bond had been badly injured and also gassed during the First World War and as a result he was never really a well man for the rest of his life – although he did go on to survive well into his nineties. I can only begin to imagine what it must have been like for him to have such an obnoxious German soldier living under the same roof with him and his family.

Daphne having had a strict Salvation Army-style upbringing, it was perhaps fairly predictable that she would fall for the first good-looking rogue to sail into St. Peter Port. My father, Joseph Robert Heal Pitchford, had spent the war in the Royal Navy, having previously made a living as a merchant seaman. Although he came from a well-to-do family and enjoyed a fairly privileged upbringing that included a good private education, he was a bit of a maverick and ended up owning a small boat in which he and a matelot colleague would make regular round trips from Guernsey to Belfast with a cargo of tomatoes, chugging up around the Cornish peninsular and then returning with a hold full of whatever merchandise they thought they might be able to sell back in Guernsey, an occupation that they resumed once the war ended. To brighten up the proceedings, he and his shipmate would consume large quantities of alcohol along the way, which, as he would later tell me, helped to make the voyages much more agreeable.

Joe and Daphne married in Portsmouth on 17th April 1948. Joe's father, a comparatively wealthy industrialist, bought the couple a seventeen-acre smallholding at Ford Heath, on the outskirts of Shrewsbury, as a wedding present. The place came complete with a selection of farm animals, including twelve Friesian cows, six pigs, a dozen Aylesbury ducks and twenty-four Rhode Island Red chickens, plus a Fordson Major tractor and a plough. It seems this was probably my grandfather's final attempt to get his rather wayward son to settle down and build a secure future for himself.

Joe and Daphne had absolutely no experience of working with livestock or farming, but they managed to make a go of it for a while, during which time I arrived on May 26th, 1949, followed two years later by my brother. By then, however, the honeymoon was already well and truly over. As I have already indicated, Joe had become an enthusiastic supporter of the beer, wine and spirit industry during his time in the Royal Navy and also on his own boat and he continued his appreciation of its various products as a young farmer. At first, he managed to keep his drinking under control, but once Daphne had two young children to look after she was no longer able to accompany her husband to the local pub in the evenings and, more importantly, couldn't be there to drag him home from the Hare and Hounds at closing time. Sometimes he would go missing for days on end – "going abroad" he used to call it. The animals and the farm, generally, were neglected and the marriage rapidly deteriorated until, sometime around 1952, Joe finally walked out for good.

Left on her own, with a three-year-old and a six-month-old baby to care for, Mum soon found herself in really dire straits, struggling to survive. Not only did she get no financial support of any kind from Joe, she also lost her home. For reasons that I have never fully understood, the smallholding was sold off and she had to leave, without ever receiving any of the proceeds from the sale. As far as her father-in-law was concerned, the smallholding had literally been the last chance saloon for Joe, an opportunity to pull himself together and make something of his life, and when the marriage fell apart the old man washed his hands of all responsibility not only for his son, but also for his daughter-in-law and his grandchildren. He sold the smallholding, which had always remained in his name, and, as a result, Mum ended up with no income, no job and no home for herself and her children at a time when attitudes towards single mothers, even those who were divorcees, were very different from what they are nowadays.

The benefit system at the time was certainly very harsh by modern standards, and in order to make ends meet Mum had to go back to work full time in a series of fairly menial jobs in shops and offices. And to keep a roof over our heads, she was reduced to lodging with friends and neighbours in and around the area for several years, even having to resort to social housing for short periods at one point, before eventually being able to afford to rent a place of her own, big enough for the three of us. Most of my family – and particularly my gambling buddies – will be aware that 11 has always been my lucky number, but not many of them know that the reason for this is that I had lived in eleven different places in and around Shrewsbury before I finally left home at the age of fifteen.

My memories of some of the earliest moves are extremely vague, as I was still only about three when we were evicted from the smallholding at Ford Heath Villa. We lodged for a time with local farm labourer named Bridgewater and his family in their very modest house in the nearby village of Cruckton and there were also brief spells at a place called the Parsonage at Lea Cross, which I believe was a charitable housing trust of some sort, and also at a former army barracks that had been converted to provide temporary accommodation as part of similar sort of social housing scheme.

My first really clear recollections are of the time we spent at another smallholding known as Wood Green. This was located just across the road from Ford Heath Villa and was home to Bernard and Phyllis Maw, a Yorkshire couple, originally from Rotherham, and their son, John, who was about the same age as me. Mum had got to know the

Maws well as neighbours and when her marriage started to fall apart they were very supportive, providing a safe refuge on those occasions when Joe returned home in a drunken rage and became abusive. At one point after the split the three of us moved in with them and although we didn't live there as a family for long, my brother and I continued to spend most of our time there, especially in the school holidays when Mum was out at work, to the extent that it was almost as if the Maws had adopted us. My brother actually addressed Bernard as 'Dad', while I called him 'Uncle Bernard'.

John Maw became my best friend, with whom I am still regularly in touch today. Growing up, we spent every spare moment together, even after Mum had got back on her feet financially and had moved with Joe and me into rented accommodation in Shrewsbury. As youngsters, we would roam the Shropshire countryside together for hours on end – if it wasn't the bird-nesting season, then it would be fishing. In the early evenings we would walk two miles from his place into the village of Ford to meet other boys of our own age and later, as teenagers, to meet girls. As we got older, we would cycle further afield, but nearly always to pursue an interest connected in some way with the countryside.

As a legacy of my bird-nesting days, I can still spot a siskin, a stonechat or a tree-creeper and can talk for ten minutes on each one, describing in detail their plumage, habits, the type of nests they build and the colour of their eggs. I suppose that these days I should be ashamed of having searched out nests and collected eggs and to a degree I am, but it was what boys of my age did in those days and it gave me a love of birds and nature in general that has remained with me all my life and is still a source of great pleasure to me.

My two sons, Sam and Alex, used to enjoy taking the Mickey out of me when they were children because whenever they said something like: "Look, Daddy, there's a seagull", I would insist that there was no such thing as a seagull, before launching into a lecture about the fact that there are common gulls, herring gulls, greater black-backed gulls, lesser black-backed gulls, kittiwakes, fulmars and a variety of different terns. But such things have a way of coming full circle and I can't help smiling to myself these days when I hear Sam and Alex explaining to my wonderful grandchildren that there is no such thing as a seagull, that there are common gulls, herring gulls…!

John Maw and I made our own bows and arrows and never went anywhere without a catapult, sheath knife and, later on, an air rifle. By the age of eleven, I knew how to use a chain saw and how to snare a rabbit and skin it, ready for the pot. I could check, with two fingers, whether a hen was going to be a good layer. And I was already strong enough to hold the back legs of a hog while John's dad, Bernard, would castrate it with one of his '7 O'Clock' Gillette razor blades. I would hold a goose or duck at Easter and Christmas while it was stunned, had its throat cut and was hung upside down and bled. Then, after the bird had been left hanging for a suitable length of time in order to mature the flesh, it would often be my job to pluck it, the period of time for which it was hung depending on the weather and the temperature at that particular time of year. And so it was that, one way and another, I learned a great deal about food when I was growing up that was to prove very useful in later life.

It must have been around the late 1950's that the Forestry Commission, having become increasingly concerned about the rapid proliferation of the imported grey squirrel that was causing the demise of our indigenous red variety and wanting to encourage a cull, offered a reward to anyone who sent in the tails of greys. John and I used to shoot them with his Webley .177 air rifle, eventually earning enough from the proceeds to buy a more powerful .22 version. We would wait until we had five tails before sending them into the Commission offices, receiving two shillings for each one by return of post. I can't recall now why we stopped doing it; perhaps we shot all the squirrels in our area, or maybe the Commission stopped the reward system. Either way, we got a newer and much better rifle out of it!

That young boys of the age we were then should have been allowed to walk around with guns, albeit only air rifles, as well as quite powerful catapults and sheath knives, may seem strange today, but the attitude that existed back then, particularly in the countryside, was very different from what is now, when it sometimes seems to me that children are overly protected.

Phyllis and Bernard Maw didn't feel it necessary to protect us in any way when, with the aid of nothing more than a heavy stick, we helped to escort the huge and potentially quite dangerous boar along the road from the neighbouring farm to 'serve' their sow, Josephine. We watched and understood the whole process. And when the piglets arrived we would bring the runt of the litter into the house to bottle feed it and prevent it being rolled on by the sow. All the farm animals – the geese, ducks and chickens as well as the pigs – were treated like pets. We were often with them when they were born or hatched, we fed and watered them every day, locked them up safely every night and were mostly with them when they died. And when the time did eventually come to ship them off for slaughter at the local abattoir, or to dispatch them ourselves to be eaten at Christmas or some other festive occasion during the year, we accepted that this was the way it had to be. What all this did was to give me an enormous and lasting respect for, and appreciation of, animals. It is something I have often had to explain to the young chefs in my kitchen, so that they can understand why I get so angry if part of any animal is wasted or not respected.

Of course, everyday life back in the 1950s, especially out in the country, could be quite hard in many ways compared with today, with few of the mod cons we now take for granted. But even my memories of some of the hardships have been softened by the rose-tinted spectacles of time. For instance, the toilet at Wood Green was a very basic outside facility, located at the bottom of the garden, seventy yards away from the house. There were lots of back numbers of comics like *The Beezer*, *The Dandy* and *The Eagle* down there; and also, hidden underneath the floorboards, some well-thumbed copies of early 'top shelf' magazines such as *Parade*, *Health and Efficiency* and *Men Only*. We three kids enjoyed finding any excuse to look at them, but were not exactly queuing up to help poor old Bernard with the fortnightly job of cleaning out the toilet, which involved digging a hole and burying the contents.

Bernard was a quiet man, incredibly hard working and very loving. He used to envelop us in his arms and scrape his whiskers against our cheeks to make us laugh. As with most men in the countryside in those days, he was very practical and could build or repair virtually anything. And if he couldn't do a particular job himself, he would find someone local who could, and would repay them in kind by doing a job for them.

Phyllis was a true matriarch and pretty much controlled everything that happened. She was undoubtedly a kind and loving person, but sometimes her unshakeable rules were difficult for me to understand as a child. But there was one rule that I did come to appreciate; at meal times you had to eat everything that was put in front of you, regardless of whether or not you liked it. Your plate had to be cleared – not even fat could be left ("It's good for you," she would insist. "It will keep you warm in the winter."). Mind you, I love all food now. There is not one single thing that I dislike, and I think I am maybe indebted to her for that.

Looking back, there is much else for which I have to thank Phyllis and Bernard, so many wonderful childhood memories of times spent with the family, among the most vivid of them being trips to the seaside in Bernard's Jensen-bodied Austin A40 convertible. Bought brand new in 1952, the car was his pride and joy. The registration, I can still remember, was HUX 985. The smallholding was just a sideline for Bernard, who worked as a storekeeper in a local garage and was a keen car enthusiast and also a more than competent motor mechanic. He always had his head under the bonnet of that Austin, fine-tuning the engine. And four or five times during the summer months he would drive us all to the seaside at one of the resorts on the Welsh coast. We used to get up at 5.30 on a Saturday morning and would be on the road by 6.30, as soon as we'd had breakfast and all the animals had been fed and watered. We each had our specific jobs to do around the farm before we left and it all went like clockwork, not to say military precision.

The drive across the middle of Wales to the coast at Fairbourne, Rhyl or Barmouth was as much a part of the day's enjoyment as anything else. Back then, motoring was definitely much more fun than it is now, not only for us kids, but for everyone, I think. The hood would be down, except in the most extreme weather conditions. Bernard always did the driving, with Phyllis by his side in the front and John, Joe and me huddled under the tonneau cover in the small seats at the back, where John and I would probably be tormenting my poor little brother.

At this point I should say that my one overwhelmingly negative recollection of that time in my life has to do with the way that I treated Joe. I don't know why it is that when there are three children in a family or a group, two of them often seem to gang up on the third. I'm afraid to say that John Maw and I sometimes gave Joe a hard time and although I wouldn't go so far as to say that the memory haunts me, I am certainly uncomfortable with it, even to this day.

Anyway, once we got through Welshpool on the A458, and just

before we joined the A470, Bernard used to pull over in the same spot every time and roll back the tonneau cover. The weather would have warmed up a bit by then and, with the tonneau right down, us kids could appreciate the beautiful scenery as the car climbed up into the mountains at Dinas Mawddwy.

The excitement would begin to mount at this point, because we all knew what was coming next, although none of us would say a single word; we just used to look at each other and giggle. Once we got through Dinas Mawddwy Pass to the other side of the mountain there were some long, flat straights and Bernard would seize the opportunity to put his foot down and wind the car up to 100 mph. Not a word would be said until the needle hit 100, at which point we would let out a loud cheer. We would then ease back down to 40 or 50 mph as we continued our trip through Dolgellau to the coast. Bernard was our hero. There weren't many cars capable of clocking up that sort of speed in those days – certainly not family cars, anyway. And you couldn't simply slam your foot down as you can today – you really did have to wind the engine up. For some reason, Bernard never attempted 'the ton' on the way home.

I loved those trips, especially the ones to Fairbourne. On arrival, we would set up camp between the sand dunes and the railway line. Bernard's first job would be to fire up the primus stove with methylated spirit in order to make a cup of tea. As with most childhood memories, it seemed the sun always shone and we boys spent most of the time playing around in those incredible dunes, or fishing for dabs in the estuary. If we went in the earlier part of the year we would be off looking for gulls' eggs.

We were never told what time to return to 'camp' – we somehow instinctively knew when it was lunchtime or mid-afternoon, time to come back for a shandy and a piece of parkin, the delicious gingerbread cake made from oatmeal and black treacle. On the way home we would always stop somewhere for fish and chips, eaten out of a wrap of newspaper – a bit of a novelty for us at the time and another real treat that we looked forward to with eager anticipation.

In the early days, we would be accompanied on these trips by the Maws' black spaniel, Sheila, who loved the day out as much as we did. When she died, the Maws could never bring themselves to have another dog. The family also had a pet bantam, called Clara, who had originally been brought into the house as a chick and had somehow never left, and she too would come to the seaside with us, happily pecking away among the dunes and never straying far from where we were camped.

Back at Wood Green there was always work to be done on the farm, digging out the ditches in the winter or going about the lost art of hedge laying. Hedges prepared in the proper traditional way lasted for years and looked beautiful as well as being animal proof. They also cost nothing except the labour involved. Us kids were more than happy to muck in and help out with the jobs that needed doing, in a way that would probably be frowned upon in our modern health and safety climate. There was one thing in particular that Bernard would have been horrified about in hindsight, knowing what we all know today and remembering how, when he was building the deep litter henhouse, he had thrown down all the off-cuts from the asbestos roofing for us to play with. Nobody then had any idea about the potentially lethal health threat posed by asbestos.

Meanwhile, my time at St. George's School for Boys in Frankwell, Shrewsbury was, I think, largely wasted. The only thing that I was interested in was a game of marbles during break and playing football for the school team, for which I was a half-decent goalkeeper. During lessons my mind was on what John and I would be doing that evening or weekend. On summer evenings we would perhaps go walking over the Caradoc or Carding Mill Valley, while Phyllis and Bernard went to the Green Man at Church Stretton for a couple of drinks.

By this time my brother and I were back living with Mum in a flat on the Springfield estate, on the outskirts of Shrewsbury, the last of my eleven childhood addresses. Although Mum was now better off financially, things were still not easy for her, and yet Joe and I would reflect in later life that we never remember ever feeling at all poor or disadvantaged during our childhood.

Having said that, there is still one story that makes me smile, even though it shows how hard-up Mum must still have been at the time. The ice cream van used to come around the estate, playing the tune that they always seemed to play in those days – the nursery rhyme *Oranges and Lemons (Say The Bells of St Clements)*. Joe and I would hear it from inside the flat and would run to Mum to ask if we could have an ice cream, whereupon she would explain to us that they only played that particular tune when they had run out of ice cream.

She worked tirelessly, enduring many hardships over the years in order to make sure that we had everything we needed, not only holding down a full-time job as well as looking after everything at home, but also devoting much of her spare time to making and mending clothes for us. An accomplished knitter, she made every jumper that my brother and I ever wore, along with bobble hats, scarves, football socks and even gloves – and I'm not talking about mittens here, but proper four-fingers-and-a-thumb gloves. Using three needles for each glove, she could knock up a pair in a single evening.

I recall going with her many times to the wool shop at the bottom of Clermont Bank in Shrewsbury town centre, where she would only ever buy two balls of wool at one time because of the cost. At the start of each new knitting project she would choose the wool she wanted, which from memory came in brown paper parcels containing twelve balls. The shop owner would write her name on the cover and put it on the top shelf and she would pay for just a couple of balls, popping in to buy more whenever she felt that she could afford it. Such was her skill with a pair of knitting needles in her hands that before long she went on to expand her output into quite a lucrative little cottage industry.

I clearly remember the day that all began. We were visiting the shop together to get more wool supplies and I happened to be wearing a white Fairisle jumper with a very complicated pattern around the neck and shoulders. Mum had made this specially for me to wear on a school trip to Switzerland that I was about to go off on the following week. The lady shopkeeper was very impressed with it and suggested that she should do some commission work, explaining that she had a friend who owned a knitwear outlet somewhere in London. Mum agreed to make a trial garment, which was duly sent off, and a week later she received a postal order for £8 – which was more than her usual week's wages at the time – along with a request for more of the same. It was the start of a business relationship that was to last more than thirty years

Mum made many hundreds of items in that time, the garments changing with the fashions of the day. For a while she used to specialise in heavy Guernsey sweaters, worn originally by the island fishermen, and she could hardly bash them out quickly enough, such was the demand. She used to knit all the time, whilst chatting or watching TV, never less than three hours every evening. And as time went on she graduated to more sophisticated items. I particularly remember her telling me about a cardigan-style coat, made from a very expensive sort of wool, for which she was delighted to receive £100 – until some weeks later, that is, when she spotted a photograph of the coat being worn by a model on the front cover of a women's fashion magazine, with a price tag of over £500. She actually taught me to knit, and whilst it was a skill that I would never have admitted to when I was younger, I am actually very proud of it now – although I never did master the circular three-needle stuff.

In the mid 1960's, by which time both Joe and I had finally flown the nest, Mum was able to resume her original career as a telephonist, re-joining what was then still Post Office Telephones, later British Telecom. By the time she retired she had been promoted to an executive position within the company, commanding a high salary and a decent pension, her only regret being that she hadn't had that sort of money earlier in life when she really needed it.

It wasn't until the 1970's that she finally got to own a home of her own for the first time, purchasing a three-bedroom detached house in the Monkmoor area of Shrewsbury that was a source of great pride to her. At around the same time she also realised her earlier, thwarted ambition to join the Women's Auxiliary Air Force by becoming a member of the Royal Observer Corps, a branch of the Royal Air Force.

I'm afraid to say that while my mother was slaving away and making so many sacrifices in an effort to ensure that I got a decent start in life, it never really occurred to me that I was at school to learn anything and so, not surprisingly, when the 11-plus exam came along, I failed it – rather spectacularly so, by all accounts. After the long summer holiday of 1960 most of my mates went off to the Priory Grammar School, whereas I started at Meole Brace Secondary Modern. Going from a school of a few dozen pupils to one of over two thousand came as a bit of a shock. The first person I saw there was a girl called Christine Mound. She was the most beautiful thing I'd ever seen and I fell madly in love with her. I spent the next year dreaming about her, until Anne Blain arrived. Then it was Zena Payne and after that it was Diane Millington. I also had a big crush for a time on celebrity gardener Percy Thrower's daughter, Susan.

On the subject of my schooldays, I often play a silly game with people whom I suspect of being ex-public schoolboys and who ask me where I went to school. "Oh, Shrewsbury," I reply nonchalantly, and they immediately sense a kindred spirit and start telling me how they were at Eton, or Harrow, Marlborough, Stowe and the like. Only if they ask me, more correctly, *which* school I went to do I tell them that I was actually at Meole Brace Secondary Modern *in* Shrewsbury.

At Meole Brace, still more interested in football than schoolwork, I somehow made the transition from goalkeeper to centre forward and for the first two years in the junior school team I was bashing in goals from every part of the field. As a result, I became the blue-eyed boy of the sports master, a great guy called Tom Lunt – not the happiest surname for a schoolteacher!

At morning assembly one morning in 1962 the headmaster, Tom Barnes, who was later to become a major influence in my life, announced that one of the players from Shrewsbury Town Football Club, then in the old Third Division of the Football League, was coming to coach our school team. We all gathered on one of the pitches on the morning of his first visit and were all absolutely astonished to discover that the team member allotted to our school was actually the club's player-manager, Arthur Rowley. Although not exactly a household name today, he certainly was back then. He had been a prolific goal scorer for Fulham, Leicester City and West Bromwich Albion, three absolutely top notch teams in those days, before dropping down the divisions to manage Shrewsbury, something unheard of for a top player in those days. He still holds the record for the number of Football League goals scored – 434 in 619 games. And I think there were thirty or so FA Cup and League Cup goals on top of that. It is a record that will never be beaten, due in part to the fact that the Football League and the Premiership are now separate entities.

During the coaching sessions, Arthur got to know the nicknames of some of the better players in the school team, who included Paul Bould, Sam Hoyle, Toby Tyler and Charlie Weaver as well as myself, known simply as 'Pitchy'. Later in the season, during a big FA Cup 4th round match down at Gay Meadow, as Shrewsbury Town's ground was then known, the ball was kicked into touch and found its way onto the terrace from which I and my mates used to watch all the home games. It bounced around on the terracing before coming to rest at my feet and I bent down to pick it up, before then looking up to see Arthur Rowley coming towards me to take the throw in. I tossed the ball to him and he called out: "Thanks, Pitchy". For a 13-year-old boy, surrounded by my friends as well as a few girls that I fancied, to be acknowledged in this way by such a local sporting hero was a really big deal. I am now a director of Shrewsbury Town Football Club and I suppose that the origins of my loyalty to the club date back to that day.

I don't know whether it was because I discovered girls, or maybe I just lost the plot generally, but I dropped from the school's 'A' stream, through the 'B' stream and eventually into the 'C' stream. I even lost interest in football. I cannot, to this day, explain why. Even Tom Lunt, bless him, told me sadly that I was the biggest disappointment that he'd ever had in the whole of his sports coaching career. Not, perhaps, the best way to have motivated me!

Meanwhile, I had got myself a spare time job with a local butcher, Ron Smout, who was based in the awful, newly-erected market building that still stands in the town centre to this day. When one thinks of the beautiful original market building that was demolished to make way for it, one can only conclude that it was a crying shame. It was just part of the enormous amount of architectural vandalism that took place at that time, but at least Shrewsbury is lucky in that so much else has survived. I used to deliver meat all around the town on three evenings a week after school and on Saturdays I would do more deliveries in the morning before helping out in the shop in the afternoon. This was when it began vaguely to dawn on me that anything to do with food interested me.

For my delivery rounds I had one of those bikes with a big iron frame on the front, into which was fitted an enormous wicker basket that would be filled with parcels of meat. It was the cycling equivalent of a Centurion Tank and was particularly difficult to manoeuvre, especially around some of Shrewsbury's famously hilly streets. But, at least, I did get seriously fit.

At fourteen I was big for my age – already six foot tall and well on my way to my peak of six-foot-three. This had its advantages. One Saturday morning, I called in at The Wheatsheaf pub for a pint of bitter and a fag towards the end of my delivery round, hot and thirsty after pedalling my way around the town. Most of the local publicans in Shrewsbury in those days weren't particularly fussy about serving minors and because of my height I certainly looked over eighteen. Anyway, I had no sooner raised the foaming pint to my lips than I heard the unmistakable bellowing voice of my headmaster, Tom Barnes, behind me, shouting: "Pitchford! My office, 8.30 Monday morning." He then turned to the landlord and told him: "You, sir, will also be hearing from me."

I was terrified and spent the whole of the weekend in state of panic, certain that I was about to be expelled. However, the storm that I was expecting when I presented myself at the headmaster's office didn't materialise. A strict teetotaller himself (as indeed I am now), Mr. Barnes sat me down and talked to me quietly about the evils of drink (and fags!). I later discovered that he had had a word with my mother before our meeting and that she had explained the lack of a father figure and that in her opinion I was to be commended for working hard in my spare time. He seemed to agree and treated me with a degree of sympathy, although he did also see fit to give me six of the best at the end of our little chat. I have no idea what happened with the landlord, as I obviously didn't venture into that particular pub again.

As a result of this episode, Tom Barnes took an interest in me that I don't think he might otherwise have done. I will explain more of that shortly, but suffice it to say at this stage that our relationship lasted until he died, only quite recently. We wrote to each other regularly over the years and he always maintained a keen interest in my career.

I had lots of adventures on that delivery bike, not many of them worthy of mention here. However, there was one other recollection that does remain vividly imprinted on my mind. I was taking a meat delivery to a fairly wealthy area of the town at the bottom of Sutton Lane, the last drop-off before my short journey home to the council estate at Springfield where we were living at the time. I went through the gate into a walled garden and round to the back door – always the back door for tradesmen in those days. Here I was greeted by the vision of an absolutely gorgeous young lady in a bikini. She was in her mid-to-late twenties, I'd guess, and she was in the process of watering some plants in the back yard. She thanked me for the delivery and asked me if I would like a drink, saying that she thought I looked as though I could do with one and adding that she had some Vimto in the fridge. I readily accepted and while I enjoyed my drink on the back doorstep she tried to make conversation with me. Unfortunately, being an acne'd fourteen-year-old, I could barely string two words together and hardly contributed to the conversation at all. After a few minutes I thanked her, rather awkwardly, and left.

The following week I had a delivery for the same house and arrived there at more or less the same time of day, hoping that I might see her again. There was no one to be seen in the garden, but as I approached the back door it opened partially to reveal the face of the same girl. Being careful not to open the door any further, she extended a bare arm and a glimpse of bare shoulder and said: "Shall I take that?" I handed her the parcel of meat and was about to turn away when she added: "Would you like to come in for a Vimto?" For some unknown reason, and without engaging my lentil-sized brain, I replied weakly: "No, thank you. I've got to get on." And I simply turned around and walked away. There was hardly a week that went by in the next five years when I didn't think about that girl and what might have happened had I said: "Yes, please!" From that day onwards I never again had a meat parcel for that address.

Back at school, I wasn't considered to be CSE or GSE material, but in spite of this I decided to stay on for a fifth year. I remember a meeting at the end of the fourth year with the so-called Careers Advice Officer. Before the appointment I had filled in a form with interests and hobbies and so on and my teachers had listed my rather sparse academic achievements and abilities. My mother was also invited to the meeting. The Careers Officer opened the session with the words: "Well, this won't take long." He then proceeded to suggest to Mum that I should hang on to my butcher's delivery round. OK, I didn't expect him to suggest I might become Prime Minister, but he could have been a little more encouraging. I would love to find out where he lives now, drive my Bentley up to his front door and ask him if he had any other useful advice for me!

Although it didn't make academic sense to stay on at school, it turned out to be the best thing I ever did in my young life. Tom Barnes was one ofthose very forward-looking headmasters who got all the girls doing woodwork and metalwork and all the boys doing domestic science, as it was then called. I remember my acute embarrassment when I turned up for my first cookery lesson dressed in a little pink apron (my mother had washed my brand new white one together with something red!), all the girls giggling at me as I walked along the corridor.

To this day, I still don't understand why women have to wash new things before they use them for the first time; same reason that they clean the house before the cleaner arrives, I suppose.

At the end of that first lesson, much to my amazement, what I cooked turned out to be better than anything produced by the rest of the group. And from then on my offerings continued to be best-in-class every time. Admittedly, we're only talking bread rolls or rock cakes, apple pie or a Victoria sponge, but for the first time ever in my school career I found myself consistently top of the class, doing the only thing, apart from playing football, that I had ever been really good at. As a result, I couldn't wait for Wednesday mornings to come around.

Up until that point, my school reports had been uniformly bad. Even on the rare occasions when they started well ("David tries very hard…), momentarily raising my hopes, those hopes would then be shattered by the time I had read on to the end of the sentence (…to give the impression that he is trying hard). But in that final fifth year it was as if someone had injected me with an intelligence serum. All of a sudden I seemed to wake up and realise what it was all about. My grades in every subject rocketed and I actually started paying attention to what was being said around me. But, most important of all, I knew, without any doubt, that I wanted to be a chef.

2 : Horses and Courses

Inspired by my newly discovered career ambition, I wrote off to Wolverhampton College of Technology, applying to be enrolled in the City and Guilds professional cooking course. To my delight, I was accepted and in September 1965 I moved into student accommodation on the college campus, then located in the old mining village of Featherstone that lies just outside Wolverhampton.

For me, it was quite a culture shock. One minute I was at school, living at home and getting 2/6d-a-week pocket money, the next I had left home and some nice person from Shropshire County Council had handed me a cheque for around £600 to pay all my college fees, travel expenses and accommodation for the whole year. Shamefully, I have to confess that I didn't at first adjust very responsibly to this sudden change in my fortunes.

The problem was that by this time I had become fascinated by horseracing, particularly National Hunt racing, mainly because of a horse called Arkle. Generally accepted as having been the greatest NH racehorse of all time, Arkle became a national favourite and was quite a character, with some unusual tastes. I wonder, for instance, what today's trainers would make of giving their star horses half a gallon of Guinness along with their breakfast feed each morning, which is what Arkle enjoyed. It certainly appeared to put a spring in his step because National Hunt racing rules had to be changed to accommodate this wonderful horse, with one set of rules when he was running and another set when he was not. He regularly used to carry an amazing three stone more than his rivals in handicap chases, and yet still managed to beat them by a distance.

Arkle was not the only equine star of that era; there were also the likes of Mill House, Flyingbolt, Stalybridge Colonist, Dundalk and Dunkirk, to name but a few. It was a golden era for horseracing, not only over the jumps but on the flat, too, and I had become hooked on the sport. Up until the time I went to college I only used to bet the odd sixpence each way from my pocket money. But with a bit of cash in my pocket, courtesy of my Shropshire County Council further education grant, I became a regular punter. Every morning I would go down to the local newsagents to buy a copy of Sporting Life, forerunner of Racing Post, along with some cigarettes – the first time I'd ever been able to afford the luxury of a packet of twenty Peter Stuyvesant or Three Kings rather than just five Woodbines! And then, at lunchtime, it would be into the pub, where I would enjoy a pint of Banks's bitter and study the form before moving on to the betting shop.

It took me no more than about six weeks to lose my entire grant, meaning I was in deep trouble as I had not paid a single bill and debts were starting to mount up. I made a valiant attempt to earn some cash by getting a job in a pub in the evenings and also as a waiter at any weekend wedding receptions that I could find in and around Wolverhampton, but my desperate efforts were doomed to failure. In the end I had no option but to go home one weekend and tell Mum what I'd done, and like most mothers, I suppose, she blamed herself for what had happened. She had actually asked me several times how I was managing my finances, but had made the mistake of believing me when I told her everything was OK.

We made an appointment to travel to Wolverhampton together to see the Principal of the college. Just like the year before, when I'd been summoned to see headmaster Tom Barnes after the pub incident, I was expecting to be turfed out, if you'll pardon the pun. But no! Once again, I was reprieved. The Principal phoned the head of the catering department, a stern German chap named Leobold, and asked for a report on my progress. To my great relief, and that of my equally anxious mother, he clearly got some positive feedback from old Leobold, because when he put the phone down he proposed that we should work out a plan to repay the money when I started work at the end of the two-year course. It eventually took me over four years to clear my debts..

That episode remains one of the most valuable lessons that I have ever had, and in a strange way I am pleased that it happened. It instilled in me a value of money that I was to find useful later on in life and that, in some respects, put me ahead of my peers.

My partner in crime in those gambling days was a chap named Jim Harris, a fellow student on the cookery course who became a life-long friend. Jim and I shared everything (except Judy Millard!). If we weren't at the bookies or the racecourse, then you'd find us at the Monmore Green greyhound racing track in Wolverhampton.

Much later, when we were both busy 'empire building', Jim was one of those friends who I sometimes wouldn't see for two or three years at a time, and yet when we did accidentally bump into each other, usually on Gold Cup day at Cheltenham, we would always pick up again from exactly where we had left off. To this day, we still don't spend that much time together, but we do occasionally meet up to go to a football match, or something similar, and we always get together when anything important happens in either of our lives. I still gamble, sometimes quite heavily, the only difference now being that I only ever gamble with money that I can afford to lose; and I never, ever chase losses as I did when I was a teenage student in Wolverhampton.

Back in 1966, Jim, with his Vespa, his short hair and his Parka, was obviously a Mod. I hadn't got a clue what I was at that age, but with my Brylcreemed hair, jeans and winkle-pickers I suppose I leaned more towards the Rockers. In spite of this, Jim and I became great mates and decided that we would spend that summer doing a holiday job together, along with another pal from the cookery course, Brian Maddocks, who was also from Shrewsbury.

We ended up working on a big caravan site on the outskirts of Tenby, in South Wales. The site included a country club with a grill room style of restaurant and the three of us used to take it in turns to cook and wait on table. The caravanners used to frequent the club and restaurant during the early and middle parts of the evening, but because it was situated a little off the beaten track, halfway between Tenby and Saundersfoot, it also used to attract the local business 'mafia'; you know the type – slot machine arcade owners, publicans, bookies and fast food restaurant owners. They didn't begin to arrive until midnight, or even later, and things often used to go on well into the early hours, particularly at weekends. We loved every waking second of it.

1966 was, of course, the year in which England won the World Cup. There was a ladies' hairdressing 'salon' on the site, housed in a caravan and run by two great girls whose names I'm ashamed to say I can't now remember, but who allowed us to watch the game live on their television, even though they were busy coiffeuring up clients at the time. It was a memorable day for soccer-mad England fans like us, and even though we were in Wales there was a fantastic atmosphere in the restaurant and the club that evening, with people spontaneously breaking into chants of: "We won the Cup, we won the Cup!"

We loved that summer in Tenby, so much so that when Mrs. Davies, the site owner, asked us if we would like to return and do the same thing the following summer we nearly bit her hand off. When I say that I wish that I could re-live a particular moment, hour or day in my life it is usually because I had messed up in some way or other first time around and would love to be able to go back and put things right. I had maybe said something stupid or thoughtless and wished I could eat my words, or perhaps I'd behaved rather badly and longed to erase the incident from my past. However, when it comes to those two summers of '66 and '67, the reason why I would love to go back and do it all over again is simply that they were just such brilliant times.

There was a posh section on the site reserved for people who owned their own caravans and who regularly visited several times a year and, to be honest, that area was a bit sedate, with one or two exceptions. The rest of the site was given over to groups of holidaymakers who used to come down and rent, usually in multiples of four, but sometimes in twos or threes, mainly from Birmingham and the surrounding areas of West Bromwich, Walsall and Dudley. This was around the time that Brits were starting to holiday abroad, but there were still many, mostly younger people, who spent their annual break in the UK. And for lads like us working there, holiday camps like the ones at Tenby and Saundersfoot were like a conveyer belt of girls. There would be quite a few families with young children, but because these were quite buzzy places, and relatively cheap, they were especially popular with groups of young people in their late teens and early twenties bent on enjoying themselves away from home. Jim, Brian and I returned to Wolverhampton at the end of that first year in order to complete our course and, thankfully, we passed all our first year exams with flying colours, even the boring associated subjects such as housekeeping, nutrition and hygiene. Somehow, though, it all seemed rather tame after Tenby and we couldn't wait to get back there. Unbelievably, 1967 was even better than 1966, maybe because we knew what to expect and didn't need to waste any time learning the ropes, but also because we were just that little bit older and marginally more mature.

As it happened, Brian Maddocks didn't return with us the second year for some reason that I can't remember now and his place was taken by a guy named Les Simpkiss. Up until then I hadn't known Les that well, but Jim assured me that he was a good bloke, so that was fine with me. In fact, he fitted in perfectly and the three of us got on like a house on fire.

Most of the girls used to come down for two weeks, with Saturday morning being the changeover day. Out with the old and in with the new! Les and I used to be in tears in the car park, waving goodbye to our departing girlfriends and trying to placate Jim's, because he himself was nowhere to be seen. He would be on the tractor, supposedly helping Aubrey, the site manager, to empty the bins and tidy up the public areas. But while the cleaners would be frantically sorting out the caravans, what Jim was actually doing was checking out the new arrivals.

The 'Oscar' for the best group of girls has to go to Jan, Gill, Jackie and Jane, who pitched up in July '67. As there were only three of us blokes, Jan was the unlucky one – or lucky one, depending upon your point of view – who didn't pair off. I fell madly in love with Gill and Jackie fell madly in love with Les. However, Gill didn't want to know anything about me once she got back to her boyfriend in Birmingham and Les wasn't interested in continuing to see Jackie. The result of that was that Jackie and I used to write consoling letters to each other for some time afterwards, becoming regular pen pals. Years later, I often thought about trying to contact her or Gill again to find out what had happened to them, but chose in the end not to do so, which was probably wise. Anyway, they were all fabulous girls and I hope they went on to have great lives.

At the end of the Tenby summer we returned to Wolverhampton, where we discovered that we had each passed our final year exams. Jim returned to his hometown of Dudley and went to work for Joseph Lucas, where he carved out a good career for himself, while I headed back to Shrewsbury and got a job at The Lord Hill Hotel, at the same time sending off applications for various jobs in London. At this point, however, Fate intervened fairly dramatically to scupper my plans. I was on my way to the Lord Hill on my bike one morning when I was hit by a car that was being driven up Sutton Lane into very low, dazzling, sunlight that must have momentarily blinded the driver. I was crossing a junction when the car smashed into my rear right side, throwing me into its path and causing my head to hit the bonnet with such force that my nose was broken just about as badly as it possibly could be, or so the doctors later told me.

Still just about conscious, I tried to stand up in order to remove myself from the middle of the road, where I had come to rest. However, my right foot was trapped between the cogs of the crown wheel, which had penetrated the arch of my foot and was held in place by the chain. Apart from being quite literally attached to my bike and unable to move, I remember the horrible sensation of blood literally gushing down the back of my throat. I was coughing it up and was convinced that I was going to die. I wasn't in a great deal of pain at that stage, but the blood loss was made to look even worse because it was raining heavily, even though the sun was shining. Amid all the chaos, one of my other lasting memories of the accident is of two ladies who had obviously heard the crash and had come rushing out of a nearby house – actually next-door-but-one to where I had encountered my bikini lady. One turned to the other and said: "Oh, my God, go and put the kettle on."

Thankfully, someone had obviously decided that calling an ambulance was more important than having a cup of tea and in no time at all I found myself in the Royal Salop Infirmary. As I said, there wasn't much pain at the time, despite the fact that as well as breaking my nose, I had also broken my leg and some ribs and had suffered severe bruising down the whole of my right side. And once the pain did inevitably kick in, it was considerable and lasted several weeks.

The accident meant that my plans to go to London had to be put on hold for quite a while, but once I was eventually able to walk again without crutches I travelled down on the train for an interview that I had managed to get at the BBC Television Centre in Wood Lane for a position in the catering department there. My mother had given me five shillings to help with my expenses and I, in my wisdom, decided to spend some of it on a very large jar of pickled onions, which I proceeded to munch through on the way down to Euston. The BBC must have been fairly desperate for staff because the interview wasn't nearly as arduous as I had anticipated. In fact, it turned out to be little more than a formality – the equivalent of holding a mirror up to my mouth to check if there were any signs of life. Luckily, the mirror misted over, so I was in.

Meanwhile, there had been a plus side to the accident, insofar as I got £250 in compensation from the car driver's insurance company. That was a considerable sum of money back then and I used some of it to start paying off my debts. Considering the discomfort, pain and problems the injury to my leg and foot has caused me ever since, especially as I have got older, what I got was woefully inadequate. Had I known then what I know now, I would have been after £25,000 rather than £250. It's funny how often these days I find myself thinking: "If only I had known then what I know now", and wondering how my life might have changed as a result. My teenage encounters with Christine Mound, Diane Millington and Gill Atkins might certainly have had very different outcomes!

One of the first things I bought with the insurance money was a 1959 Hillman Minx, complete with column gear change and bench seats, for which I paid the princely sum of £30. I must confess to having had some great times in that car. It gave me freedom and opportunities in my late teens and early twenties that I wouldn't otherwise have had. The registration was either KRB 350 or KR 35, depending on whether you were looking at the front or the rear number plate. I don't know where or when I lost the B and the zero from the back plate, and it didn't occur to me to replace them at the time. In fact, not replacing them came in very handy one evening when I happened to be up North, driving to a nightclub in Sheffield with Jimmy Thickett and Taffy Jones, a couple of mates from the Dorchester, where I was working by then. Also in the car with us were three girls from Rotherham that we had picked up somewhere. Along the way, I was pulled over by the police for not having an efficient silencer on the exhaust system. I must admit that it did make the car sound like a passing Spitfire and so it was no great surprise, on reflection, that I was flagged down by the patrolling Panda car.

There were three officers on board, one of them a policewoman, who, luckily for me, was obviously a rookie. While going through the process of booking me, she was constantly ridiculed by her two male colleagues in a way that would never be tolerated today, at least not publicly. Clearly flustered, she only took down the registration number from the rear of the car and also copied the address incorrectly from my driving licence, putting it down as 8 rather than 80 Penton Place. The combination of these two mistakes meant that I was never prosecuted for that particular misdemeanour. At the time, the policewoman also reprimanded me for the car being overcrowded, which I thought a little harsh, to say the least, as there were only six of us – and the three girls were not particularly buxom as I remember!

I used to travel to work at the Dorchester every day in my beloved Hillman. At that time one could still park for free on the roads next to Rotten Row, on the south side Hyde Park. The march of parking meters, and then the devastating Hyde Park bomb placed by the IRA, put an end to that long ago.

Being a proud but nevertheless rather naive Salopian youth, I found the transition from Shrewsbury to London extremely difficult and suffered a severe culture shock when I first moved down to start my job at the BBC. Shropshire, in those days, was very much a sleepy farming community by comparison and the last bus from the town centre to where I lived used to leave at half past eight in the evening. In London, I shared a bed-sit in Penton Place, near the Oval cricket ground in Kennington, with my Shrewsbury schoolmate and fellow Wolverhampton cookery student Brian Maddocks, who was, by then, working at the Mayfair Hotel before later moving on to Claridge's. I travelled over to the BBC TV Centre at Shepherd's Bush every morning on the tube and compared to how hard I was to work later in my life it was an absolute doddle. It hardly seemed worthwhile, really, going all that way for just a nine-hour shift. What was then the fairly new circular building next door to the old White City stadium consisted of four floors, with a restaurant on each one; the higher up the building you went, the better the restaurant.

For a newly arrived hick from the sticks like me it was a very exciting place to work. I regularly bumped into TV celebrities, both in the corridors and in the fantastic BBC Club, of which all employees, even lowly kitchen hands, automatically became members.

In the fast food restaurant on the lower floor, I was put in charge of making omelets, which I would cook to order, on the spot, as they were ordered. I would make fifty or sixty of them each and every lunchtime and, as a result, I reckon that I became – and still remain to this day – the best omelet maker the world has ever known!

Being able to enjoy the facilities of the BBC Club, which was open twenty-four hours a day, was a fantastic perk of the job, especially for an all-round sports fan like me. Thanks to the BBC's live feed, I was able to sit there in the early hours of the morning and watch world title fights, Grand Slam tennis finals and other events as they were happening somewhere on the other side of the world. That was a very big deal in those days.

Looking back, the food at the Beeb was quite ordinary and, generally speaking, certainly didn't reach any great gastronomic heights. However, one day the head chef, Mr. Abel, called me into his office and announced that he was assigning me to work with a girl named Gill, who had her own kitchen in VIP Hospitality and was responsible for cooking for the many famous visitors who arrived at the BBC from all over the world. They included Royalty, major political figures and genuine International superstars from the worlds of film, theatre, television and sport. These people couldn't eat in the regular restaurants, mainly for personal security reasons, so they would dine in private rooms. And what they were served with was a cut above what was on offer in the other restaurants. It was the first time I had cooked with very expensive ingredients such as caviar, lobster and foie gras. I learned a lot in a short space of time about things I'd never seen or even heard about before, let alone prepared. It was also the first time that I was required to cook for customers with special dietary requirements, religious or otherwise.

The BBC was good for me and I learned a great deal – and not only about cooking. During this time I also made a fair amount of headway in the transition from country bumpkin to city dweller. I used to speak so slowly compared with the natives that people often used to say: "Wake me up at the end of your next sentence"!

I really wanted to get myself in at the sharp end of where top-notch cooking was taking place, and in those days that meant one of the five-star hotel kitchens. After eventually leaving the BBC in 1968 I spent six months at the Mayfair Hotel, but if you wanted to be a really serious contender as a chef you knew that you had to get yourself into one of the "Big Five" – the Dorchester, Savoy, Ritz, Claridge's or, rather surprisingly, what was then the recently-opened Hilton on Park Lane.

At the Mayfair I got my first taste of working in a big hotel 'partie' system, inevitably making mistakes but learning from them and gaining invaluable experience that was to stand me in good stead for when

I started at the 'Big D', as the Dorchester was known.

My six years there began in late 1968, when I was fortunate to fill one of the vacancies left by two guys who had been sacked for (to put it euphemistically) getting their property and the Dorchester's property mixed up. A lot of 'shopping' – nicking items of food from the kitchens – used to go on in those days. Anyway, I happened to be on duty in the main kitchen at the Mayfair when one of these two guys, who had managed to get a job there despite his ignominious dismissal from the Dorchester, popped in for his staff meal just before the lunchtime service. He was a pastry chef or 'sponge monkey' as we used to call them. They're all mad as hatters – it must be all that flour they've breathed in! Actually, joking aside, those of them at the top end of our industry are among the most talented people in the whole world of professional cooking.

Anyway, I struck up a conversation with this chap and mentioned that I was desperate to get in at the Dorchester. He told me that there were a huge number of young lads like me who wanted to work there and that if I tried by the more conventional means of queuing up at the back door on my day off, or writing letters of application, I was unlikely to get anywhere, as the odds would be seriously stacked against me. He advised me to put on my best bib and tucker, walk straight through the front door on Park Lane, through reception, into the Grill Room, diagonally across the restaurant, through the left-hand service door, turn left down the stairs and then right into the kitchen and ask for Mr. Alec Riddell, the senior sous chef.

The idea of boldly walking through the front door of a hotel like that would never have occurred to me, and even when he suggested it I didn't really think I would possibly be able to pull it off. However, I plucked up a huge amount of courage and did exactly as instructed. He had told me to keep looking straight ahead, to avoid making eye contact with anyone who seemed about to come up and challenge me and to continue walking purposefully as if it were my business to be there. To my amazement, it worked like a dream and I found myself in the cavernous basement kitchens of one of the very best and most famous hotels in the world. Purely by chance, it was Mr Riddell himself who then came over and confronted me and, once again acting as instructed, I told him that I was there to be interviewed for the vacant job as a commis chef.

We then had what could perhaps be laughingly described as an interview. It went along the lines of: "I don't know nuthin' about no f***in' interview. How'd you get in 'ere anyway? And where you workin' at the moment?"

"Mayfair Hotel, Chef."

"Only poofs work at the Mayfair."

"I know, Chef that's why I want to come and work here, Chef."

"What you on?"

"£14 a week, Chef."(I was actually on £12).

"How much notice you gotta give?"

"One week, Chef."

"OK. Start a week next Monday. 7.00am. £12-a-week. GOT IT?"

"Yes, Chef."

"Then get yer arse up to personnel. I'll phone to tell 'em yer comin'."

I was elated. Although Mr. Riddell behaved like a sergeant major and frightened the life out of me at first, I later discovered that he had a heart of gold. He would explain to me that the only reason he had given me a job was because I had managed to bypass all the back door security to get into the kitchen in the first place, something that was thought at the time to be impossible.

I finished at the Mayfair and duly turned up at the 'Big D' the following Monday, as directed. But because the laundry at the Mayfair Hotel came back on a Tuesday morning I didn't have a clean chef's hat. I approached Mr. Riddell with an enthusiastic "Good morning, Chef", proceeded to explain my predicament regarding the hat and asked if I could possibly borrow one. To which he replied: "F*** off and come back next Monday when you've got ALL your whites."

I was living from hand to mouth back then and going unpaid for a whole week was going to be a serious problem for me. However, one of the lads in the kitchen who had seen what had happened came over as I was leaving, disconsolately, and told me that when walking up from Charing Cross railway station that morning he had noticed a sign in the window of the nearby Lyons Corner House, announcing that they were looking for staff. I went straight down there with my hat-shy whites and within ten minutes I was at work in the kitchen. That week's work saved my life, making it possible for me to pay my rent. At the end of the week the manager offered me £16-a-week to stay. I went all wobbly bonkers for a minute at the thought of earning that much, but I was certain that it wasn't really an option for me. The Big D was the only place I wanted to be.

3 : The 'Big D'

I arrived at the Dorchester the following week, complete with all my whites, and was promptly placed on the Vegetable section. The way the kitchen worked in those days was that almost everyone started on the Veg, but after four months you were then permitted to look for a commis chef on another section to do a swap with you. The two of you then had to go to Mr. Riddell to get his approval for the swap. The problem in trying to arrange such a swap was that you actually found yourself in a Catch 22 situation, because almost everyone had to start on the Veg, so hardly anyone wanted to go back there. The only way to get around this snag was to find someone who was thinking of leaving and get the swap sanctioned before that person actually handed in his notice.

At the Dorchester, as in most major restaurant kitchens at the time, the section responsible for producing and serving vegetables worked in a rather different way from how they mostly operate today. Chefs nowadays generally dictate what vegetables and garnishes will accompany the main course dishes, but back then customers were normally left to choose their own vegetables and order them separately and this required large amounts of mise-en-place – previously prepared component parts.

As well as about twenty different seasonal vegetables or vegetable compositions, there would also be a choice of about ten different potato dishes, all of which would need to be prepared and cooked to order. Vegetables and potato dishes were often batch-cooked, which meant that they were prepared in advance in anticipation of estimated customer demand, and this could be a very wasteful system if not managed carefully.

At the Dorchester there were, altogether, over a hundred chefs, or 'white hats' as the Swiss Chef Eugene Kaufeler used to call them.

If you completed every section within the partie system then you emerged as a reasonably well-rounded cook, how good you actually were depending on your individual drive and ability. I know that the system is still alive in the big hotels, but generally I see young chefs today flitting from one Michelin-starred restaurant to another, building up a repertoire of dishes without ever understanding the underlying principles of good cooking.

The currency within the Dorchester kitchen in those days was beer. Everyone got a daily allocation of two large cans of bitter – Courage, I seem to remember. There was an early shift and a late shift and they used to overlap in the afternoon, meaning that there were around a dozen commis on the Veg section alone. The Chef de Partie on the Veg section when I joined it was a guy named Ray Kenny, an Irishman who had worked in Germany. He used to make all the commis on the section put one of their beers in the centre of the table and when he gave the word each commis started to pick the inedible ends off his box of extra fine Kenya beans (haricot verts). Whoever finished first would take all the beers.

For some unknown reason I was an exceptionally quick bean picker, albeit a slow talking one, and so I would regularly win the 'pot'. The same thing was done with fresh leaf spinach (epinards en branche), which involved taking out the central stalk from the leaf before it was washed five separate times in clean water in huge sinks. The Chef de Partie would closely check everyone's work to make sure there was no cheating, such as chucking a couple of handfuls from your box into the pig bin or into another commis' box when he wasn't looking. Anyone whose 'strigs' were longer than a quarter of an inch was disqualified. And any cheats were also made to deal with the odd few boxes that remained after the team had done the majority.

Taking into account the large banquets of up to a thousand covers in the ballroom, as well as maybe ten different parties of up to a hundred in private rooms, there would regularly be thirty boxes of beans and twenty boxes of spinach to pick each afternoon, even more when the hotel was working at full capacity. It would take you 15-20 minutes to pick a whole box of Kenya extra fine beans on your own. Ray only organised the competitions to motivate people to get a move on and it certainly worked. These days there are companies that specialise in supplying hotels with prepared vegetables, so things are very different.

Because most people tend to imagine cooking in a restaurant or hotel as being simply a glorified extension of cooking at home there is no concept of just how complicated and difficult the vegetable and garnish section could be, with so many different vegetables and garnishes having to be delivered to the other sections precisely when the main course from that section was ready to go to the table. As sections go, it is usually at the bottom of the kitchen hierarchy, which is a shame, because the skill required in order to run it properly is immense. Bear in mind that as well as servicing the two main restaurants at the Dorchester along with the private dining and banqueting rooms, the kitchen also had the considerable extra task of feeding the four hundred hotel staff.

I had my eye on a move from the Veg to the Soup. Rollo, the guy I was planning to swap with, had once referred to Irishman Ray Kenny as 'the Killkenny Kraut' because of his German connections, and as a result Ray was not especially well-disposed towards him and tried to block the move, thankfully without success. I had negotiated with Rollo to pay him twenty beers to do the swap and after we shook on the deal he tried to upset me by saying he would actually have done it for ten. I always did my best to have the last laugh in those days, so I replied that I would happily have paid thirty.

Having graduated from the Veg to the Soup – more correctly termed 'Potage' – I was on my way. The soup section was responsible for serving twenty-one different types of soup each day. There were veloutes, crèmes, bisques, chowders, broths, purees, consommés and miscellaneous others, all made from scratch. An example of a miscellaneous soup would be soupe a'loignon gratinee, which didn't fall into any particular category. Potage 'Lady Curzon' was a strange concoction comprising cream of fresh peas combined with turtle soup and topped with a lightly curried sabayon cream.

Because kitchens were far more traditional in those days there was none of the innovation and individuality that you get now. You did what you were told to do and you did it the French way. The system of ordering was French and all food was referred to by its French name. If customers wanted a fresh asparagus soup (crème d'asperge) then than that's what they got. At the same time, you had to be prepared to make customers' special, individual requests to order – there was no such word as 'no' at the Dorchester.

As well as soups, Potage was also responsible for producing all rice, pasta, farinaceous and egg dishes. Complex egg dishes were far more popular then than they are now. As well as straightforward boiled, poached, coddled, fried or scrambled eggs and a full range of omelets, orders might include oeufs frites à la Francaise, oeufs mollet, farci, sur la plat, durs or cocotte, to name but a few variations. And there were not just hens' eggs, but also gulls', ducks', lapwings', pheasants', goose and quail eggs. A lot of what went on in that section is pretty much a lost art these days.

Turtle soup was generally made from consommé and 'turtle herbs' and was more correctly termed mock turtle soup. I only ever got involved in the making of genuine fresh turtle soup once, and that was not at the Dorchester but for a banquet at the Guildhall, where I was 'moonlighting' for the specialist livery hall catering company Ring and Brymer and where the cavernous underground kitchens included the largest ovens I have ever seen – each one large enough to accommodate three whole barons of beef. A live turtle was used and it was a genuine horror story. This was back in the late 60s and you would quite rightly end up in prison if you attempted it now. We followed Escoffier's recipe from his *Guide to Modern Cookery*, which starts: "Take a turtle weighing between 120 and 180 lbs. and let it be very fleshy and full of life. To slaughter it, lay it on its back on a butcher's block with its head hanging over the side. By means of a double butcher's hook, one spike of which is thrust into the turtle's lower jaw while the other suspends an adequately heavy weight, make the animal hold its head back. Then, with all possible dispatch, sever the head from the body." The recipe and method goes on for another two-and-a-half pages and let's just say that I don't think that you will be seeing it done on *Ready Steady Cook*, *Saturday Morning Kitchen* or Hugh Fearnley-Whittingstall's *River Cottage* any time in the near future.

My new Chef de Partie when I moved to the soup section was a chap called Colin Ryall, a highly accomplished cook and one of those lucky people who seem to have it all. A good-looking, smooth-talking Cockney Jack-the-Lad, he drove a white convertible Sunbeam Alpine, so there was always a queue of girls waiting to go out with him. On the other hand, there was me, fresh from the country and the exact opposite of Colin in every way, and yet we got on really well and he took the trouble to spend a lot of time teaching me and passing on tips when he needn't really have bothered.

We didn't socialise much outside of work, mainly because the gulf between a commis chef's pay and that of a Chef de Partie was vast. However, we did venture out together on one memorable occasion, along with another lovely chap called Peter Queree, who was the top commis on the sauce section at the time. They were good mates and regularly went out on the town, usually to the Orchid at Purley, the Whisky A Go Go club in Soho or the Hammersmith Palais, all of which were the happening places of the time.

On this particular occasion we found ourselves at the Orchid on a night when Desmond Decker and the Aces, who were riding high in the charts at the time with their big hit *The Israelites*, were playing live. Colin spotted a girl he fancied, sitting with two friends on the edge of the dance floor, and he instructed Peter and me to ask the other two for a dance. The apple of Colin's eye was without doubt the best-looking girl in the place and he approached her with the line: "Want to dance, princess?" Quick as a flash, she replied: "I might not be the princess, I might be the queen". Whereupon Colin, without missing a beat, came back with: "On yer feet then, darlin', you just met the king!" Of course, that sort of thing would make us all cringe nowadays, but at the time I thought he was the coolest guy in the world. That was the last Peter and I saw of Colin that evening and we were left to find our own way home.

It was at around this time that I first became aware of a young chef at the Big D named Richard Shepherd. Mr. Eugene Kaufeler, the Chef de Cuisine at the Dorchester, was approaching retirement and it was obvious to us all that Richard was being groomed to take over; and had he done so he would have been the first English chef to take a top London hotel job. The Chefs de Cuisine of all the five-star hotels in London in those days were either Swiss, German, French or possibly Italian, but never English. As it was, Richard decided against taking over at the Dorchester and went instead to the Capital Hotel, a small hotel restaurant in Basil Street, just behind Harrods, owned by David Levin. There, with Brian Turner as his sous chef, he made history by becoming the first English chef to win a Michelin star. I don't ever remember seeing Richard looking anything less than immaculate in his whites. He was an incredibly talented cook and had an authority that I don't recall seeing in anyone else his age. He was also impossibly good looking and became the darling of the press and the media generally. We all wanted to be like Richard Shepherd.

His path and mine were to cross many times during our respective careers and he was always incredibly good to me. Although he was one of the busiest men on the planet he would always make time to sit down with me over a glass of wine or a lunch and point me in the right direction. He left the Capital Hotel to go into partnership with Peter Langan and Michael Caine and the rest is history. Langan's Brasserie opened on Bastille Day 1977 – the same year and the same day as Read's, incidentally – and went on to become, in my opinion, the most successful British restaurant since the Second World War. If anyone should write an autobiographical book it should be Richard, but he has told me that he never will.

Richard is now semi-retired and spends most of his time in France. In the early days at the Dorchester and the Capital he unquestionably proved himself to be an incredible chef. I will never forget going to the Capital with Rona and my great friend Eddie McIntyre and his wife Wendy to celebrate Eddie's 30th birthday. The meal we had there that night ranks as one of the top three I have ever had in my life. As a chef/restaurateur Richard was unsurpassed in his all-round ability to produce the highest-quality Michelin-starred cuisine, while at the same time putting bums on seats. He was one of the very few chefs who understood how to do both, consistently, over a long period.

It was shortly after starting at the Dorchester that I moved from Penton Place in South East London to Cathcart Road in Earls Court, where several of the Dorchester kitchen boys shared a basement flat. Because of the shift system, we operated a sort of 'hot bunking' system, whereby you grabbed any vacant bed when you got home after work. And whoever was first up was best dressed, often nicking somebody else's newly-laundered shirt if their own was in need of washing or ironing. It was not a time that I would wish to go back to, but I suspect that most young men experience something similar at some stage in their early lives.

Amid the chaos that existed in the rather overcrowded flat there was one near-disastrous incident. The aforementioned Eddie McIntyre, one of the flatmates, had been cooking on the gas stove when the gas ran out, and as he didn't have a shilling for the meter he gave up, watched TV for a while and then went to bed. When I came in some hours later to find no gas to cook with, I promptly fed the meter. What Eddie had forgotten was that the gas fire in the communal bedroom had also been on when the gas ran out and he had not thought to turn it off, so when I put my shilling in the meter the gas started escaping. Fortunately, it must have been one of the rare occasions when Eddie hadn't gone to bed overly inebriated and the smell of gas woke him upin time to prevent a potential tragedy.

Eddie was a highly colourful character and led a life that was something of a mystery to the rest of us kitchen boys. After finishing his shift at the Dorchester, he would regularly go off to work as a croupier in one of the many illegal gambling clubs that were dotted around London in the days before the gambling laws were relaxed, when gambling licences were hard to come by and only a handful of legal casinos existed. Eddie would impress us with the slick way in which he could shuffle a pack of cards and then deal himself four aces, and he would fool us every time with his demonstrations of 'Find the Lady'. Returning to the flat at dawn from whichever club he was operating in, he would snatch just a few hours' sleep and yet still find the time and energy to sell copies of the Socialist Worker outside tube stations before reporting for work at the Dorchester.

On one occasion he came into work having not returned to the flat at all the night before and announced that he had won thirty tickets for the Manchester United v Benfica European Cup Final at Wembley in a card game. I had thought Eddie and I were good mates, but I must have been mistaken because a good mate would surely have given me (or at least sold me) one of his spare tickets for what was being billed as the biggest soccer event since the 1966 World Cup Final. But no such offer was forthcoming and I was more than a little pissed off when it became clear that he had no intention of sharing his good fortune. He obviously knew that I was a bit miffed about it because he came in the next day with a couple of the match day programs in a rather sheepish effort to placate me.

Despite my ill feelings over this perceived snub, Eddie and I went on to become lifelong friends. We still see each other regularly to this day and always spend every Christmas together. But nothing more was ever said about the ticket episode until quite recently, when I started writing this book and asked Eddie to tell me a bit more about exactly how he had won the tickets and what he had done with them all. Only then did he tell me the full story, explaining that he had won them playing poker with some of the punters at the club where he had been working as a croupier and that he had emerged from the club at about 7 o'clock in the morning, fearing for his life, as the people who frequented such places were, as one can imagine, a pretty tough bunch. He was quite relieved to get home safely, convinced that he was going to make a fortune from fans desperate to get to Wembley for the game.

He went on to recall that there was a place in Piccadilly where shady characters went to sell or trade illicit goods and he duly managed to unload eight of the thirty tickets there for a handsome profit. He then decided that he would turn up at Wembley on the night of the game with the remaining twenty-two and tout them at the stadium, making even more of a killing. That was when his hopes of riches beyond the dreams of avarice were shattered. Both Manchester United and Benfica had been allocated 35,000 tickets each for sale to their respective supporters, but Portugal, at that time, was under the military dictatorship of General Salazar, who severely restricted the movement of Portuguese nationals outside the country. As a result, only about ten thousand Benfica supporters made it over to London, bringing with them handfuls of spare match tickets to sell, ruining Eddie's market.

I had been under the impression for all these years that Eddie had made a big profit that night and it was only now that he revealed the truth – that he had sold a couple of tickets for face value outside the ground and had given the rest away. He was too embarrassed to tell me at the time and insisted that had we had mobile phones in those days, he would have called me and told me and the rest of the lads to get ourselves over to Wembley pronto. I still have in my collection the match day programs that he gave me, one of which is in perfect condition and probably worth quite a lot of money. And I have to confess that I took a certain amount of pleasure in taking them out and showing them to him when he eventually told me the whole story. So, in that way at least, I guess I can say I had the last laugh.

Unfortunately, I feel unable to recount some of the more colourful exploits and adventures that Eddie and I shared together, mainly due to the fact that he went on to achieve a great deal of success and respectability in his career, becoming Principal of the Birmingham College of Food and Domestic Arts, later University College Birmingham, and also being honoured with a CBE, again proving (according to Eddie himself) that, contrary to the old saying, you really *can* fool all of the people all of the time! He's actually being far too modest, of course. Not for nothing was UCB's new higher education and post-graduate centre named McIntyre House in his honour. There will be more about Eddie later.

My next move at the Dorchester was from the Soup to the larder or Garde Manger. This was really five sections in one. My stint in the fish part of the larder, which lasted several months, was the most uncomfortable of my entire time at the Dorchester. In a professional kitchen one gets acclimatised to heat, even to quite extreme temperatures, but I never got used to being constantly as cold as I was when working amid ice all the time in the fish prepping area. As a result of my experience there, it is no mystery to me that the high street fishmonger has become virtually a thing of the past. It is a tough business.

At the Dorchester in those days there were live lobster tanks and another one for live trout. I can't remember the last time I saw truite au bleu on a menu anywhere. The process required a live trout to be killed, gutted, gilled and placed in white wine vinegar, making sure that the natural slime was kept intact. The trout was then delivered to the fish section, often still flapping about, where it would be poached within seconds of being killed and would turn blue, hence the name. Trout cooked in this way is impossible to fake.

The cheese and fruit rooms were originally separate entities, but were combined during my time in the larder. It's a real skill keeping cheese in prime condition. Then there was the hors d'oeuvres section, which was run by Lina, from Switzerland, the only female in the whole kitchen at that time. Looking after an hors d'oeuvres section properly has become something of a lost art, the whole idea of hors d'oeuvres, so fashionable in the sixties and seventies, having long since fallen out of favour in most restaurants. No doubt, however, some chef will resurrect the old hors d'oeuvres trolley sometime in the future and claim it all as his or her own work. Just like everything else, what goes around comes around.

Caviar was kept in a special locked fridge situated in one of the cold-rooms and was served to each of the restaurants within the hotel as required, and sometimes directly to the suites and bedrooms. In the latter case, this involved a ritual that was open to a little bit of surreptitious sampling at the customer's expense. The order would come down from one of the floor waiters in the hotel and the senior sous chef on duty at the time would come down to the larder and unlock the caviar safe. The appropriate caviar (Beluga, Sevruga or Oscietre) would then be handed to me to be placed in the socle in which it was to be served. More often than not, the socle would be in the shape of a swan, carved out of a huge chunk of ice, with a space on the back, between the wings, into which the largest 1.8kg tin of caviar would fit neatly.

Once it had been weighed, I would treat myself to a little fingerfull before handing it to the floor waiter, who would then deliver it, on a beautiful custom-made trolley, to the customer up in the suite or bedroom. The floor waiter may well have had a little taste somewhere on the way up in the service lift and I certainly used to have a bit more sometime later when it was returned to me in the larder. I would then call the sous chef and weigh what was left in order to calculate what the customer would have to pay. The returned weight would then be carefully logged into the caviar book and signed by the sous chef. It is largely as a result of my time in the larder section that caviar is my favourite food in the whole world, although, sadly, I don't get to sample it so much these days. I always felt a bit cheated when the tin – that would have cost many thousands of pounds in those days – came back empty, as it often did. The number of times the swan-shaped ice socle was in and out of the freezer would determine how long it lasted. Carving a socle was a very specialist job and although I did have a go on a couple of occasions, my swan always ended up looking more like a giraffe, or the Starship Enterprise coming in to land.

Apart from the occasional illicit perk of a mouthful of caviar, I never had my hand in the fridge, so to speak, as I was far too scared of getting caught. Others at the Dorchester were not so honest. As I mentioned earlier, a lot of so-called 'shopping' went on, hence the tight security measures. The security officers at the Dorchester were mostly retired policemen, who were positioned at the rear staff entrance of the hotel, near the loading bay, and were entitled to conduct random searches on anyone they thought might be trying to smuggle something out. Many of the employees devised devious ways to get their booty past the guards and one of the most ingenious in this respect was a Scottish mate of mine who is now a captain of industry, so I'd better not use his real name. Let's just call him Donald

Donald's wife worked locally and would pop down the ramp into the loading bay when she finished work at around six in the evening, ostensibly to have a quick chat with her husband on her way home, but actually to meet him for the handover. Just prior to the pre-arranged rendezvous time Donald would nip into the toilet with a chicken that he had pinched out of the cold room and would conceal it under his chef's tall white hat. The back end of the bird had to be firmly pressed on to his skull and the legs appropriately arranged for stability. The deportment required as he then walked along the corridor to the exit was considerable – any catwalk supermodel would have been very proud of him. Even more skill and elegance was required as he ascended the stairs and turned left at the top before walking past the guard, pausing to ask in his broad Scottish brogue: "OK if I have a quick chat with the missus, Jimmy?" He called everyone 'Jimmy'. Having got the nod, he would then exit through the swing door into the loading bay where his wife would be waiting, holding her shopping bag wide open as Donald doffed his hat, allowing gravity to do the rest.

This plan worked a treat for several years until one day when, after consuming two or three more beers than was wise, Donald rounded the corner at the summit of the stairs and caught his toe on the top step. He took a dive and the chicken briefly flew once more before slowly rolling to a halt in front of the security guard. With considerable presence of mind, Donald rose from his tumble, turned to the empty staircase and shouted in his most menacing Glasgow accent: "Which one of you c**** threw that f****** chicken at me?"

Donald also perfected the art of suspending a side of smoked salmon from an "S" shaped butchers hook that he attached to the waistband of his underpants, so that it dangled down his inside leg. Again, the skill here was to be able to walk past the guards without adopting a rather unnatural gait, but Donald somehow managed it. I often wondered whether those who ate the contraband were informed about the manner in which it had been acquired – and transported!

Although I did miss my little caviar perk, I was very happy when the time came to move on to the butchery section. I loved my time in the larder there and consider myself very fortunate to have learned my trade at a time when it was part of a chef's education and training to be able to break down a carcass of lamb, pork or even a hindquarter of beef. I try very hard not to knock young chefs these days, because in many ways they are every bit as good, and in someways much better, than we were. But it is fair to say that they are often useless at butchery. Now that accountants run kitchens, most meat comes portion-controlled and all ready for the pan or oven. There are exceptions, of course, but generally butchery is a lost art as far as most young chefs are concerned.

Among my less memorable exploits on the butchery section was when one of the sous chefs, Maurice Bozzinni, caught me larking around with the lads on the butcher's block, sitting astride a large saddle of venison with a white table cloth wrapped around my head and a huge cleaver in my hand, shouting: "On to Akbar". He didn't appreciate my Lawrence of Arabia impression, although I think that I might have got even more of a bollocking than I did had he not been surreptitiously enjoying the spectacle himself.

From Butchery I moved on next to the Roast, which was also a very enjoyable time for me. For a start, I was back in the warmth of the main kitchen. That the move also happened to coincide with the game season was more by luck than judgement. I learned about woodcock, grouse, snipe, partridge, quail, pheasant, teal, widgeon, pintails, mallard, capons, geese, turkeys and Aylesbury and Rouen ducks. The fact that I was familiar with most of these birds from my childhood and could talk at some length about each one gave the senior chefs on the section the impression that I knew everything about them, which was mostly true. The one thing I didn't know was how to cook them. As a result of my ornithological knowledge the Chef de Partie spent more time with me than with any other commis on the section and I benefitted enormously from that extra attention.

As well as the feathered variety there was also furred game, of course, and because of my country bumpkin upbringing it was no hardship for me to skin a hare or wild rabbit – although I do remember being quite shocked when confronted for the first time with one of the commercially reared white rabbits. I learned about the different sorts of venison, such as roe and red deer, and also acquired the considerable expertise involved in roasting large joints – barons, fore ribs, wing ribs, whole sirloins and fillets of beef, plus equivalent cuts of pork, lamb and veal.

The roast section also included the art of grilling, which is not quite such a simple process as most people think, their idea of a grill being what you normally have in your kitchen at home, where the heat comes from above. Well, no – that's a salamander; a grill is where the heat comes from underneath, as in a barbecue. The two processes are entirely different and the results are nowhere near the same.

Understanding meat is also very important. Supermarkets have a lot to answer for when it comes to ruining the art of butchery. Butchery is not only about cutting meat up, it is also about hanging it. What you need is fish that's fresh and meat that isn't, but try telling that to a supermarket 'butcher' as he hands you a lamb chop from an animal that was killed just three days earlier. Most of them are not real butchers, at all – they're mad axe murderers, who've been given a minimal bit of supermarket training! One notable exception is Graham, at Tesco's Whitstable branch.

I felt that I was beginning to be noticed by the Dorchester's Head Chef, Mr. Kaufeler, because he had started talking to me on a comparatively regular basis, something he had not done before. He would usually arrive around 9.00am every morning and would then go directly into the washing-up area, where he would first greet and shake the hand of the kitchen's chief washer-up – or plongeur, to use the proper term – a massive Italian named Mario. Despite the apparently menial nature of the task, a plongeur plays a vital role in the smooth running of any large kitchen. Mario, whose brother happened to be Head Banqueting Manager at the Grosvenor House Hotel, just up the road along Park Lane, commanded enormous respect, and you didn't mess with him. The only words I ever heard him utter, other that when he was talking to the Head Chef, were: "Pud 'em in 'ere" – referring to the enormous copper cooking pans that he would want placed in his huge sink and which he would then spend all day cleaning. In the whole of my life, I don't think I've ever seen anyone work harder than that man. Only after talking to Mario would Mr. Kaufeler then go to shake hands with the early shift chefs de partie, such was Mario's stature in the kitchen hierarchy.

The kitchen porters were also incredibly hard working, and generally came from Poland or Pakistan. The only English that the Poles could speak was: "Brum Brum, Mister". This presumably derived from "Broom Broom, Mister" and meant: "Get out of the way while I sweep and mop your section." The Pakistanis, in particular, were very badly treated by some of the not so bright young British boys in the kitchen, who were guilty of casual racist abuse.

I had a dusky girlfriend from Singapore at the time and was often on the receiving end of racial prejudice when we were out and about together, so I had a certain amount of sympathy for the Pakistanis. Although there was a staff canteen for everyone working in the hotel apart from management, they chose to prepare their own meals and would eat them in the potato room. When I was working in the larder of the fish section I would give them salmon heads, with which they used to make the most delicious curry. After I left the section they still continued to get given the heads and would always invite me to share their meal. It was only later in life that I came to realise that these guys were only working in such menial jobs in order to support their families back in Poland and Pakistan. Many of them were educated men and, looking back, I like to think that by treating them with respect I maybe helped to make up a little for the disrespect shown by some of my peers.

One day, Mr. Kaufeler invited me into his office and for a moment I was anxious, wondering what I'd done wrong. So it came as a pleasant surprise and boosted my confidence no end when he told me that I was making good progress and encouraged me to keep my head down and carry on working hard. Shortly after this I was invited to move to the sauce section, without having to arrange my own swap. The sauce and the fish sections were where every ambitious young chef wanted to get to, being without doubt the top two departments in the kitchen – so much so that even if a commis managed to arrange a swap into one or other of them, it wouldn't necessarily be sanctioned by Mr. Riddell. It was accepted that only the best and most promising commis in the kitchen were allowed on the Fish and the Sauce, and everyone had to respect the hierarchy of the kitchen.

My Chef de Partie on the Sauce was a lovely guy called Roy Raiman, with whom I got on extremely well. He was very good to me and spent a lot of time teaching me. I also made some great friends among the people I worked with on the section, including a couple of Scots, Robert Young and Robert Armour. The two of them were both passionate Rangers soccer fans and in 1971 Robert Armour took me up to Glasgow with a coachload of fellow fans from the London branch of the supporters' club to see Rangers play Celtic in the Scottish Cup Final at Hampden Park, in from of a crowd of 134,000. The match program is one of the most prized in my collection.

The night before the match we went around to Robert's house in Kilmarnock and his mother cooked haggis for us. It was fantastic. I've had it cooked by supposed professionals a few times since then, but it has never been as good as Mrs Armour's. The next morning I was taken out by Robert and a mate of his called Iain on a bit of a crawl around some of the city's Protestant pubs. I've never been a great beer drinker and after a couple of pints of 'heavy' I ordered a glass of white wine in order to pace my way through what was clearly going to be a hard day's drinking. On hearing my request the barman leaned over the bar, grabbed me by the lapels, lifted me clean off my feet and growled in a barely understandable Scottish brogue: "This is a man's shop, son". It was all very good-natured, though, and everyone had a good laugh at my expense. And those Glasgow meat pies! I still remember the taste of those fantastic meat pies.

We arrived at the ground with about an hour and a half to go before kick-off. Robert had bought each of us three cans of McEwen's Export to drink during the game, but as we were going through the turnstiles and into the ground we were searched for alcohol. It was only then that I realised that Robert was no longer carrying the bag containing the cans of beer and that Iain had disappeared somewhere. When I asked where he'd gone Robert just grinned, led me to a precise spot about fifteen yards along from the turnstiles and muttered: "Wait here and pay attention!" A few seconds later nine cans of beer came over the twelve-foot-high wall, one at a time at three-second intervals. We caught each one and stuffed them in our pockets. All this took place in full view of the stewards who had searched us just a minute or two earlier. And when I looked around, everyone else was doing the same thing. A few minutes later Iain re-joined us.

I won't even begin trying to explain the sectarian nature of the football in Glasgow. Let's just say that I have been to local derbies in Manchester, Newcastle and London and nowhere else comes close to Glasgow in terms of the vile, filthy language and the blasphemous religious chanting that I heard that day. As I think I mentioned earlier, I am not a religious man and not easily offended, but I have to confess that I was quite taken aback. And yet I have to say that if you take the time to learn a little about William of Orange and why the Catholics and Protestants hate each other so much, it helps to explain the level of tribal hostility. Some of the humour, if you can call it that, was surprisingly clever and if one detached oneself from taking sides and the prejudice of it all, it was hugely entertaining. The football match was pretty good, too. I have not been to an 'Old Firm' match since then, but I find it hard to imagine that in these more enlightened times the level of abuse could possibly be quite as violent as it was that day.

Visiting the fantastic Turnberry Hotel in 2015 for our annual Academy Golf Day, which is held there every September, I was introduced on the first tee to the starter, Peter McCloy, who, it turned out, was actually the Rangers goalkeeper on that memorable day back in 1971. He was from Girvan, a small town just down the road from Turnberry and, due to his exceptional height, his Glasgow Rangers nickname at the time was 'The Girvan Lighthouse'. He seemed to enjoy talking about the match and everything that happened all that time ago. As for the Turnberry Hotel itself, I'm afraid that I still find it impossible to refer to it as Trump Turnberry, which it became when the American President bought it in 2014.

I spent six months on the Sauce and enjoyed every minute of it so much that, to be perfectly honest, I didn't really want to move on. I had planned to complete a full year on that top section so that I could experience all four seasons and the various foods that came along at different times of the year. Things are very different now, but in those days, when the order came down to the kitchen, the appropriate items would be delivered from the larder and cooked to order on the sauce section. For a table of three, say, there might be a cote de veau, a tournedos of beef and a poussin. The accompanying sauce was generally made in the pan in which the item had been cooked, using base preparations, with appropriate accompaniments added to complete the dish.

Some of the garnishes would be sent from different sections – asparagus, for instance, from the vegetable section. The various components of each dish would be presented on suitable silver flats, polished copper dishes or cloches and would be taken upstairs and silver-served to the customers in the various restaurants; I don't recall anything being plated and served directly to a customer – everything would have been put onto the customer's plate by a waiter. That seems strange now.

There were also the daily specials. I don't know whether or not the Dorchester still does this, but at that time there used to be a variety of dishes, usually of a fairly traditional nature, that would appear on any given day. These were served to the customer in the restaurant from a silver domed trolley known as a voiture. There were the obvious items, such as roast sirloin of beef at Sunday lunchtime, along with some more unusual dishes, such as boiled leg of mutton with a caper sauce that used to be on offer on Thursdays and Scotch broth, which always featured on Wednesdays.

Now, from the kitchen management point of view this didn't make a great deal of sense, as if it was done the other way around the mutton stock from Wednesday could be used to make the Scotch broth for Thursday. But when the head chef eventually changed the two items around, a lot of regular customers complained bitterly, having timed their visit specially to sample these particular dishes, sometimes travelling from quite a distance. This was my first experience of learning not to mess with the expectations of customers, something that is always going to be risky.

The same thing has happened at Read's many times over the years, with dishes that have been on the menu a long time, sometimes from day one, being dropped from the menu and then having to be reinstated because of the resulting outcry. Examples have included soft herring milts on granary toast at lunchtimes and the mature Cheddar cheese soufflé on a bed of smoked haddock glazed in a creamed Parmesan sauce. You would be surprised how unpleasant people become if dishes like these are suddenly taken off the menu or changed in any way.

The mechanics of cooking have changed dramatically since those days and so has the way food is served. Consequently, the role of the waiter has changed virtually beyond all recognition. Most chefs I know have little or no knowledge of how a restaurant works on the other side of the hot plate and yet but for the skill, ability and understanding of the long-suffering waiter the system would simply break down and become totally unworkable. The so-called 'hot plate war' between chefs and waiters has existed for as long as I have been in the industry, but is probably not as vicious now as it once was. These days silver flats are not used in quite the same way as they were back in the silver service days, but many is the time I have seen a young kitchen commis place the waiter's side of the salver underneath the salamander, deliberately getting it so hot that the waiter's fingers would stick to it when he tried to pick it up. It was considered fair game and good for a laugh to try and play this painful trick on a waiter in this way.

Many of the prominent chefs I have encountered tend to be so totally focused on the food they produce that they care little about what happens once it leaves the kitchen. On the other hand, most waiters and restaurant managers I have worked with care deeply about the customer's experience. The combination of the two skills should make for a successful restaurant – one is certainly of little use without the other.

The problem, sadly, is not helped by the fact that in this country the perception of someone in service has always been very low, as if there were something demeaning about the job, and this shows no sign of changing. But the truth is that although dramatically different, the commitment, skills and knowledge required of a waiter or sommelier in a high-end restaurant are immense and equal in every respect to that of a chef. In the mind of an often not very bright young chef (and many older ones, too, I am sad to say) a waiter does not actually make or create anything; he simply delivers to the customer something that someone else has made – and how difficult can that be? Well, actually, it can be *extremely* difficult. As a chef who owns his own restaurant, I have sometimes had to help out front-of-house as well as in the kitchen, particularly in the early days when we were often short-staffed, and as a result I have a much better understanding of the difficulties a waiter encounters every day, and a greater appreciation of the skills required.

The totally dominant position that the modern-day chef adopts is both unfair and also detrimental to the overall image of our industry – and, especially, the future recruitment of top quality front-of-house staff. The rise of the celebrity chef over the last thirty or forty years is partly to blame. Up until then, customers in a top restaurant were far more likely to have known the name of the head waiter, the restaurant manager or the maitre d' than the chef. Maybe that's where the deep division between kitchen and dining room staff took root. I am not suggesting that, we should try to turn the clock back that far, but I do believe there should be a better balance between the two.

The legendary Silvano Giraldin, for many years the restaurant manager and now a director of Le Gavroche and the Roux empire, has fought tirelessly over the years, alongside Sergio Rebecci, Didier Garnier and John Cousins, to gain more recognition for waiters and sommeliers. Talking to him as I often do in my capacity as chairman of the MCA (Master of Culinary Arts) for all three disciplines of the Royal Academy – kitchen, pastry and service – I am slightly saddened to hear Silvano say that things have not improved significantly over recent years as far as service is concerned. In fact, he underestimates what his efforts have achieved in this respect, having been almost single handedly responsible for the inclusion of the service discipline under the heading of Les Arts de la Table back in 1985, setting an example that was followed a few years later by the highly esteemed Academie Culinaire de France.

I should add that it is not a good idea to incur the wrath of Silvano. Many is the time I have been to a function where the evening culminates in the well-known tradition of 'Sante du Chef' – raising a complimentary toast to the chef. I would advise anyone leading the tribute to be prepared for an extremely difficult time afterwards with Silvano if no mention is made of the service; and rightly so.

As I say, I was reluctant to move on from the Sauce, but Mr. Riddell suggested that it was about time I progressed to the Fish, so that was that. Geoff Hale was the Chef de Partie in that section and his first commis was a guy called Pat Grigsby. Although Pat and I had not worked together before, we knew each other well as members of the Dorchester's football team, which was in the second of the three divisions that made up the Catering Trades Football League. We played in the afternoons on the pitches alongside Rotten Row, in Hyde Park and, surprising though it may seem, the standard of football was actually very high, quite a few of the many foreign chefs, waiters, kitchen boys, hotel and restaurant staff included in the various teams having been professional or semi-professional players back in their home countries.

The best teams in the top division in those days were those from the Hilton, Grosvenor House and Oddeninos hotels. Some of the hotels used to take the football so seriously that the first question for junior kitchen staff at job interviews would not be about the level of their cooking experience, but how good they were at football and what position they played. They would then be invited to attend the next practice match or trial and their performance would determine whether or not they actually got the job. This did not happen at the Dorchester, however, which is one reason why we had only ever been in the second division of the league.

If you were a member of the Dorchester team you were automatically given time off to play. Eddie McIntyre, who played in goal for us – I had become a sweeper by this time – injured his leg really badly during a game one afternoon and reckoned he might have broken it, but because he had a rather unfair reputation for exaggeration, he was ordered to return to work that same evening by his Chef de Partie. He was in such pain that he couldn't even stand properly, so he was made to sit in the potato room and pick beans for the rest of his shift. It wasn't until we finished work and I took him down to St. George's Hospital, then situated nearby at Hyde Park Corner on the site of what is now the Lanesborough Hotel, that it was confirmed he had indeed broken his leg. I was fortunate enough to captain the international side that was made up of players from all the London hotel teams when we played our French counterparts from Paris in 1972. The annual match was usually played at Highbury, still very much the home of Arsenal in those days, but that year it moved to Crystal Palace for some reason. The English chefs tend to hate French chefs because of their pompous, supercilious attitude to English cooking and we took great delight in totally outplaying them and stuffing them 4 - 1, if you'll pardon yet another pun.

My enjoyment of what was undoubtedly one of the highlights of my sporting career was slightly spoiled by our manager telling me immediately after the game that as winning captain I would be expected to speak at the post-match dinner held at the Grosvenor House Hotel that evening, in front of an invited audience of 400 people, including the guest of honour, Sir Stanley Rous, the chairman of FIFA. I can't remember exactly what I mumbled – or, to be more honest, perhaps I should say that it was a performance I've actually chosen to forget.

It was while I was on the fish section that I eventually accepted the position as 1st Commis that Pat had vacated – but not before I had, quite rightly, been seriously reprimanded by Geoff Hale for taking my eye off the ball, so to speak, as a result of becoming so heavily involved, as captain, in running the Dorchester football team. We were at last on the brink of promotion to the top division for the first time ever and I was spending too much time on trying to ensure that we maintained our challenge. Geoff put me in the picture in no uncertain terms about where my priorities needed to be

Pat Grigsby and I had meanwhile become very good friends. He was a skilled craftsman and had a great sense of humour, but his Achilles' heel was that he drank a bit too much. There were no rules on drinking in that kitchen – how could there be when you were given beer for free. The problem was that when all the beer was gone Pat used to drink wine, and when that was gone he would drink some of the spirits that we were allocated to cook with. I must confess that in later life I sometimes reflect that I may have contributed to his alcoholic demise. Along with another good mate, John Hornsby, Pat and I used to run around to the locker room at the start of our 20-minute 'tea break', quickly get changed into our civvies, charge out of the back door, run up the ramp and sprint the 250 yards to The Red Lion at the back of the hotel in Duke of York Street. There, we would each down three pints of bitter before legging it back to the Dorchester, changing back into our whites and returning to our respective sections. Crazy! Why on earth did we do that? Young men can be so stupid!

It was at around this time that I had an unfortunate experience that I still blush to recall. I had finished my shift one night at 11.00pm and, after getting changed, went racing out of the hotel, intent on catching the number 36 bus down to Victoria. As I came dashing up the ramp at the back of the hotel and ran out into Deanery Street I crashed headlong into an elderly and rather distinguished looking gentleman, who was dressed immaculately in a dinner jacket, having obviously been to a function close by, maybe even at the Dorchester itself. I guessed he must have been about seventy years of age and he was with a beautiful, much younger lady in her mid-to-late twenties. As I bent to help him up off the pavement I was shocked to realise that the man I had just flattened was none other than David Niven, one of the greatest Hollywood film stars of his era.

The great man was most definitely not amused and cursed and swore at me, albeit in the most gentlemanly way. He called me a yob and a hooligan and I was genuinely distressed and upset by the episode, especially as he was so unforgiving towards me. I apologised profusely, of course, but to no avail. The only good thing that I could say about the episode was that he appeared not to be badly hurt in any way and we both went our separate ways. I always had a very strange feeling whenever I saw David Niven in a film after that.

Some years later I was to let Pat Grigsby down very badly. Shortly after I won the Chef of The Year title in 1986 I was asked to do a tour of the USA, promoting British food and cooking. I was allowed to take someone with me to help with the television appearances, restaurant guest spots and demonstration work that the tour itinerary entailed, and although Pat was the obvious choice I was worried about taking him because of his drinking. Instead, I offered the gig to Colin Stone, who was then teaching professional cookery at Westminster College, after a career in the kitchens at Claridge's. Colin was brilliant, but I should really have taken Pat. We hardly spoke after that. Pat died a few years ago and just talking about the way I snubbed him still makes me feel guilty.

I found it quite difficult making the transition to 1st Commis because it meant that one day I was laughing and joking as one of the lads and the next day I found myself having to give orders to the six fellow commis who had been, and indeed still were, my mates. There is a great skill involved in getting people to do things in an authoritative way while at the same time remaining on friendly terms with them and it takes time to learn it. I have often heard females complaining that people won't listen to them just because they are girls, but I think it can be the same for guys in some situations. It's all about respect and you just have to learn how to gain it. I have always respected females in the workplace if they are good at their jobs, just as I have not respected males if they are not.

Following my stint in the fish section I was promoted to Tournant, the title given to whoever takes over the running of a section on the Chef de Partie's day off. It's a tough job, because not every Chef de Partie would be conscientious when it came to mise en place – the French culinary phrase that literally translates as 'everything in its place' and which refers mainly to the vital prepping, well in advance, of certain components of various dishes – so that sometimes you would come in to find yourself hopelessly behind schedule before you'd even started, struggling to sort out everything that had been left undone.

Probably the most enjoyable time I spent at the Dorchester was when I was on Night Guard. As the name implies, you would find yourself there on your own, sometimes until the breakfast chef came in just before 5.00am, cooking for any resident hotel guest who might order from room service. Incidentally, the breakfast chef was called Bev; I can't now remember his surname but he was like a sports statistician whose encyclopedic knowledge of football and football stadiums, even those in the lower divisions, was immense.

A Night Guard obviously had to be someone who was familiar with every section of the kitchen, knew where everything was and could work alone. Occasionally, if things were busy for some reason, it could be quite demanding to be left on one's own to do everything, but to be perfectly honest, it was generally quite easy. Elizabeth Taylor and Richard Burton, who were undoubtedly the two most famous people in the world at the time, used the Penthouse Suite at the Dorchester as their London home. They would often arrive back very late at night, sometimes individually, sometimes together and occasionally with other people, and every now and again they would want something to eat. But as was also the case with Peter Sellers, another big name for whom I regularly cooked late at night or in the early hours, I never actually got to meet them. Probably just as well – I wouldn't have known what to say to them.

My mother used to think it was quite romantic for me to be cooking for such famous people. I remember one occasion when, at about two-thirty in the morning, King Hussein of Jordan arrived in the hotel and wanted to eat. I cooked for him several times and whatever he ordered he would always want loads of fresh leaf spinach with it. On this particular occasion I was busy cooking away when I suddenly became of someone standing in a corner of the kitchen, watching me intently. I was a bit startled, as I would normally expect only the floor waiter to be there, and he wouldn't have been standing in that exact spot. This was a foreign-looking gentleman, very smartly dressed in a silvery grey suit, and for a moment, unsure about who it could be but suspecting that he must be something to do with the royal entourage, I panicked slightly and executed a bow of sorts – more of a curtsy, really! – just in case. I later found out he was the king's bodyguard-cum-taster, there to keep an eye on what was going on, at which point I felt rather foolish.

During the early hours, usually when everything had died down, an immaculately dressed floor waiter named Jimmy, probably in his late twenties or early thirties, would appear. I would know immediately now that he was gay, but still being a relatively naïve Shrewsbury lad at that time, such things were a mystery to me. We had a couple of 'close encounters', at the end of which I learned that he was gay and he learned that I wasn't.

Although it's very common these days for a gay guy and a straight guy to be friends, back then it was more unusual because of the prejudice that prevailed at the time. Nevertheless, Jimmy and I became good friends and he would come down into the kitchen around 1.30am for his staff meal and ask: "What have you got for me tonight, Chef?"

This was in the days before the accountants started to keep a beady eye on the kitchens and checks on exactly what went out of the larders were not quite so stringent, so we would chat about what I thought would be really good to try. He was a true gourmet, very keen on the seasonal dishes, and would want to know if there was anything particularly interesting on offer. He might express a fancy for the first of the new season English asparagus or spring morels, or maybe the first of the wild sea trout or partridge, depending on what time of year it was.

I would prepare whatever he chose and when he returned at an allotted time he would bring with him a half bottle of wine. Sometimes it was an unopened half bottle of red or white, sometimes a half-consumed bottle of something left by a customer – even, occasionally, a quarter of a magnum. But, whatever it was, it would always be something fairly exceptional. Moreover, It would always be an appropriate accompaniment for whatever dish he had chosen and with it he would also bring the correct glass to drink it from. I learned a lot about wine from Jimmy and started to read up about it, something that would stand me in good stead in later years. In fact, virtually everything that I was doing at that time was to prove hugely useful for my future role as a chef/proprietor.

Once Jimmy had eaten, and if there was nothing else pressing that needed to be done, I would retire to the potato room to eat my own supper. I always prepared two portions of whatever Jimmy had requested, one for him and one for me. It was a great joy to be left alone to enjoy the food and well-chosen wine together, maybe a Poo-lig-knee Mon-tra-shet or a Do-croo Boo-cal-ooh, as I used to pronounce them back then.

Meanwhile, I was coming to the end of a three-year advanced cookery course at Ealing Hotel School, which I had been attending each week on my day off, having realised as soon as I started at the Dorchester and found myself surrounded by so many talented and ambitious young chefs that in order to keep up with them I needed to learn a lot more about advanced culinary principles and techniques; the practical experience gained through the everyday slog of working in the Dorchester's kitchens was not, by itself, going to be enough. Sometimes I would not be confident about what I was going to be cooking at college the following week, so I would turn the tables on Jimmy and explain that I really needed to practice, say, a Lobster Newburg – would that be OK? Of course, it always was.

Head of Ealing Hotel School in those days was Victor Ceserani, who lived on to the ripe old age of ninety-seven and who was one of the most respected people in the industry at that time. He had written a book with Ronnie Kinton called Practical Cookery, which was used as the culinary bible by every decent catering college in the country. Although it was aimed at young students making their way in the world, I have to say that I still use some of the recipes to this day. Unusually for a cookery book, all the recipes actually work.

Among the staff at Ealing was a professional cookery lecturer called Brian Price. He was a quietly-spoken, thoughtful man and he became my mentor. The advanced course lasted three years and included the study of the chef's three key culinary disciplines – pastry, larder and kitchen. Brian taught me kitchen throughout the three years. Any chef knows that, contrary to popular belief, actual perfection is impossible to achieve in our profession, but Brian used to insist that just because it was impossible to achieve didn't mean you shouldn't try.

Everyone in that particular class was a top-notch craftsman, having come from some of the very best hotels and restaurants in London at the time. Brian told me some years later that it was the best class he had ever had in nearly forty years of teaching. And as I myself was soon to discover, in order to teach people of that calibre you have to be at the very top of your game. Towards the end of the three-year course I remember that we were all preparing a turbotin, or small turbot. It had to be tunnel boned in order that the fish retained its shape. The cavity was then filled with a mousseline of Dover sole and poached whole in a white wine fish stock. It is extremely difficult to get the mousseline and the thicker parts of the turbot perfectly cooked whilst not overcooking the thinner parts of the fish. It then had to be glazed with a Bercy sauce in an earthenware dish and served on a silver flat, with an oval dish paper separating the flat from the earthenware. Because he had intentionally filled us with the confidence that only youth can have, Brian challenged us to present him with the perfect turbotin dish. And he promised that if anyone managed it, he would take us over to the pub across the road and buy us all a drink after the class had ended.

My turn came to present my dish. He always talked each student through every aspect of the dish they had cooked, its presentation and saucing. He waxed lyrical about my offering, saying that he could get emotional just looking at it. I was convinced I'd finally got him, that I'd achieved the elusive perfection, only for him to fail me for having my dish paper upside down!

Knowing Brian and respecting him the way I did started me thinking that maybe teaching professional cookery in further education might be the job for me, too. A teaching vacancy came up at Ealing at the end of the course and Brian recommended me to apply for it. I made an appointment to see Mr. Ceserani to talk it over and he made it clear to me that if I really wanted to succeed long term in cookery education then I would need to go to teacher training college. I managed to persuade myself that I didn't want to work every evening, weekend, bank holiday and Christmas Day any more, which, as a chef, was exactly what I would have to do for the rest of my working life. I wanted a comparatively conventional job with evenings and weekends off, the same as everyone else – or so I thought at the time. So I went ahead and applied to the teacher training college at Roehampton and succeeded in gaining a place to start the one-year London University degree course known as a Cert. Ed. in September of 1973.

When I handed in my notice at the Dorchester, Mr. Kaufeler called me into his office and told me how disappointed he was that I was leaving, a feeling that I myself have since experienced on many occasions during my time as a restaurant chef/patron when I have lost a promising member of the kitchen staff. He said that although I might enjoy the freedom of teaching for a while, he was of the opinion that, ultimately, I would only be fulfilled by working as a chef; and in the end, of course, he turned out to be absolutely right. Despite the reservations he expressed about the path I had chosen to take, I made the necessary preparations to go to Roehampton, but even as I did so, there was something about it deep down that didn't seem quite right, a niggling doubt in my mind. Was I a chef, or was I a teacher?

4 : When David Met Rona

When I started at teacher training college I was living at Forest Hill in South London and still mostly getting around on my bike, just as I had in Shrewsbury on my 'Centurion Tank'. It was twelve miles, door-to-door, from Forest Hill to the college in Roehampton and although that wasn't much fun when it was wet, it was actually easier and less time-consuming than going by public transport.

Arriving on the first day of term, I was directed to the Common Room for a coffee and a chat before going into a lecture theatre for an explanation of how the course would work. It felt a bit like going back to school. There in the Common Room, slightly to my surprise, I immediately bumped into two Dorchester kitchen boys, Richard Martland and Laurie Mills, who, unknown to me, had both come to the same conclusion as I had about their future careers. I didn't know either of them particularly well as they had been on the opposite shift to me at the Dorchester. But I knew from their reputation that they were both good cooks.

There were about four hundred people on the course that year, but only six or seven of us were intending to teach professional cookery. I was standing in the Common Room chatting to Dick and Laurie when, just as I was taking a last sip of coffee, I noticed, over the rim of my cup, a particularly attractive girl sitting on the diagonally opposite side of the room, just about as far away from me as it was possible for her to be. Working on the assumption that faint heart never won fair maiden, I left Laurie and Dick standing where they were and made my way towards her, just as the announcement was being made for us all to move in to the lecture theatre. I followed her into the next room and politely muscled at least one guy out of the way in order to be able to sit next to her.

I introduced myself as 'Blue', the nickname by which I had become known to everybody at the Dorchester, and found out that she was named Rona – Rona Caroline North, as I discovered later. We chatted for a few minutes while waiting for the briefing to begin and, despite the fact that I had been in a relationship with a Singaporean girl for five years and had had no particular inclination to change up until that moment, I was instantly besotted. Even so, I could never have imagined at that first meeting that she was destined to become the most important person I would ever meet in my life.

During the briefing we were informed that at the end of the first week we would be asked to choose which two subjects, from a choice of four, we wanted to specialise in, the options being educational psychology, educational sociology, the philosophy of education and the history of education. Having registered my choices on the Friday, I went back in on Monday morning to check what Rona had chosen. By then everybody had been allocated their respective groups and classes and, to my horror, I found that Rona had opted for the opposite two subjects to me. I went straight to Ronnie Kinton, the course lecturer, and told him that there had been a misunderstanding and they had got my requests wrong. I explained that the subjects which I had marked with a cross were the ones that I did NOT want to do. Luckily, he believed me and allowed me to change, so I was now in every class that Rona was in. All that was left for me to do was to persuade her that she liked me as much as I liked her.

One of the guys that I'd barged out of the way as we were going into the lecture theatre on that first day was from Cornwall and he seemed to have stolen a march on me when, within two weeks, he invited Rona down to the West Country for the weekend. I would later discover that Rona had spent many childhood holidays down in Cornwall and was quite tempted. Fortunately for me, however, she couldn't go because she had already arranged to visit her parents at home in Kent that weekend. Or, at least, that is what she told my rival.

Quickly realising that I was up against some serious competition for Rona's affections, I decided that I needed to make my move sooner rather than later and straightaway left a little 'Smiley Face' card in her pigeon hole, asking her to go out with me the next weekend, making sure that it would be waiting for her first thing on the Monday morning when she returned to college after seeing her parents. That morning I waited anxiously for her reply and was delighted when she said yes to my invitation.

We arranged to meet at five o'clock the following Friday, an hour after classes finished. She turned up looking even better than usual, dressed in one of those Afghan coats that were so popular in the sixties and early seventies. As I found out later, after we got caught in the rain, those coats smelled a bit like a wet dog when they got damp. But being on Cloud Seven by then, I found even that rather attractive!

I had thought long and hard during the week about where I would take her to ensure that the first date was a success. I changed my mind several times but finally decided that it had to be a big night out in the West End, with a theatre show followed by dinner. I booked seats for *Godspell*, the hit musical starring David Essex, Julie Covington and a young Jeremy Irons.

The slightly awkward problem I still faced concerned suitable transport. I didn't have a car, just my pushbike, whereas Rona actually had her own little Citroen 2CV. I decided I would have to swallow my male pride, suggesting that if she didn't fancy going by public transport then it would have to be a choice between riding the crossbar on my bike or going in her car. Not surprisingly, she offered to drive.

We arrived in the West End a little early for the show, which was on at Wyndham's Theatre, just off Leicester Square, so we went to a pub just around the corner while we waited, completing the Evening Standard crossword together. *Godspell* was great – an inspired choice, even if I do say so myself – and Rona genuinely enjoyed it.

Afterwards, we settled for a pizza and a bottle of wine in a little Italian restaurant opposite the theatre, going on from there to the Vauxhall Tavern, just south of the river. In those days this was a very busy, fashionable pub, famed for its drag shows featuring transvestites who paraded up and down the bar in all their finery, singing and telling highly risque jokes – a bit like a Cockney Lily Savages, only better. It might sound weird now, but it was wonderfully entertaining and great fun at the time.

By now it was about 11.30pm and I didn't want the evening to end, so I suggested that we could maybe go and catch the *Midnight Movie*. Rona seemed to think that this was a good idea, but then, as I was directing her towards the Camberwell Green area from Vauxhall, she began to look rather puzzled and asked which cinema we were going to. At that point I had to explain that what I had in mind was watching the regular Friday night *Midnight Movie* on TV, back at my place! There was an awkward silence for a moment – the first of the evening – and I said I would quite understand if she wanted to change her mind. She replied that, no, that would be fine – and that, actually, she would like to see where I lived.

The movie turned out to be rubbish and we soon gave up on it, instead spending the next few hours talking endlessly, getting to know each other's past history and what had led us both to Roehampton. I learned that Rona's family background was very different from mine. She and her brother, Alan, had grown up as part of a very close family, living first in Gravesend, where her father, Bert North, an electrician by trade, had started his own electrical contracting business after the war, before also opening up a high street shop that was run by his wife, Eva, and then moving with the family to Teynham, between Sittingbourne and Faversham.

Having marginally failed the 11+ (as a lot of the best people did!) Rona started her secondary education at Collyer Road Secondary Modern School in Sittingbourne, but after a year her parents, not happy with the progress she was making there, decided to move her out of state education and into the Convent of the Nativity convent school. The Mother Superior ruled the school with a rod of iron and explained to Rona's parents that if she were to be accepted as a pupil then extra elocution lessons would be essential in order to tone down her strong local Kentish accent. Having complied with this rather unlikely requirement, Rona went on to do well at the school and towards the end of her four years there made up her mind that she wanted to pursue a career in the hospitality industry and applied to join the Hotel and Institutional Management Course at Thanet College in Broadstairs.

She then got an early insight into some of the joys that awaited her in her chosen career when, during her final summer holiday, she got a job as a silver service waitress in the restaurant at Riceman's, the up-market department store in Canterbury. On her first day there she went into the kitchen to inform the chef that the people on Table 4 were ready for their main course. When the order was not immediately forthcoming she repeated the request, to which the chef responded by telling her that if she said another single word to him he would "shove this f****** frying pan right down your throat", which came as something of a rude shock to a 15-year-old convent schoolgirl.

She went on to achieve good passes in all the eight 'O' levels she sat, so it was a great disappointment to the Mother Superior and all the nuns at the convent when she decided not to stay and do 'A' levels, especially when she announced that she had opted instead for a career in catering, which they clearly looked down upon as a rather unfortunate choice. However, she was welcomed very positively as a boarding student at what was the first HCIMA course to be offered at Thanet, where the senior lecturer, Peter Barrett, was to become a major influence in her life.

Rona sailed through the two-year course, becoming one of the stars of the group before leaving to take up a position on a management training scheme run by the in-house catering department at what was BP's head office at the time in Moorgate, in what was the first skyscraper in the City of London to exceed the height of St Paul's. Training was thorough but slow, to the extent that after a month she had got no further than qualifying to act as head tea lady. Feeling that progress was a little bit too slow, she did not complete the course, leaving to join Lloyds Bank at Canon Street, firstly as assistant catering manager before moving to the directors' dining section at Threadneadle Street as catering manager. After two years with Lloyds she moved to the Thomas Delarue School in Tonbridge, where she was employed as housekeeper-cum-caterer.

Run by what was then known as The National Spastic Society, but which later changed its name to Scope, the school cared for about 120 permanently residential students, ranging in age from seven to sixteen, all of whom suffered from cerebral palsy and were in need of constant attention and physiotherapy. The job involved Rona, too, in being resident on site and she loved her time here, making many good friends and becoming very emotionally involved with the work. The school closed for six weeks in the summer each year, and wherever possible the resident youngsters would return home during that time; those who couldn't go home for any reason would be sent to a suitable alternative establishment where the same appropriate care could be provided.

During this six-week break at the end of her first year there, Rona and Carol, her lifelong best friend, drove to Greece in Rona's little Citroen 2 CV. They boarded the ferry in Dover and crossed to Dunkirk before driving from there to Brussels. They then motored on to Germany, where they met up with a golf pro whom Rona had befriended during a family holiday with her parents at the Atalaya Park Golf complex in Spain the previous year. They spent a few days with him, cruising on the Rhine and visiting the vineyards, and then continued on through Germany and into Austria, either staying along the way in modest hotels or camping in the tent they had taken with them.

In Austria they stopped off in Salzburg and then went on to Lubyana in what was then still Yugoslavia, now Slovenia, heading on from there to the Adriatic coast where they spent a couple of relaxing days before attempting the long drive along the winding Yugoslavia coast road to Dubrovnik in order to make the ferry crossing from there to northern Greece. They got as far as Split, at which point the temperature started to soar and the terrain became winding and repetitive, like a lunar landscape. At this point the two girls got talking to a guy who told them it would be madness to try and drive all that way in the searing heat, suggesting instead that they should take what was a rather makeshift ferry from Split down to Dubrovnik. They still vividly remember watching nervously as the boatman placed two railway sleepers under the car, with ropes attached to form a cradle, before precariously winching the 2CV on board with a small crane. However, the change of plan proved to be a wise decision, because although the ferry voyage took a whole day, it was still quicker and a lot less tiring than driving would have been.

While on board they got chatting to a guy from Chicago who invited them to stay with him on a trip to the USA that they were already planning for the following year. Having eventually arrived safely in Greece, they spent a few days travelling down the coast to Athens, then took another ferry to Corfu, where they again spent a couple of days before moving on to Brindisi in Italy. From there, they drove across the country to Rome, where they stayed for two nights as guests of the parents of one of the disabled youngsters from the Thomas Delarue School, who had come home for the summer accompanied by one of the house mothers from the school.

They then set off on the long journey home, going via Florence into the south of France and then right across northern Spain from Barcelona to Bilbao, where they boarded the final ferry back to Dover. Altogether, they had driven over 4,000 miles in the little Citroen 2CV, not including the ferry journeys. This was all at a time when travelling through Europe by car, particularly in the Communist countries, was nowhere near as easy as it is now; and yet the two girls planned and executed the whole thing themselves, without any help from travel companies or agencies.

Rona has an incredible steely determination to succeed in everything that she attempts – something that I see every day at work. Many years later, following her mother's death, she and her brother decided to climb Kilimanjaro together to raise funds for research into motor neurone disease, from which Eva had suffered towards the end of her life. Within striking distance of the summit, Rona started to suffer badly from altitude sickness and severe, blinding headaches and was advised by her guide not to go on. She and Alan decided that at least one of them should make it to the top, having got so close, so Alan continued on with his guide. Having reached the summit, he spent twenty minutes there, watching the sunrise and saying a prayer for his mother. But then, on the way down, he was astonished to see Rona continuing her climb, having refused to give up. The two of them were too exhausted to speak to each other as they crossed, but just touched hands and trudged on in opposite directions. It took Rona over an hour to cover the final 100 metres, but she did eventually make it to the top, which came as no surprise to me, knowing her as I do.

The final part of her story, leading up to the moment our paths crossed at the college in Roehampton in 1973, involved the trip to Chicago that she and Carol did indeed make after she had completed her two years' employment at Thomas Delarue. The two of them tracked down the guy they had met on the ferry from Split to Dubrovnic and stayed with him for a couple of days while looking around for employment in the USA, something they wouldn't be able to do quite so easily today.

They each ended up getting jobs as nannies, Carol with a wealthy Jewish couple and their three children and Rona with Corky and Nancy Rich, who had a Honda and Suzuki dealership selling motorbikes and snowmobiles and who were well on the way to becoming wealthy themselves. Nancy already had one child, Amy, and was pregnant with her second, who was to become Heather. Heather was actually born in the car on the way to the hospital and on her passport her place of birth is listed as Kennedy Freeway, Chicago. Nancy and Corky went on to have two more children, Ryan and Christopher, as well as later adopting a further two. Rona worked for the family for over six months, during which time she enjoyed a number of great experiences, including seeing Elvis perform live in Las Vegas. She and the Riches have remained in touch to this day, and we have visited each other here and in Chicago.

Corky and Nancy were keen for Rona to stay in the US indefinitely and she might well have done so but for a promise that Carol had made to her parents that she would return for her grandparents' 50th wedding anniversary. Rona felt that she couldn't desert her friend and the two of them returned together. Back in England, Rona applied to Leeds University to do a home economics teaching course, but at the last minute she happened to visit Peter Barrett, her old college lecturer from Broadstairs, who persuaded her to apply to Roehampton to do the teacher training course there instead. Thankfully, from my point of view, she took his advice.

Having virtually swapped our entire life stories at the end of that first date, talking long into the early hours of the morning, we eventually just flopped down on top of the bed and fell sleep. The next morning I was awake before Rona and just lay there quietly, looking at her sleeping. I couldn't believe my luck. When she finally woke up we had a coffee and I explained that I was supposed to be playing football later that day for the local team with whom I had become a regular, adding that I would be happy to call in and say I was unwell and unable to play if she would like the two of us to do something else together. I fully expected her to go back to the college at Roehampton, where she had a room in the student hall of residence, instead of which she chose to come along and watch the football. I usually went for a couple of beers with the rest of the lads after the game, and although I would have been more than ready to give it a miss on this occasion she insisted that I should carry on and do whatever I normally did, adding that she would be happy to tag along.

What happened next was very, very strange indeed. As we left the pub to go back to my flat we passed the local bookies and as I happened to know there was a horse I fancied running at Kempton Park I suggested that we pop in and place a bet. I don't think that Rona had ever been into a betting shop before. I could easily imagine her at Ascot, but not at the Forest Hill branch of Ladbrokes! I placed an each-way bet at odds of 100 to 6 that you don't see any more, but which equated to about 16 to 1. We got back to my flat and switched on the TV just in time to see the start of the race.

Sadly, despite being in contention all the way round, our horse just failed by a nose to get in the frame, finishing fourth. Rona asked if that was any good and I had to explain that unfortunately it was not – unless one of the first three horses was to be disqualified. As I then went on to explain exactly how an each way bet worked, it was announced over the Tannoy at the racecourse that there was to be a Stewards Enquiry. And no sooner had I finished explaining to Rona what that meant than a further announcement came that as a result of the enquiry the first three horses past the post had all been disqualified and our fourth-placed horse had been declared the winner. An extraordinary, quite unbelievable stroke of luck! We skipped back down to the betting shop, giggling all the way, and collected just over £60, a tidy sum back then.

Someone on the teaching course was holding a party that Saturday evening and Rona had been invited, so we decided that we would go along together. But before that, owing to the lack of sleep the night before, we decided to go back to my flat for a nap. Again, I woke before she did and, just as I had done earlier, lay there for a while, simply staring at her with the most tremendous feeling of elation.

I had a quick bath and got changed for the party and we drove back over to the college so that Rona could do the same. The block where she lived was exclusively female and there were strict rules about visiting males, but there didn't appear to be anyone around, so she was able to smuggle me in. We got to the party around about 10.30pm, had a few drinks and just talked the whole time. I think there may have been one dance, but I can't really remember. I do remember that 'Cornwall Man' was at the party, but apart from saying hello, that was it. I don't think he asked Rona out again – if he did, she didn't tell me.

We got back to her residential block somewhere between three and four in the morning. As we approached it, I could see that my bike was still where I had left it on the Friday, when Rona had driven us into the West End, and I remember thinking that I almost wished that someone had stolen it so that I wouldn't have to cycle back to Forest Hill. Thankfully, Rona didn't make me go home and sneaked me into her room. For me it had been pretty much the perfect weekend; we had spent every second of it together and I didn't want to do anything to spoil it.

That perfect weekend was followed soon afterwards by a very painful one, when I suffered the complete opposite of the euphoria I had experienced over those first few dates with Rona. It didn't take us very long to decide that we wanted to stick together and that meant I had to sort things out with my Singaporean girlfriend. I don't think it is appropriate to explain in any detail how I went about the unhappy task of breaking the news that I had met someone else and that our relationship was over, but suffice it to say that I made a complete and utter mess of it. I wish I could go back and change that day, but I can't. Sorry, La.

Rona and I weren't exactly flush with money during that year at college and so, through the Dorchester, I arranged to do regular part time work on Sundays for a Jewish caterer named Joe Oberlander. In those days the Dorchester used to cater for a lot of Jewish weddings and Bar Mitzvahs, under the jurisdiction of the London Beth Din, always on a Sunday. And although I used to go and help out mainly for the much-needed extra money, it also provided an opportunity for me to learn another culinary discipline; because if you worked in a Jewish kitchen you had to know the ropes when it came to what could and could not be eaten or used in any part of the cooking process, being careful never to get your 'meaty' and 'milky' pans mixed up. There would be a rabbi present in the kitchen, keeping an eye on things and making sure that it was all 'kosher'.

The events that Joe Oberlander catered were what the kitchen staff at the Dorchester called 'outside jobs', not because they were in the open air but because they tended to be in a lot of different venues most of the time. Brian Price used to organize the staff alternately with Charlie Chase, who was the Chef de Partie on the roast section. Brian always used to phone me to help him because he knew that I needed the money. I would leave home at 5.30am and often didn't get back until the early hours of Monday morning. Despite their reputation for being ruthless in business, I have always found Jewish people to be very fair; they expect you to work hard, but in return they pay very well. I used to get the best part of £100 for my extended day's work, which used to go a long way towards getting Rona and me through the week.

While I was out working for Joe on a Sunday, Rona would write an essay. The course at Roehampton consisted of three, three-month-long study periods and in each of these we had to submit two essays, one for each of our chosen subjects. Rona used to submit her essay at the beginning of the study period and then, towards the end of the three months, I would submit the same essay, copied out in my handwriting. I used to add a couple of spelling mistakes and a few grammatical errors just to make it more likely to have been from me. The only annoying thing about it was that while Rona always got a mark of 90% or more for hers, I would get only 65% or 70% for mine. Explain that one to me, please! I suspect that it is something that a lot of teachers are unwittingly guilty of – a sort of 'self-fulfilling prophecy', based on how favourably they view different pupils or students and how they expect them to perform. However, I wasn't really in a position to complain, was I?

One morning, while enjoying a coffee in the student Common Room during a break between lectures, I picked up a discarded newspaper and started to glance through it. I don't normally read tabloid newspapers, even when I find them lying about, but something made me pick this one up. I think it must have been before the 'Page Three Girls' became a regular feature because I turned the front page only to be confronted, to my horror, by a photograph of my friend Jimmy, the floor waiter at the Dorchester whom I had befriended, alongside a murder report with a headline that read: 'Notting Hill Gay Tryst'. I was completely shocked to find myself reading about Jimmy's violent and untimely death. He had been really good to me and I was genuinely very depressed about it for some time. The tabloid had sensationalised the murder without really giving any details, but on reflection it was perhaps better that I didn't know.

Incidentally, I mentioned in the previous paragraph that I happened to be enjoying a coffee break, something I rarely did once I left college and started working fulltime again. Chefs are used to working very long hours, often under intense pressure, and to have something as simple as a coffee break or a lunch hour is often a real luxury. Throughout my years in the kitchen I have relied on cups of coffee to see me through the day, but I never dreamed of stopping work whilst I drank it. And to have lunch, sitting down and taking a whole half an hour off during a normal working day, was almost unheard of. The same goes for having evenings and weekends off – on the rare occasions when this was possible it was absolute heaven. In the restaurant and hotel trade you would get two weeks holiday a year and time off in lieu for Christmas Day and Boxing Day, if you were lucky; Bank Holidays were disregarded as a complete irrelevance.

Because I submitted essays written by Rona as my own, you may think that I didn't take my teacher training very seriously, but, actually, I did. The fact that I knew or didn't know about the 1662 Act of Uniformity, which allowed religious dissenters to set up academies for those who did not wish to subscribe to the articles of faith of the Church of England, or the Education Act of 1944, which introduced the tripartite system of grammar schools, secondary modern schools and technical schools, didn't seem to me to be that important. Such knowledge was all well and good, but it was not going to make me a better teacher, was it? It's also worth bearing in mind that I did not want to be studying the history of education in the first place – I had only chosen it so that I could be in the same class as Rona.

I was always far more interested in the practical applications of teaching, learning about Pavlov's Dogs and how, by studying them, I could then move on to "reinforcing a series of successive approximations", which would enable me to teach a chimpanzee how to make an omelet, something I've metaphorically had to do many times since then in my career! Another thing that fascinated me was learning the art of demonstration and how to present a particular subject in such a way as to make it interesting, while at the same time being able to ram home the key important points, something that would again stand me in very good stead when I came to take part in the Chef of the Year competition many years later.

As it happened, it was during my year at the college, in January 1974, that Brian Price entered and won the annual Chef of the Year title at Hotelympia. It remains the only time it has ever been won by a teacher rather than a working chef and I was so delighted for him. It just proved what a great craftsman he was, something we all knew, of course. He was also the first Englishman to win the title.

Towards the end of our year at Roehampton, Rona and I started to apply for jobs. I only ever wanted to go back to teach at Ealing, so that was easy for me. Rona was a little more flexible. She was always being directed towards the subjects that were considered to be more suitable for females to teach, such as housekeeping. However, she was very stubborn, which she had to be at a time long before gender equality in the workplace, and insisted that she was only interested in teaching professional cookery or food service. This severely narrowed down her job options, but she kept at it and eventually secured a job at Westminster College, as it was then known. Four people from our class applied for the single vacancy that became available at Ealing and I was fortunate enough to get it. We both secured our jobs subject to examination results being positive, which, thankfully, they were.

At the end of the course Rona's mum and dad, whom I had met many times at their home in Faversham, came for dinner at what used to be *my* flat in Forest Hill but was now *our* flat, a development in our relationship that I could not have been happier about. Within two hours of arriving there, Bert and Eva had planned the total redecoration of the place and the following weekend a little army of us set about transforming the first floor, two bed-roomed flat into something more habitable. What had started out as a simple painting and decorating exercise soon turned into a total refurbishment, with new carpeting and furnishing throughout. All of a sudden, the flat was transformed into what we considered to be quite a desirable little residence.

However, things were soon put into perspective. In those days it was possible to hire a television set rather than buying one outright. That seems silly now, but that's the way it was when TV sets cost a fortune and renting was so much more affordable. It was said that even the Queen rented her set! Rona and I went down to the main street in Forest Hill, where there was a branch of the TV rental chain, DEF. We had chosen the set we wished to rent, had agreed all the payment terms and the deal was going ahead smoothly until it came to the point of signing the agreement. The salesman suddenly noticed the address and promptly tore up the contract, announcing: "We don't rent to people living in Devonshire Road." Well, it may not have been Mayfair, but we never thought the area was that rough!

After finishing at the college we had a week of holiday left before starting our full time teaching jobs and decided that we would go to Alderney, where my mother had lived as a child and where I had spent many happy childhood summers. We flew there in on one of those Islander aircraft, a real boneshaker that only had about ten seats, as I remember. You could touch both sides of the aircraft at the same time simply by stretching your arms out. The weather was perfect as we came in to land, with deep blue skies above and even the sea below the bluest I'd ever seen it. We had borrowed a tent and a couple of sleeping bags from Rona's brother and as soon as we arrived we hired a couple of bikes on which to get around.

We set up camp near the lighthouse, beyond the fort at the other end of Bray beach, and when that was done we walked over the sand dunes to a little semi-circular bay, where about eight Jersey or Guernsey cows were paddling in the sea. How we laughed! I've never seen anything like that before or since. Rona loves cows, for some unknown reason, and for a moment I thought that it might be a good moment to ask her to marry me – but for some reason that I can't now recall, I held back.

That evening we went and had a drink in The Divers Inn, which my mother's family had owned many decades earlier. The weather had begun to deteriorate by this time and a heavy mist rolled in. We found our way back to the camp just as the foghorn on the lighthouse started to groan. We had pitched our tent about fifty yards away from it and with that noise going on we didn't sleep a wink all night. After a misty start the following morning the weather cleared and it was just as it had been when we arrived, so we spent the day riding around the island, going to all the places I had frequented as a child.

By late afternoon, however, the breeze had started to freshen and by bedtime it had become a howling gale. It continued to get even worse and by 2.00am I was seriously concerned that we were going to lose the tent completely. Rona lit the Camping Gaz lantern so that we could see what we were doing and I went down to the beach looking for a few heavy stones that I could use to anchor the flaps inside the tent. Struggling back with a particularly heavy boulder, I bent at the knees and slowly lowered it into position. I was only wearing a pair of brief underpants and as I slowly subsided under the weight of the stone the tenderest spot of my bare thigh came into contact with the surface of the Gaz lantern. I let out a scream, dropped the stone on the very same foot I had injured so badly when I was knocked off my bike in Shrewsbury, and leapt up with the lantern literally stuck to my backside.

I have suffered a number of injuries at various times during my life. I have broken my nose (twice), my arm (twice) and my leg, as well as several ribs; I've had two hernia operations and I've had five dental implants drilled into my lower jaw in the same afternoon; and yet I can't recall anything more painful than that burn at the top of my thigh. I have been back to Alderney many times since and thoroughly enjoyed every visit, but by the end of that week I must confess that I couldn't wait to get off the Island.

Back at home, we started our new jobs at Ealing and at Westminster College's Kensington branch, respectively. Public transport across London was very difficult and cycling wasn't really an option for both of us, so we invested in a Honda 50 motorcycle on which the two of us would ride to St Albans Grove, Kensington, where I would drop Rona off before going on to Ealing. There were occasional difficulties when our late teaching evenings and early morning starts didn't always coincide, but we made the best of it and it generally worked out quite well.

Teaching is really hard work if you do it properly, which a lot of people in further education unfortunately don't. We were very lucky at both Ealing and Westminster as these colleges were generally regarded as being the best two in the country at the time and the quality of the teaching was top notch. Some of the cookery lecturers I met on teaching practice at certain colleges that shall remain nameless were downright poor cooks, meaning that even if they were good teachers, the students suffered; on the other hand, there were some really good cooks who were poor teachers. Well, that's life, I suppose. Interestingly, I did also observe that some students were able to prosper despite poor teaching.

One of the difficulties of teaching as far as I was concerned was that while I was a pretty good cook, I found myself having to teach related subjects that I was not really qualified to teach, such as hygiene, nutrition and accounts. Although I had a basic knowledge of those subjects, it required a lot of extra work on my part to be able to stand up in front of a class of students and teach authoritatively for an hour at a time, once every week over a twelve-week term. In this respect, Rona and I had an advantage in that we could work together to formulate our lesson plans, as we were teaching the same courses and therefore the same subjects and at the same level. We built up a library of lesson plans fairly quickly and, as with anything else, the more we did it, the easier it became. But we reckoned that with those subjects that we found more difficult, it took at least four hours of preparation to teach properly for one hour.

When it came to the practical cookery classes, we could handle those without having to think too much about them. The biggest problem was adjusting to working with students who often did not know quite what they were trying to achieve. Our students were actually servicing the college restaurants that were open to the general public as well as the staff and students, and although outside customers understood the concept of a training situation to a degree, they still wanted something decent to eat and they didn't want to wait too long for it. There were many occasions when I had to chuck the students' stuff in the bin and quickly cook something myself that was acceptable. As far as the students were concerned, this could be seen as a useful learning exercise in itself in some ways – but only up to a point. If a student burned fifteen portions of beef bourguignon with only ten minutes to go to before it was due to be served, then there was not a lot that could be done about it. One just had to console oneself with the thought that people learn by making mistakes – I guess that's why they put rubbers on the ends of pencils!

There are lots of funny stories from my teaching days – at least, they seem funny when I recall them now. There was, for instance, the student who managed to cut himself really badly while poaching an egg. Don't ask me how! Or the girl who was refreshing thirty portions of spaghetti under running cold water in the sink and managed to lose the lot down the plughole. Yes, every last strand!

The Mary King Room was the name of the training restaurant and on one occasion we were serving a private party with hot canapés that included vol-au-vents of fresh white crabmeat. One of the young student waitresses, who was from Poland, had been told what the filling for these vol-au-vents was, just in case a customer were to ask. Like any foreigners, Poles often have a slightly different way of pronouncing some words because of their accents and when one of the customers did indeed inquire about the filling the poor girl smiled and announced brightly: "Crap". Then, when she saw the shocked expressions on the customer's face, she added helpfully: "Fresh crap".

While I was on the advanced cookery course I befriended a great chap called Sid Halsey and we ended up nearly always working together. He was a genuine pastry specialist, having worked for Lyons in their product development kitchen at Cadby Hall, and was so good that he was being groomed to take over from Percy Cross, the long established head of the college's pastry section, who was nearing retirement. There was literally nothing that Sid did not know about pastry, but he was a bit weak on the savoury stuff, while I, like most chefs, was a bit weak on the pastry side, so we used to help each other out.

Occasionally, a lecturer would not turn up for one reason or another, through illness or a family crisis, and when this happened someone would have to stand in, often at short notice, as Mr. Ceserani would not allow any classes to be cancelled. I remember having to cover a block release class one day when the task to be taught was savarin paste. This is used to make rum babas and is a bit tricky because it is a temperature-sensitive, yeast-based product. It's fairly easy to make an OK savarin, paste, but very difficult to do it really well, so I sought Sid's help. He helped me through a quick refresher course, which involved weighing out all the ingredients and placing them on a tray in the correct order so that I could perform my demonstration in front of the class before the students were allowed to go and do their own. Each item was specifically placed in precise order – warm flour, yeast, warm milk, eggs, melted butter, sugar, salt and so on. If anyone had turned my tray around I would have been in trouble.

It was another block release group that was involved in what was initially shaping up to be the worst experience of my entire four-year teaching career until, quite by chance, it unexpectedly turned out to be one of the most memorable. Block release groups did eight weeks in industry and eight weeks at college. They were usually OK in the kitchen situation, but weren't really interested in classes that they did not see as being relevant or important. They were mostly rejects from the education system and some were tough kids who had no qualms about letting you know that they did not want to be there, an attitude with which, as I have already hinted, I myself had a certain amount of sympathy.

I had been assigned to teach this group basic accounting, considered by nearly all aspiring chefs to be one of the most boring of all the related subjects, and by the end of the first lesson it was clear that with this particular bunch, I was headed for disaster. They were all totally disinterested and made no effort to hide the fact that they were bored to tears. They had no respect whatsoever for teachers, even at the best of times, secure in the knowledge that there was no way they would be disciplined or expelled. If you did expel them the college lost the funding; and, anyway, you couldn't expel the whole class.

After the debacle of the first lesson I genuinely worked really hard at trying to make the next one as interesting as I possibly could and asked some of the experienced senior lecturers for help. I was dreading the next hour as I walked into the classroom and spotted one of the real hooligans from the previous week reading a copy of *Sporting Life*, which was, as I mentioned earlier, the forerunner of *Racing Post*.

I asked him casually what horse he fancied and, together, we started to look at the form. The whole class, all fourteen of them, had gathered around by this time. My lesson plan immediately went out of the window as I spotted an opportunity. I suggested we all put 10p into a kitty and go and put the money on a horse. They thought that this was a great idea, so we chose our nag and someone popped to the bookies just over the road to place an each way bet. By the time he returned with the betting slip we had about half an hour to go before the race was run and I suggested that we work out what our winnings would be if the horse either came in first or was merely placed, in which case you get only a fraction of the odds. We then calculated what percentage our returns would be on our total outlay in each case and what our gross profit margin would be.

I know you are going to find this difficult to believe after my earlier betting story with Rona, but our horse romped home at 14/1. One guy went over to collect our winnings and came back with the cash and the broadest of smiles on his face. As a teacher, I had gone from zero to hero in an instant. I know it was unethical, but I am still convinced to this day that it was better than the regulation way of teaching, which had been such a failure the previous week. We spent the next six weeks doing exactly the same thing and by the end of the block they were pretty good at calculating percentages, gross profit margins and so on. Unfortunately, we didn't trouble the payout desk again, as that first horse proved to be our only winner.

In the meantime, Rona had stuck to her guns and was doing very well teaching professional cookery, but she always felt a little inferior to her colleagues because she had not come from the same big hotel background as many of the others. However, she got an unexpected chance to put that right thanks to Anton Mosimann, who by now had taken over as Chef de Cuisine at the Dorchester.

There had been big changes there in the two years since I had left. The whole hotel and restaurant industry was on the verge of momentous change and Mosimann was at the forefront of it all. The old guard was disappearing and the cooking of food, its presentation and service was changing dramatically. Mosimann had visited Ealing several times, obviously with a view to taking our best students at the end of their courses. At the same time, he also let it be known that any lecturers who fancied returning temporarily to the industry during the summer vacation in order to experience and keep up with the changes that were taking place would be welcome at the Dorchester. Not every teacher was happy about spending his or her summer holiday working back in a commercial hotel kitchen and only a handful took him up on his offer. Rona was at the front of the queue and I went along too, just to keep her company and show her the ropes. And so it was that we spent the summer working with one of the most innovative chefs of his generation.

Rona was also keen to do the advanced cookery course, but didn't want to be taught by her Westminster colleagues, so she applied to do it at Ealing instead. By this time it was a two-year course, as the pastry discipline had been dropped and had become a specialist two-year course in its own right. The course now consisted of just kitchen and larder. I was also teaching an evening class on the same day, so things fitted in quite nicely and we were able to travel home together on the Honda.

Everything was going swimmingly until the bi-ennial National Cookery Competitions at Hotelympia came around. The Ealing larder chef lecturer, a lovely man named Vic Renaud, was so impressed by Rona's skill that he persuaded her to enter one of the senior cookery competitions – as opposed to the junior competitions that were for college students.

Senior medals at the National Cookery Competitions were extremely difficult to win, the standards being very high indeed. There was also a huge amount of rivalry at the event between the two premier colleges in the country and it was a major coup for whichever one managed to win more medals than the other in any given year. Rona achieved a fantastic Silver Medal for her pâté en croute and was absolutely delighted, as we all were. But there was then a twist in the tale. When the overall medal tally was totted up it revealed a tie between the two protagonists at twenty-eight medals each – until Vic Renaud gleefully pointed out that Westminster had mistakenly included Rona's medal in their tally when she had actually entered under the Ealing umbrella. The revised medal tally now read Ealing 29 Westminster 27. And while Rona was hailed as an absolute hero at Ealing, she was not, as you can imagine, quite so popular at Westminster!

5 : A Place Of Our Own

By the time of her triumph at Hotelympia, Rona and I had been happily settled in the flat at Forest Hill for about a year, and having made up my mind that I wanted to spend the rest of my life with her, I started to think about how I might propose. I thought long and hard about it, just as I had with our first date and came up with several options, which included taking her away somewhere romantic for the weekend, or maybe arranging a really big night out in London. I definitely had visions of doing things in style, but ended up simply popping the question in bed one night! My biggest regret about doing it on the spur of the moment like that was that I never got to ask her father beforehand for permission to seek his daughter's hand in marriage in the traditional way.

We named the day – August 2nd, 1975 – and the wedding took place at Lynstead Church, near to where Rona's parents lived in the small village of Teynham, in Kent. The reception was held at their home.

Most of the men I know complain about their wives taking ages to get ready to go anywhere, but Rona has always been absolutely brilliant in that regard. We prepared the food for our wedding reception together and only then did she go upstairs to change, by which time there was just an hour to go before she was due to walk up the aisle. Even so, she almost beat me to it!

My lasting memory of that magical day, for which we were blessed with beautiful weather, was discovering at the last moment that while everyone else had been allocated a seat in the transport that had been laid on to get everybody to the church, I had not been included in the plans for some reason. And so it was that, dressed in my morning suit, I found myself being driven up Lynstead Lane to the church gate in the back of a mate's open Mini pick-up, perched on bags of sharp sand and Portland cement.

Another memorably funny moment came during the ceremony when my brother Joe, who was best man, dropped the ring as he handed it to the vicar. There was an audible intake of breath among the congregation as it rolled in a perfectly straight line back down the aisle for about fifteen yards. I looked at Joe, as if to say that it was his job to retrieve it, but he didn't move. You'd think that someone would have stepped forward to pick it up, instead of which everybody just froze, so that in the end I had to go back and get it myself.

Finally, when we all got back to the house, my mother pointed out that in the rush of doing our own food and getting everything ready, I had forgotten to have a shave. On reflection, I suppose you could say that the whole day had actually been quite a close shave!

By the time of the wedding, Rona had changed her Citroen 2CV for a little red soft top Triumph Spitfire, and although we didn't particularly want to leave the reception, as we were having such a good time with our family and friends, we eventually waved everybody goodbye sometime around mid-evening and drove the few miles to Dover with the hood down, staying overnight in the local Holiday Inn before catching a ferry very early the following morning. As anyone who knows Rona well will be aware, she is prone to suffer migraines after any really big occasion, and, almost inevitably, the wedding brought on an attack. These episodes normally last for at least twenty-four hours, but with her usual determination she almost willed herself to be well enough to travel the following morning, despite still feeling very fragile

We spent the best part of a whole month driving around France on our honeymoon, sometimes staying in modest accommodation, once or twice in a really nice hotel and occasionally camping in the Alderney tent, although thankfully without a repeat of the Gaz lantern trauma. We still have the little red book that Rona religiously filled in after every meal, detailing each aspect of the dishes we chose to eat and the wines that went with them.

These days, sadly, France isn't quite what it was as regards food. A Michelin-starred restaurant is going to be pretty good whichever country it's in but, generally speaking, the everyday restaurants in France have deteriorated, failing to keep up with rising standards elsewhere in the world. Much of this can be put down to the 35-hour week, along with the gradual disappearance of the genuine, old-style family-run restaurant. And far from trying to live up to the great French culinary reputation of a time gone by, it seems that today's younger generation are just as likely as their counterparts anywhere else in the world to settle for convenience food bought in a supermarket on the way home from work.

Returning to London after what had been a wonderfully relaxing, extended holiday, Rona and I started the new college year and eased back into our teaching routine, although by now we were both starting to question whether we wanted to make teaching a long-term career. I, in particular, was beginning to realise that Mr. Kaufeler, my old boss at the Dorchester, had been right when he predicted that I would only really find true fulfilment working as a chef. And, once again, both Rona and I found ourselves dreaming of maybe one day having our own restaurant. It then turned out that we weren't the only ones thinking that way.

We had gone down to Kent one weekend to spend a couple of days with Rona's parents. Albert Samuel 'Bert' North and his wife, Eva, were both very keen golfers – respectively Captain and Lady Captain of Faversham Golf Club at the time – and, as a result, most of our activities whenever we went to visit them revolved around the club. On this particular occasion the four of us were having a drink together in the clubhouse between rounds when Bert, whose work as an electrical contractor took him all over southeast England, suggested that we go and have a look a house he had spotted for sale in the picturesque local village of Doddington. It was an attractive Georgian property that had been operating as a local post office and village store and, before that, as a tea room, with living accommodation above. However, the business had closed some months earlier and it was now on offer, freehold, with vacant possession.

Bert had obviously thought things through carefully and had realised that the property could operate as a food outlet of some kind without the need to apply for change of use. We went along to the estate agent and were horrified to discover that the asking price was over £11,000, well out of our reach at the time. Had it been a straightforward purchase I am sure that Bert and Eva would have made some money available to help out with the deposit so that we could have bought it, but it turned out there was a complicated structural problem and so we didn't pursue it any further.

Although we'd said nothing specific to him, Bert had clearly picked up on where our ambitions were headed and had taken it upon himself to set the ball rolling. And with his tacit support and encouragement, Rona and I soon became hooked on the idea and started to think seriously about the possibility of opening up our own restaurant together rather than continuing to teach cookery.

Back at Ealing, the teaching actually continued to get a little easier as our library of lesson plans increased and I was 'promoted' to teaching a supposedly more intellectual group of Ordinary National Diploma (OND) students, although I still didn't enjoy it that much. The one major plus side of my involvement here was getting to know Dan Jenkins, one of the students in my class who went on to become a key member of our staff at Read's in the early days and a lifelong friend. Difficult to believe, now that he has gone on to become a hugely successful IT businessman in his own right, but when he first arrived at Ealing Dan was a shy young man from Wales; more about him later.

By this time, I was also teaching advanced cookery, which I found very demanding. It made me realise how difficult teaching could be at this much higher level, with students who weren't happy simply to accept everything they were told and wanted to analyse and query everything, just as I had done a few years earlier with Brian Price.

Meanwhile, in the early months of 1976, Bert spotted another property for sale that looked as though it might be suitable for conversion to a restaurant. This time it was an old run-down bakery in a Sheldwich, a little village near Faversham. We pursued it for a while, but, again, it wasn't quite right for various reasons. Shortly after that, Bert then returned from a job he had been working on with all the component parts of a small walk-in cold room type of refrigerator that had been discarded and thrown out on the scrapheap. He had loaded it up in the back of his Transit van, complete with the condenser and refrigeration unit, insisting: "This will come in handy one day."

A few weeks later he got to hear about yet another place that was rumoured to be coming up for sale, this one in the village of Painters Forstal, just a stone's throw away from his golf club. Located in the centre of the village, Mummery Court, as it was rather grandly known, comprised a two-storey flat-roofed house attached to a large single storey building that had been a operating as a mini-market shop and, before that, as a mail order distribution centre. Overall, it was a very unattractive, totally characterless early sixties structure, the house itself partly brick-built, with three layers of painted shiplap boarding around the top half. It reminded me that there were two groups of people I used to think should be publicly executed – 1950's dentists and 1960's architects. However, it seemed to have the potential for relatively straightforward conversion into a restaurant, with family accommodation attached.

Although there was no 'For Sale' sign outside, we made some enquiries and established that it was indeed available, the mini-market business having recently gone bust. The asking price was £28,000 and almost before we knew where we were, Bert, Eva, Rona and I, between us, had made an offer for the full amount. In what was an enormous leap of faith, Bert and Eva put their own house on the market and sold it almost immediately. Rona and I had had a couple of pay rises since we looked at the Doddington house and, as a result, had managed to save some money towards a deposit. Rona's parents put in £14,000 and we managed to secure a mortgage for the rest. As well as the house and mini-market, the property also included about an acre of land and our eventual aim was to get planning permission for a bungalow on the site, so that Bert and Eva could again build their own house, as they had done fifteen years earlier in Teynham. In the meantime, the idea was that we would all live together while we tried to get our restaurant business off the ground.

However, there were some anxious moments before the sale finally went through when, having made our offer and with the finance all set up, we became aware that we weren't the only potential buyers. The owners of a small caravan and camping business were also very interested, the site lending itself perfectly to their needs, with the mini-market being converted into a shop and office and with tents and caravans on display on the surrounding land.

We approached the land agents with an improved offer in an effort to gain an advantage, but were informed that as the property was bankrupt stock any increased offer would only muddy the waters and somehow make things more complicated. Our improved offer was therefore refused and we were advised that the place would go to whoever could arrange to complete first. Thankfully, we were able to get in ahead of our rivals.

No sooner had we finished celebrating this momentous development than Rona hit me with the best possible news – that she was pregnant with the baby who was to become Sam. Amid all this excitement, we set about handing over the rental of the Forest Hill flat to my brother and moved lock stock and barrel to our new home at Painters Forstal. Bert and Eva had done the same and the four of us started trying to organise ourselves as best we could. Rona continued to work at Westminster for the next few months, but handed in her notice after one more term.

We then nearly lost the whole shooting match within weeks of moving in when Eva and my mother, Daphne, came up with a bright idea for clearing the four-foot-high hayfield that had grown up over what had once been three quarters of an acre of lawn behind the house. They decided that instead of trying to mow it, it would be much quicker and easier to burn it, just as farmers used to burn the stubble in their fields after the harvest. Well, anyone who remembers the non-stop heatwave summer of 1976 will not be surprised to hear what happened next. The hay was tinder dry as a result of the drought and as soon as Eva and Daphne put a match to it the fire took hold as if they'd doused everything in petrol. The flames were visible for miles around and the blaze was so fierce that it burned out within a matter of minutes. It was only by the grace of God that the wind was blowing in the right direction, away from the house, otherwise we could easily have ended up homeless almost before we'd had time to settle in.

I continued to work at Ealing, the only problem with that being that it was obviously a considerably longer commute than from Forest Hill, so that for the next six months it seemed like I lived in the car. Dan Jenkins, who was in his second year at the college by this time, had become aware of what we were intending to do and said he would be happy to come down and help out at weekends in any way he could, an offer that was gratefully accepted.

Meanwhile, Bert had already started work on adapting the property to our needs. Although an electrician by trade, he could turn his hand to just about anything from bricklaying and carpentry to plumbing. He truly was an all-round handyman. He was also an incredibly hard worker. There was something in his make-up that wouldn't allow him to sit down and relax for very long. I have often reflected that Rona is similar in many ways and our elder son Sam, now that he has grown up, has inherited some of that same North family work ethic.

Bert had had an unusual upbringing. He never got to see his father, who, tragically, was killed at Arras in the last few weeks of the First World War, when Bert was just ten days old. As his mother had to go out to work to support them both, he was then mostly brought up by various aunties, as was often the case in those situations at the time, returning to live full-time with his mother only when she re-married. He himself went on to become a sergeant major in the army during World War II, and he could frighten the life out of most people, including me when I very first met him. But I soon came to realise that he had a heart of gold.

However, although normally the most good-natured of characters, he was prone to sudden furious outbursts, sometimes about things that would seem trivial to the rest of us. Fairly typical was an incident that took place when we were playing golf together one day. Bert absolutely loved his golf and was a fairly decent player off a 14 handicap, modelling his swing on that of his idol, Gary Player. On this particular occasion he was in great form and everything was going smoothly. He hit a superb drive at the first hole, followed by a long iron to the heart of the green and then a fifteen-foot putt for a birdie. On the second hole he hit another great drive to the centre of the fairway, a mid-iron approach to about three feet and another birdie. This was followed by a nice par 3 on the third, a tricky short hole. At the fourth he again hit a fantastic tee shot straight down the middle, only to astonish me by then hurling his club quite a considerable distance over a fence and into the neighbouring apple orchard with an anguished cry of: "That's another bloody tee peg I've lost!"

You would think that playing near perfect golf would have made him happy, but no. The totally inconsequential loss of a tee peg was enough to cause a momentary and totally disproportionate meltdown. We all accepted these little temperamental outbursts as part of his character and in their own way they were actually quite amusing. But they could be very difficult for an outsider to understand.

Back at Painters Forstal, there was a smaller room at one end of what had been the mini-market that had been used to house the post office section of the business and, size-wise, this lent itself perfectly to becoming our restaurant kitchen. That was where we started work on the conversion. During the week Bert would toil away and at weekends Dan and I would be there to do the menial labouring stuff, such as digging holes and trenches for the drainage and sewage pipes.

Bert was not really one for rules and regulations; for instance, he thought it totally unnecessary to apply for planning permission before changing the entrance to the building along with the entire facade, adding a porch to protect the diners inside from feeling a draught of cold air as other customers came in. This was just common sense to him and he felt no need to bother the local planning officers, only reluctantly agreeing to seek permission for major extensions. Of course, we wouldn't have got away with any of that sort of thing nowadays.

Rona was also busy slaving away, planning everything to do with the opening right down to the last detail and making all the arrangements as well as organising the interior décor and furnishings that, we hoped, would add a bit of style and character to what could only be described as a wholly unprepossessing building. Strangely, the very plain and unpretentious outward appearance of Mummery Court was to become a major, rather quirky plus when the food guides eventually discovered us some years later.

As we all beavered away we could at last begin to focus on a possible opening date somewhere around mid-June, 1977, although the inevitable last minute hold-ups meant this eventually had to be put back a month. In the meantime, there was one other little event that we all had to deal with and that was baby Sam's arrival. The day that he was born – June 4th – started much like any other. By then I was no longer working at Ealing, so I made us all an Irish stew for lunch. I don't know quite why I picked that particular dish. It may have been something to do with me thinking about whether I would put it on the lunch menu when the restaurant opened and, as I hadn't made one for years, wanting to remind myself how it was done. Rona's contractions started mid-afternoon and when I phoned the hospital for advice they told me to time the contractions and when the intervals between them had reduced to a certain point, only then to take her in to Kent and Canterbury Hospital.

I remember Rona saying that being pregnant was a bit like being up in an aeroplane; everything is fine whilst you are up there, but you know that at some stage you will have to come in to land – and it could be bumpy! This was in the early days of husbands being allowed to be present at the birth and we decided that I should be there.

As any man who has gone through the experience will tell you, it is horrible to see someone you love in so much pain, knowing that there is absolutely nothing you can do about it. Towards the end of several gruelling hours of labour, Rona was unable to make the final push and it was decided that an incision would have to be made – and I don't mean a Caesarian! It was probably just as well that Rona couldn't see exactly what was going on, but I could, and it was, to say the least, unnerving. The midwife produced what I can only describe as a large pair of shears and instructed the doctor (yes, it was that way round!) to make one big cut, not lots of little ones.

At this point I really just wanted to run away, but somehow managed to stay put. I just sat there up at the pretty end, smiled encouragement at Rona and said rather unhelpfully: "Nearly there." It was only later that I realised Rona could not see me because of my mask. The dreadful deed with the shears was done and Sam literally popped out covered in blood, which was spurting everywhere. Being there at the birth of your child is a totally unique experience – on the one hand a genuine horror story and yet somehow beautiful at the same time. We both shed a little tear as we looked at our newborn son and Rona was sewn up. During the whole process she had been throwing up continuously and since that day she has never been able to face an Irish stew again!

In those days one didn't have the option of knowing the gender of a baby in advance, not that we would have wanted to, anyway. As soon as we were presented with a boy, he was named Samuel Joseph – Samuel being Bert's middle name, and Joseph a Pitchford family name. I left the hospital in the early hours of the morning and drove home to give Bert and Eva the news. The two of them also shed a few tears, especially when they heard that their grandson was to be named Sam.

In spite of what I considered to be major surgery, Rona spent just two more nights in hospital and then brought Sam home with only a month to go before the restaurant was due to open. The turmoil caused by the arrival of a new baby is well documented, but add to that the daily deliveries of kitchen equipment, tables, chairs, cutlery, crockery, glasses, tea and coffee cups, carpets, curtains, tablecloths, napkins, ice buckets, cruets, wines, spirits, beers, liqueurs, soft drinks, mixers and so on and you can imagine the frantic pressure we were under. On top of all that, Dan and his girlfriend, Sherry, had thankfully decided to come and work for us full time and were living in the caravan at the back of the house while, just to complete the mayhem, my mother also came to visit, obviously excited to see the new baby, her first grandchild.

We had all spent a lot of time thinking about a good name for the restaurant, usually whilst enjoying a drink over at the Alma, the country pub just across the village green. The locals couldn't really understand what we were trying to do and considered us to be slightly weird. They were all of the opinion that nobody from the village was going to be frequenting the restaurant and that consequently we would very quickly go bust. When we walked into the pub during the evening, usually quite late because we all had been working hard to finish our jobs across the road, they would all stop talking, exchange glances and then start to snigger. Many of those villagers were good, honest, hard-working people and I wouldn't wish to belittle them in any way, but some of them had never been to London in their lives and one or two had never been further afield than Faversham. That seems strange now that everyone is more mobile and most people have been abroad at some stage, but back in the seventies rural village life was very different and many members of the older generation, particularly, rarely ventured much beyond the nearest big town.

Everything about the restaurant scene at that time was still heavily influenced by the French style and we were anxious not to go down that road. Bert felt that it was obvious that we should call the restaurant Rona's, plain and simple, and we very nearly did. However, we eventually decided on Read's, which was made up from the first letters of each of our names – Rona, Eva, Albert, David and Sam. We even thought about calling our dog Apostrophe at one stage!

Meanwhile, in the last few months leading up to the opening of the restaurant, we had all begun to notice a change in Bert. He had started to show uncharacteristic signs of extreme tiredness after a day's work and Eva later confided that she had noticed for some time that he wasn't quite himself. In particular, he was having difficulties sleeping, mainly because of waterworks problems. However, he had kept toiling away, turning his attention to the key job of fitting out the restaurant kitchen. British Gas had been offering a free planning service that we initially decided to take advantage of, but it soon turned out that they didn't have a clue. The kitchen they proposed might have been OK for a hospital or for a large works canteen, but was totally inappropriate for an à la carte restaurant, so we decided to do it ourselves.

Purely by coincidence, I happened to be teaching a day release basic cookery class one Friday afternoon, just prior to finishing my teaching career, and the class included a dinner lady employed by Ealing Borough Council. She alerted me to the fact that her school, which was just round the corner, was having a new kitchen fitted and that at that very moment they were throwing out all the old equipment. As soon as the class was finished I went straight round to the school and, having been introduced by my student pal, paid the nominal sum of £30 to the demolition crew for what they were about to chuck out onto the scrap heap. I got two Stott Benham solid-top gas stoves, complete with ovens, plus a deep fat fryer, a large sterilising sink, two double kitchen sink units, a hotplate, various stainless steel tables and pot racks and a collection of pans and sundry other small items of equipment.

I phoned Bert and told him all about it and he arranged for us to borrow one of his vans in which to collect it all the following day. Dan and I drove up from Kent early on the Saturday morning and, with the help of a couple of passers-by, loaded half the stuff into the vehicle and drove it back to Painters Forstal, before returning to get the other half. Bert was very impressed when he saw what I'd bought, saying approvingly that he reckoned it would prove to be the best £30 quid I would ever spend. Any sort of compliment from Rona's dad was something special and I basked in the warmth of what, for him, was high praise indeed. Those Stott Benham stoves were very heavy and my lasting memory of that day is of Dan and me driving back along the M2 with the front wheels of the van hardly touching the ground because of the weight of the stoves in the back.

We spent the whole of Sunday dismantling the stoves, cleaning every single one of the component parts and reassembling them, while Rona and her mum concentrated on the fryer, sinks and stainless steel equipment. When we looked at what we had all achieved at the end of the weekend I remember feeling that I had never been more proud of two days' work. The following week we put our own kitchen plan into operation, with Bert doing all the skillful work and me and Dan doing the numbskull stuff.

We were now in the extremely satisfying position of knowing exactly what equipment we had and where it was going to go. Dan and I chased all the electrical cables into the walls and bashed holes where the gas pipes would come into the building and run under the floor.

You might remember that we already had a walk-in cold room. The only bits of equipment we had to go out and purchase brand new were a freezer for the ice creams and sorbets and a new salamander, so that the total cost of our restaurant kitchen added up to less than £500. Of course, if one had taken all Bert's work into account then it would have been a lot more, but what we actually paid out was a tiny fraction of what it would normally have cost to fit out an entire commercial kitchen.

It was now time to get the supposed professionals involved and so we contacted British Gas to come and commission Bert's work and connect us up to the mains. We then contacted the equivalent of what is now the Environmental Health Officer to approve everything we had done. In those days each regional health authority had their own rules and regulations and we just needed the nod as to which floor and wall surfaces they would require us to install now that all the electrical cabling and pipework was in place. Bert laid the quarry tile floor and I did the ceramic tiles on the walls, but only after he had given me a little test area to complete in order to make sure that I wouldn't make a complete mess of it. Once the Environmental Health Officer had given us the thumbs up and the gas was turned on, we tested everything and were delighted to find that it all worked perfectly; it was a truly great and memorable day.

Dan would occasionally have a weekend back in Paris to see his mother and would always return with the gift of a little parcel of meat especially for Rona. France was the only place where you could buy calves' liver in those days and this was one of two things that Rona craved during the final weeks of her pregnancy. The other thing she became addicted to was spinach. That just goes to show what a wonderful thing the human body is, because the doctors were telling us at the same time that she had an iron deficiency.

We had finally settled on Friday 15th July 1977 as the date for the opening of the restaurant, but we then had an enquiry from the local Rotary Club, asking if we could possibly cater for a private party of twenty-two people two days earlier on the 13th. We thought about it and decided that although it would interfere with our last minute plans, it might actually be rather a good idea, serving as a sort of preview that would effectively put us through our paces. We served them with a set menu that included a seafood avocado starter, with a beef fillet Tournedos main course and a strawberry tartlet dessert to follow. The first course was to be accompanied by six bottles of Golden Oktober Liebfraumilch at the VAT exclusive price of £5.85, while the main course wine was to be chosen on the night. The party went well, but we were all only too well aware that the real test would come on the Friday, when we would be serving a full house from an à la carte menu.

Any chef will tell you that starting from scratch in a new restaurant is the most difficult thing in the world to do. Eddie McIntyre and Wendy came down to help out over that first weekend, Eddie working with me in the kitchen and Wendy out front with Rona, Dan and Sherry. Despite Eddie and I working together throughout the night we still didn't manage to get everything ready in time.

In carefully planning our menu, we had deliberately decided to offer a choice of just eight first courses, eight main courses and seven sweets, plus a selection of British-only cheeses. Very much Rona's innovative idea, this was all fairly revolutionary at a time when people were used to going to Italian restaurants that would offer over a hundred choices, and when nobody anywhere that I knew of had ever thought of having a British-only cheeseboard. Rona had devoted a huge amount of time and energy to sourcing some outstanding cheeses from various local cheese makers around the country.

It is easy to forget how very different the British restaurant scene was in the 1970s to what it is today, certainly outside Central London. Leaving aside the Indian and Chinese restaurants that had been springing up everywhere, there were the Italian and so-called 'French' restaurants, plus the steak house venues that also played their part in the development of the restaurant scene at the time. And in these establishments the menus mostly consisted of the same items wherever you went. For starters, customers expected to see a prawn cocktail, a wedge of melon, a slice of pate, and a French onion soup on the menu; there might also have been corn-on-the-cob, whitebait and smoked salmon, but basically that was it. The main courses were invariably steaks cooked well done with 'all the trimmings', plus a chicken dish and maybe half-a-duck with most of the bones left in and topped with either an orange or black cherry sauce. There might have been a fish dish, but whatever fish it was would probably have come out of the freezer rather being been fresh.

Even in the Italian restaurants, those big menus were deceptive.

There would simply be ten Dover sole choices, ten steak dishes, ten chicken dishes and so on, and all the garnishes would be a combination of the same ingredients. And the sweet trolley would feature bought-in cassatas from the freezer, unwrapped to order, along with fresh fruit salads, crème caramels and a bought-in Black Forest Gateau that was cut into twelve portions in advance so that when someone ordered it the waiter would simply have to pour a bit of double cream over it. So, in reality, it wasn't quite such a splendidly varied menu as it might appear at first sight, but the relatively inexperienced British public, many of whom were only just getting used to the idea of going out to eat on a fairly regular basis, had come to think that offering such a supposedly huge selection was the thing to do.

All this gastronomic goonery was invariably washed down with beer or lager, but for the really adventurous there might be a bottle of Mateus Rose in those lovely old Bocksbeutels that wouldn't fit in any wine rack that I ever saw. Sauternes was often served with a main course, or maybe a Liebfraumilch Blue Nun – what a successful bit of marketing that was! For the very posh, it could have been Beaujolais, with those who were not quite the connoisseurs they liked to think they were wrongly complaining when it was correctly served at cellar rather than room temperature.

By these standards, the dining experience we were aiming to offer at Read's was both fairly sophisticated and, for a small restaurant well off the beaten track in the wilds of Kent, pretty adventurous. However, despite all our meticulous planning, we didn't get off to the greatest start.

When people go out to eat on a Friday or Saturday night they almost invariably want to book for precisely 8.00pm. This is especially true out in the country, so it was no surprise to find ourselves standing around in the kitchen at 7.45 looking out on an empty restaurant, with nothing to cook, only to be working frantically half and hour later in an effort to keep up with a sudden avalanche of simultaneous orders. This can be inconvenient at the best of times, but even more so on a first night when everyone is tense and there are the inevitable teething troubles.

On this occasion, one of the problems was that the lemon sole we had ordered for the main fish dish had been delivered late and with everything else that was going on, Eddie and I had not had time to skin

(Above) My mother, Daphne, as a young woman, pictured walking in her hometown of St Peter Port, Guernsey; and my father, Joe, in his Royal Navy days at the end of the war.

(Below) Me, as a bonny and toothsome baby; and with my brother, Joe, (on the left) during a holiday in Guernsey.

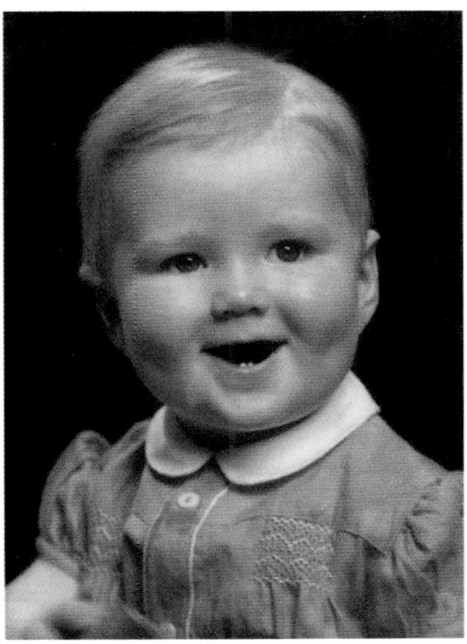

'Uncle' Bernard Maw and his wife Phyllis (holding pet bantam Clara), neighbours who became like family to my mother, Joe and me and helped us through some hard times. (Below) John Maw (on the left) and me posing with the Austin A40 convertible in which Bernard would regularly do 'the ton' on the way to the seaside.

(Left) Me, on the right, with Joe and John Maw (centre) on one of those fondly remembered Welsh seaside trips.

(Right) The three of us on the Maws' smallholding with the family's pig, Josephine, and, (below), John takes pet bantam Clara for a spot of gentle waterboarding! Clara went everywhere with us, including the seaside trips!

Armed and dangerous! Me in my grey squirrel hunting days. John Maw and I boosted our pocket money with two-shillings-a-tail bounty from the Forestry Commission.

The young Rona, with whom I fell in love at first sight. Not a day goes by when I don't wake up and thank my lucky stars that I met this girl.

Rona on our wedding day, arriving at the church with her father, Bert, and cutting the cake with me. And (below) on holiday with her parents and brother Alan at Butlins.

(Above) Fooling around with lifelong friend Eddie McIntyre during our Dorchester days, (right) together again at the opening of Read's in 1977 when Eddie came to help out in the kitchen and (below) more recently – still best mates but not quite so crazy after all these years, Eddie having gone on to become a pillar of society as Dr Eddie McIntyre, CBE, Principal of University College, Birmingham.

(Left) Sealed with a kiss! Congratulations from Rona on winning Chef of the Year – very much a joint achievement. The judges told us later that our teamwork was the best ever seen in the competition. I certainly could never have won it without her.

With Sarah 'Windy' Miller and Dan Jenkins, many years after they played a vital role as key members of our front-of-house team in the early days.

Me (back row, second from right) with an all-star cast of chefs, brought together for a magazine feature in 1990. (Back row, l to r) John Hornsby (ex-Dorchester, head chef at the Four Seasons, Washington) Brian Turner (top restaurateur, President of the Royal Academy of Culinary Arts, star of Ready, Steady, Cook) Paul Gayler (The Dorchester, Inigo Jones and then Executive Head Chef at the Lanesborough), Marjan Lesnik (Executive Head Chef at Claridges and then Harrods), David Nicholls (Executive Head Chef at the Mandarin Oriental now Group Director of Four Seasons Food and Beverage) Michael Bourdin (The Connaught), me, Anton Edelman (Head Chef at the Savoy for 21 years). (Front row) Victor Ceserani (The Ritz and Boodles and then Head of Ealing Hotel School, where both Rona and I trained), Eugene Kaufeler (legendary Head Chef at the Dorchester for 30 years) and Louis Virot (Head Chef at the Savoy Grill).

With two of my 'proteges' – Mark Sargeant and James McLean, who won Young Chef of the Year in 1996 and 1997 respectively. Mark went on to become National Chef of the Year in 2002.

and prep all of it in advance, so we simply stuck a hand-written label over the price on the printed menu, doubling the price in an effort to deter people from ordering it. Nevertheless, Sod's Law being what it is, seventeen of the first twenty-one people to order chose the lemon sole.

Amid the frantic activity that ensued, things then got even worse when Dan burst through the kitchen swing door at 20mph, having dropped a whole load of stuff on the floor at the bar, and the sudden draught blew all the orders off Bert's home made 'tab-grabber' – the board with numbered pegs under which the order slips for each table are pinned – scattering them all over the floor, so that we no longer knew which table each one belonged to. Chaos was not the word for it. While Rona tried to get the orders sorted out, Eddie and I just carried on cooking as much as we could as quickly as was possible on our two little solid top stoves.

While all this was going on, Eric Bland, a friend of Bert's, had been helping out by fixing the five letters of the name of the restaurant to the wall outside. He'd managed to get the R and the E up by himself, but then made the terrible mistake of coming into the kitchen to ask if either Eddie or I could pop out and give him a hand. As you can imagine in the circumstances, the torrent of abuse that came his way in response to this rather badly-timed request sent him reeling back out into the car park in a state of shocked surprise!

There were so many more things that went wrong that evening, but it would be boring to go through the entire list. Suffice it to say that although it was the done thing in those days for the chef to go into the dining room and chat to the customers towards the end of the evening, by the time I had the breathing space to make an appearance most of them had already gone home. And I was greeted by the unusual sight of those who were still there holding their coffee cups in their serviettes with slightly pained expressions on their faces. We had left the cups on the hotplate in order to keep them warm, but because it was the first time we had used the hotplate we had not realised that it was actually more like a very hot oven, leaving the cups so blisteringly hot that people had burnt their fingers when they picked them up.

At the same time, Eric Bland was at the bar having a drink with Bert, still smarting over the way he had been told where to go when he innocently asked for some help with the sign outside and complaining bitterly that he was not used to being spoken to like that – especially when he was only trying to do somebody a favour out of the kindness of his heart. It would be another week before we got the A, D, and S up on the wall.

So, for many reasons that evening was the worst service I had ever experienced, which was especially disheartening given that I had so desperately wanted it to be the best. I know that every chef reading this will understand what we went through on that occasion. Strangely enough, the customers were all very complimentary, apparently unaware of the mayhem that had been going on behind the scenes. That was all down to the front-of-house team, led by Rona, who had done a brilliant job of somehow managing to make everything appear as if it was going along very smoothly.

At about 1.30am we all sat down and held a post mortem over a drink, analysing the events of the evening, identifying where we had got things wrong and working out ways of making sure we didn't make the same mistakes again. We eventually got to bed at about 3.00am, only for Sam to wake us at 6.15. Rona fed him and then Eva came in and took over. It has to be said that we wouldn't have lasted a week without Eva.

Although we were officially open seven days a week for lunch and dinner we thankfully didn't have any customers booked in for that first Saturday lunchtime. However, there was another chock-a-block full house in the evening. We were a bit anxious, but we'd all learned a lot from the night before and this time things went much better. At last, after all those months of planning and hard work, Read's was finally up and running – even if the sign outside still wasn't! And the regular 'ker-ching' sound of our old-fashioned till registering another sale was like music to our ears!

That till was actually a bit special in a sentimental sort of way, having come from Bert's old shop in Gravesend. And Rona and I weren't the only members of the family who found that 'ker-ching' sound comforting – as we discovered a few years later, very nearly to our very considerable cost. Our young son, Sam, was also attracted by it and one Sunday afternoon when Rona and I were out and he was being looked after by Eva, he somehow managed to open it without her noticing – and then decided that it would be a great idea to take out all the paper money and throw it down the loo! We're talking here about our takings for the whole weekend, so several hundred pounds. Fortunately, Eva got wise to his little game before Sam flushed it all away!

Meanwhile, the week following our official opening was equally as nerve-wracking as that first evening, but in a totally opposite sort of way, as we had only eleven customers during the entire week – and seven of those were on the Saturday evening. I don't know what we had imagined would happen; did we really think that the world would be beating a path to our door straightaway? We'd been so inundated with bookings the previous Friday and Saturday that we'd had to refuse literally dozens of customers and this had lulled us into a false sense of security. Having had to turn away over two hundred customers on that first weekend, we were shocked that things had then fallen quite as flat as they did.

In those days, especially, people generally didn't understand how an à la carte restaurant worked – they seemed to think that all the food was cooked beforehand and then ladled out when the customers arrived. In fact, there are many people who still think that's how it works, whereas very little actual cooking takes place until the moment at which an order is handed in to the kitchen. However, a lot of the component parts of the various dishes have to be 'prepped' in advance – the so-called 'mise en place' – so when there are just eleven customers for fourteen services spread over a whole week there can only be one certainty, and that is that there will be a lot of wasted mise en place.

For every lunchtime and evening service we would be ready at 12 noon and 7.00pm respectively, in the hope that people would start to arrive. I referred earlier to the rather unprepossessing outward appearance of our building and this was a disadvantage that unfortunately manifested itself many times. Peering out of the window from behind the net curtains, it was soul-destroying for us to see how often people would drive up in their cars, get out and take a look at the old flat-roofed mini-market, only to get straight back in their cars and drive away again.

We hadn't done any advertising as such, mainly because of the expense involved. Most of our hopes were pinned on the golf club and the word of mouth recommendations that we thought might be generated there, and apart from that we had also written to all the local businesses we could think of, announcing our presence. We were very naïve then and wouldn't dream of doing things in the same way today.

Another mistake that we made was to offer the same menu at the same price for both lunch and dinner. That was a big mistake and it cost us dearly. By the time we got around to doing a cheaper and quicker lunch menu the damage had already been done and we had got a reputation for being expensive and slow at lunchtime. When you get any kind of negative reputation in the restaurant business, it takes a long time to turn it around.

At the end of one particular week in the very early days we had no bookings for Sunday lunch and Rona suggested that I should order a large leg of English lamb so that the whole family could sit down together and enjoy a proper Sunday lunch of our own for once. She didn't come into the restaurant that morning, spending a couple of hours with Sam and her mum and dad while Dan, Sherry and I went through the motions, just in case anyone turned up by chance. At the same time, I got on with preparing what was to be our lunch. Then, at about ten past two, a couple of cars turned up in the car park and seven people came in and asked if we were open. It was our policy never to refuse anyone unless we were fully booked and simply didn't have a free table, so I felt I couldn't turn them away. Dan then took their orders and brought them into the kitchen and my heart sank as I saw that all seven had gone for roast lamb. And so it was that I ended up selling our Sunday lunch! Rona didn't speak to me for two days.

Over the next few weeks business slowly began to pick up. There was a chap called Mr. Hamlyn, the managing director of a locally-based international company, BMM Weston, who did a great deal of entertaining. He used to arrive in his cream Rolls Royce and always drank Dom Perignon. He would regularly visit us five times a week, mostly for lunch but also, occasionally, for dinner. And he always ate à la carte, whether it was lunch or dinner. Looking back he was vital to our survival in that first year.

There were also some people who used to visit us precisely because we were quiet, somewhere they could bring their mistresses or secret boyfriends. If only we'd had rooms for rent in those days, we could have made a real killing!

I don't know what it is about the cussed Sod's Law of catering that somehow dictates that on a really quiet night there will always be the one dreaded twosome. It is hardly ever a four or a six, and if you ever have a run of four consecutive quiet nights you will never have eight people on one of those nights and nobody at all on the other three nights; it will always be just two on each night. Having just two people by themselves in a restaurant is a killer, both for the staff and the customers themselves. Nobody at all is much better than one table of two.

As our first Christmas at Read's approached, we were becoming increasingly aware that Bert's health was continuing to deteriorate, although we all clung onto the hope that maybe he was just getting older and slowing down a bit. He had virtually stopped doing any heavy work as he just could not cope physically, although he did seem to enjoy coming downstairs to the restaurant on busy nights to look after the bar for us. He also used to help enormously by taking Sam for long walks in his pram.

We tried to cheer ourselves up by promising ourselves that after Christmas we would take a short trip across the Channel to France for a couple of days, returning to Wimereux, a favourite place just along the coast from Boulogne. When Rona and I first got together in 1973 we used to pop over there for golfing weekends with Bert and Eva, along with Derek Place, the golf professional at Faversham. Derek was a lively chap and great company, and we spent many happy times together. We used to stay at a very modest little family-run hotel in the middle of Wimereux, appropriately named the Hotel du Centre. While the husband did the cooking, his wife, their son and daughter-in-law together looked after everything front-of-house. This was exactly the kind of true family-run operation that I had in mind earlier when I lamented the decline of France's great traditional culinary reputation.

Back at Painters Forstal, business at Read's was continuing to improve, most noticeably at Sunday lunchtimes. We offered four main courses, one of which was always roast beef – and always a quality cut like sirloin or wing rib rather than the usual topside that was the norm almost everywhere else at the time. In addition, the menu would invariably include a white meat, usually chicken, and a fish dish. The other main course could be anything that we wanted to get rid of. It seemed to be a winning formula and we went from a patchy start to regular full houses in a comparatively short space of time.

I think that one of the main reasons for this was that, back then, the licensing laws were quite different and pubs were required to close at two o'clock on Sundays. The word quickly spread that we did late

Sunday lunches and publicans from all over Kent would call time on the dot of 2.00pm at their own establishments, so that they could get finished up and be with us by about 2.30pm, occasionally bringing some of their customers with them. The added bonus of all this was that publicans were generally pretty heavy drinkers; the only downside was that the sessions often didn't finish until 8 or 9 o'clock in the evening. Although we said that we were open for fourteen services a week, in actual fact we rarely had any other customers coming in on Sunday evenings after the lunchtime lot had eventually gone home and it was only a matter of time before we opted to make it lunch only on Sundays. The evening became our own precious time when we would all sit down together and have a proper family meal. There would usually be seven of us – Bert and Eva, Rona, me and Sam plus Dan and Sherry.

Despite the healthy upturn in business, we were still only just about making ends meet at the time and every single penny was important. As a business, we were supposed to put our rubbish into colour-codedbin bags, for which we had to pay the council. However, we used to put the great majority of our rubbish in ordinary black bags and then spread them around the village along with everyone else's bin bags at about 1.00am, ready for the regular collection a few hours later that morning.

Another mistake that we made that first Christmas was not having our set Christmas lunch and dinner menus ready a month or two in advance. The office party types like to get their bookings in the diary well in advance and they also like to know exactly what they are going to eat. By the time December actually arrived everyone was booked up elsewhere. It was still a pretty good month for us, but not quite as good as it could have been if we had been a bit quicker off the mark. The reason I dwell on these things is because there is such a fine dividing line between surviving and going under in the restaurant business and these little things can make the difference between success and failure.

One aspect of the business that was never a problem in those early days, but which can now be a major headache, is finding staff. In the late seventies you used to be able to phone up the local job centre or employment agency and ask them if they had got anyone available to fill a washing-up vacancy, for example, and usually they would be able to send someone along straightaway. Nowadays, however, every small business has to do so much paperwork, health and safety assessment, contracts of employment and so on that hardly anyone uses the job centres anymore; but that's another story.

Washing up in a restaurant is a monumental task and a good KP (Kitchen Porter) is worth his or her weight in gold. I soon began to understand exactly why, at the start of each day, Eugene Kaufeler at the Dorchester always used to make a point of going to shake hands with his washer-up-in-chief first, before any of the chefs; a hard working KP who understands kitchen hygiene and cleanliness (they are not the same thing) makes a restaurateur's life a great deal easier than it might otherwise be. During nearly forty years of running our own business we have managed to carry on OK when short of chefs or waiters, but to operate properly without a good KP is almost impossible. There have been the odd occasions when we have found ourselves in this situation and have somehow had to cope, but it is absolutely soul-destroying at the end of a long, busy night, to have to tackle the mountain of washing up which, by 1.30 in the morning, is likely to be stacked in a pile six feet high that stretches out into the car park.

It's not just matter of sticking everything in the dishwasher, even if you do happen to have one of the industrial machines needed to cope with the sort of volume generated in a commercial kitchen, something we didn't have for many years for reasons of expense and practicality. And, anyway, dishwasher-clean glassware is simply not good enough for a top quality restaurant – everything has to be steamed and polished with a special glass cloth. Taking into account glasses for aperitifs, white and red wine glasses, liqueur glasses and water tumblers, as well as glasses used for amuse bouches and desserts, and you can be talking about literally several hundred glasses every day. At the same time, cutlery has to be cleaned, polished and silver-dipped to prevent tarnishing.

On TV and in the movies you sometimes see customers who haven't got the cash to pay their bill offering to do the washing up instead. I would absolutely love that to happen here at Read's, just once. I would happily agree to let people wash up on a busy evening, with the stipulation that they would have to do everything on their own – kitchen equipment, pots and pans, cutlery, plates, cups, saucers, flatware and glasses. If they managed to get it done in less than twelve hours I would not only let them off paying their bill, but would happily offer them another meal on the house as well!

One of the better decisions we made when equipping the restaurant was in our choice of plates. You can easily spend £100 on a restaurant plate these days and it was proportionally the same back then. We decided on a company called Dudson who were well known for producing attractive but sturdy items that were relatively inexpensive and would last forever. We ordered sixty large oval plates for all the main courses. Seventeen years later we retired them to the cellar, where I think they still are, and we had fifty-eight left, which was amazing. If you dropped a Dudson plate, it was the floor that broke!

Staff are often very careless with crockery and glassware, which they tend to throw about a bit. I remember a story told to me by Iain McAndrew, one of the finest chefs of his generation, who also happened to be one of our nearest local competitors in the 1980s when he was in charge first at Eastwell Manor and then at the excellent restaurant 74 in Canterbury. To be honest, the creative rivalry between us was actually quite fierce and we were a bit miffed when he beat us to a Michelin star. Anyway, Eastwell was then owned by the Bates family, to whom money was no object, and Iain explained how they spent many hundreds of pounds ordering twenty absolutely beautiful Villeroy Boch porcelain china coffee pots, only to find that three weeks later they had eighteen coffee pots and one lid.

Rona and I had agreed before we opened that we would do everything possible to give ourselves the best chance of surviving, and this included opening on Christmas Day and staying open all the way through to New Year's Eve. After that, we were anticipating a quiet January, but not as deathly quiet as it turned out to be. As we had promised ourselves, we closed up for three days in the early part of the month and went off to France with Bert and Eva and Sam. We had as good a time as it was possible to have, given that we knew by now that this would be our last trip away together with Bert. By now he was "tired to the bone", as he put it, very frail and pale, but he still managed to take great delight in his grandson. By March he was dead, and Sam was the only thing that could make any of us smile.

The restaurant was busy on the evening of the day he died and Rona had to work for at least some of the session to help Dan and Sherry, who would have been seriously under pressure without her. I remember coming up to the bar during the evening to collect some white wine for a fish dish I was cooking and a lady customer was explaining to Rona about what a "nightmare" of a day she'd had, getting caught in traffic on the way back from the hairdresser. I desperately wanted to put her in the picture, but somehow managed to resist the temptation. That's why I'm in the kitchen, not front-of-house. I am full of admiration for people who actually deal diplomatically with customers, however awkward, difficult, thoughtless or downright rude they are. It is something that I could never do well – I would last five minutes at the very most before losing my cool.

Rona's mum was obviously distraught at the loss of her husband. I suppose, if I'm absolutely honest, I would have to say that Eva was the least enthusiastic of the four of us about the restaurant venture, and probably, on reflection, with good reason. After all, she had reached a time in her life when she could have expected that she and Bert would be able to take things a little easier and enjoy life after all the years of running their electrical contracting business together. Instead of which she had been uprooted from her home and pitched into helping us to make our business venture a success.

Born Eva Lottie Honor Barnes, she was one of the most naturally happy people I have ever met, totally committed to family life and homemaking as well as supporting her husband in his chosen career, qualities that often seem to be belittled by some of today's feminists. She was born in Gravesend and Northfleet and had three brothers – Albert, Roy and Ronnie. Ronnie died when he was eleven years old from TB, a huge killer in those days, as it was on my side of the family, too. Her father, Herbert, and her mother, also named Eva, ran a fish and chip shop next door to their end-of-terrace house in Gravesend. Before her marriage she had been an usherette at the local Majestic Cinema, which is where she had met Rona's dad just before the outbreak of the Second World War. She was already engaged to be married to a local carpenter when she and Bert got together and when the engagement was broken off her mum was not amused, as she had thought a lot of the carpenter and had been quite looking forward to welcoming him into the family as a son-in-law

The story from there on is so romantic that you couldn't make it up. When war broke out Bert was shipped off to Gibraltar, where he would remain for two years. He and Eva wrote to each other virtually every day and in April, at the end of the second year, he wrote wishing her a happy birthday. Her actual birthday is in late December, so she knew it must be a coded message, letting her know that he was coming home. He couldn't tell her that in so many words because all communications from army personnel were heavily censored by the authorities and, for obvious reasons, any indication of his regiment's movements would have been considered potentially sensitive information.

Eva had been a plane spotter with the ATS during the war years, a job that involved being stationed next to the Ack-Ack guns, looking through a piece of range-finding equipment to work out the co-ordinates of the enemy bombers that she then bellowed to the operators of the huge guns, so that they could target the planes and try to blast them out of the sky. She was actually chosen for this job partly because of her booming voice, but also because of her exceptional ability to recognise all types of German aircraft. It wasn't an easy task. The raids were mostly at night and the searchlights would pick out the aircraft in the darkness at which point she would have to calculate very quickly both the altitude and the speed at which they were flying.

Within ten days of Bert arriving back in England from Gibraltar he and Eva were married. He was then shipped off again more or less immediately, this time to Norway to help protect the fleet, and he remained there for the best part of another two years. Eva had fallen pregnant with Rona's elder brother, Alan, almost immediately after the wedding and it was to be over a year before Bert got to see his son for the first time.

After being demobbed, Bert returned to the job as an electrician that he'd had before the war, but Eva persuaded him that he would be better off working for himself rather than someone else, and so it was that North Electrical was born. Rona arrived in June 1949 and by the mid-fifties the family had a high street shop selling cookers, refrigerators and a range of other electrical goods.

By 1959 the majority of North Electrical's work was in and around the Canterbury area and the journey along the old A2 was tedious, to say the least. The family decided to move closer to where the work was and Bert bought a plot of land in the little village of Teynham for about £400 and set about building a family home on it. The summer holiday of 1959 was spent on Trianon Beach in Cornwall, where the family would plan their own dream home surrounded by all the current design and building magazines available at the time. As soon as they got back, Bert started work on the house that was eventually to become Alrona and which still exists today in Lynstead Lane, still with the same name. The family moved there from Gravesend in 1960, the year in which Alan left school at the age of sixteen and Rona moved to secondary school at eleven, so the timing was perfect as far as their education was concerned.

Once the roof had gone onto the new house and it was weather-proof, the whole family would go and live there at weekends, sleeping on mattresses on the bare floor and all pitching in to help Bert with the building work. The house was completed in less than a year and it remained the family home for sixteen years, until 1976 and the start of the Read's venture. God knows how Eva must have felt about giving it all up for the unknown. Now that I am older and a little wiser, I can only begin to imagine what the upheaval must have been like for her.

About three months after Bert died, Rona and I experienced one of the saddest days we could ever remember when we both returned home one day to find Eva in tears, standing on a spot at the back of Read's in front of a smouldering pile of ashes. She had just burned all of the love letters she and Bert had exchanged during the war. To this day, that vivid memory still brings tears to my eyes whenever it comes to mind. It must have been her way of acknowledging the end of an era and the start of the rest of her life.

6 : Grub Tin

By the end of the summer of 1978 Read's had been in operation for just over a year and things were going pretty well, although it was still a bit of an uphill struggle at times. Finding the right staff was one problem. We did have Dan and Sherry, of course, but it was proving very difficult to get anyone else half decent. We think that it's hard enough nowadays to find any staff, let alone good staff, but embarking on a new business venture with no experience and no reputation, plus the added problem of opening up in what was the gastronomic graveyard of rural Kent, put us at a considerable disadvantage when it came to attracting staff with any worthwhile experience.

In the end we decided we would have to find and train people up ourselves – we had, after all, been professional catering teachers. We started off our little in-house training scheme with a couple of local village girls, an aspiring young chef and a washer-up, and others then followed. We would sit them down at the end of each evening session and discuss the problems that had arisen that day (weekly meetings would have been too much to cope with), and all that we can remember of those discussions were the puzzled expressions on the faces of our young colleagues as they tried to work out what these strange people who used to work in London wanted from them.

One thing that soon became obvious to us was that, quite understandably, the local youngsters we were employing in this way had no idea what it was actually like to be a customer in a restaurant like ours and were completely ignorant of the needs of the people they were helping to serve. Rona then came up with the idea that we should take them out to eat in places that would convey to them exactly what we were trying to achieve. What we wanted to do was to give them first hand experience by taking them to restaurants that were the best of their type, whether it was the best country house hotel restaurant, the best stand-alone restaurant, the best five-star hotel restaurant, the best brasserie or, for that matter, the best Indian restaurant.

The only problem was how to finance the project, because then, as now, eating in top quality places could be a very expensive business. It was eventually agreed that we would all put £2-per-week into a 'grub tin' – a figure that rose gradually over the years to £10 – and this put enough in the kitty for us to be able to go out somewhere special for lunch or dinner maybe two or three times a year. On each occasion, we would all sit down together beforehand to discuss which establishment to visit. It was then a matter of waiting for a quiet day when there were no bookings at Read's – of which there still quite a few in 1978 – and then taking advantage of the opportunity to go out for our meal. If we chose to go out for dinner we could still open for lunch at Read's, and vice-versa.

The restaurants we visited included Le Gavroche (original and present), The Dorchester (both Grill and Terrace), Langan's Brasserie, The River Room at the Savoy,The Souffle (Intercontinental Hotel), The Manoir au Quats Saison, The Ritz, Inigo Jones, Chez Nico (Queenstown Road, Rochester Row, and Great Portland street), Claridge's, and Eastwell Manor. These were the top places of the day and in later years, when Read's closed on Mondays, we ventured even further afield and visited three separate Michelin-starred establishments in France at various times.

As a learning exercise, all this proved invaluable both for the kitchen and restaurant staff, and apart from that it was, of course,immensely enjoyable. Nowadays, it would be viewed as a bonding exercise. I must also point out, particularly in view of the fact that the rise of the chef/patron was seen in some quarters as contributing to the demise of waiters' skills, that the establishments we visited were chosen as much for their reputations for excellent service as for good food. And where a menu included a dish that would allow a waiter to display his carving or flambé skills at the table, we made sure that that dish would always be chosen by at least one member of our party.

I suppose that on some occasions we must have looked a bit of a motley crew, as none of our staff were regular customers of Boss or Giorgio Armani! Some final style adjustments were occasionally necessary in preparation, one kitchen commis becoming quite distraught at the thought of having to leave both his huge earrings behind. There were also the odd embarrassing moments, such as when two young kitchen boys, having been asked if they would like an aperitif, requested a Pernod and blackcurrant and a Newcastle Brown Ale. They were quickly put right by the other members of our party. Just to be on the safe side Rona and I made a point of ordering a bottle of champagne on arrival for our first visit to Nico's, where Nico Ladenis, who ended up with three Michelin stars, famously refused to serve customers prawn cocktails, well-done steaks or more than one gin-and-tonic as an aperitif, on the grounds that such things were an offence against culinary good taste!

From our own point of view as customers, there was only one restaurant we visited where the food and service were both appalling. And yet, somehow, this proved to be the most positive learning exercise that we ever had. The post mortem on the evening lasted two and a half hours and we couldn't help but admire the determination on the faces of our young staff as they discussed ways of making sure that our customers at Read's were not subjected to a similar experience.

Fortunately, Rona and I were quite well known within the industry, having worked with many people who were, by then, in prominent positions, including a number of household names. And we made the most of those contacts when organising our little educational outings. In general, even some of the most famous chefs and restaurant managers were very kind to us, often taking the time and trouble to come to our table for a chat; and it certainly made a big impression on our young staff when the likes of Anton Mosimann, Nico Ladenis, Raymond Blanc, Silvano Giraldin, Sergio Rebbecchi, Richard Shepherd, Albert Roux, Brian Turner and John Curry, legendary maitre d' at the Dorchester, spared them a few moments of their precious time.

Towards the end of 1978 we suffered a bit of a setback in the staff department when Sherry suddenly decided that she'd had enough; whether it was enough of Read's or enough of Dan, I can't exactly remember now. Anyway, she had gone by Christmas. Dan now had the caravan to himself and terrorised the Kent countryside during the afternoons and on his days off by careering round on his 250cc Honda 'Dream'. In Sherry's absence, he remained a key member of our team and a good friend. He and I had got to know each other well in the months before Read's actually opened, when he used to come down for the weekend to help out and we would travel to and from

Kent in the car together. We were both smokers in those days and the only word he would utter on the way to Ealing on the Monday morning would be a muttered "Breakfast?" as he offered me a fag from his packet of Marlboro. On the way back down to Kent on the Friday evening, however, he would be more communicative and we chatted a lot.

Once the restaurant opened, he and I also used to find ourselves together on numerous occasions in the early hours of the morning, when all the other members of staff had been sent home and we were waiting for the last 'dreaded twosome' to get up and go. He used to get very angry with customers who lingered for ever over half a cup of coffee – not to their faces, of course, but in the privacy of the kitchen, where he would sometimes explode. I would tell him to go back to the caravan and leave me to wait until they finally decided to depart and called for the bill. Ten minutes later he would return with a smile on his face, put his arms around me and tell me everything was fine. I don't know what it was that he was taking out there to suddenly relax him like that, but there were times when I certainly could have done with some myself.

It is difficult for people who do ordinary jobs – or should I say, more correctly, people who do jobs that finish at a normal time of the day – to understand what it is like to find yourself continually working all day until very late at night and sometimes into the early hours, never quite sure when you are going to finish. I can't immediately think of many trades or professions where the customer stays as long as they want to while the staff have no option but to hang around until they decide to leave.

I can recall a waiter once having a grumble at me as he went out of the door just after 3.00am at the end of what had turned into a thirteen-hour shift, saying: "Can you imagine instructing the lazy f*****s at ASLEF or the RMT that the train drivers and conductors can only go home when the last passenger finishes his crossword and decides to disembark from the train – and, by the way, we can't tell you exactly when that might be?"

As I said before, customers used to linger a lot longer in those days. And when the last customer did eventually go you couldn't just go straight to bed. There have been many times when I have locked up and have then sat down to read for a while or flick through the channels on television in search of something to watch, not because I was particularly interested in the film or whatever it was, but just because I needed to wind down a bit before I could attempt to sleep.

Now and again Dan and I would finish comparatively early, at maybe 11.30pm or midnight, and would simply sit down and have a drink together with the genuine intention of calling it a day a few minutes later. But I'm afraid the old adage is true: "When you work hard, you play hard." One drink would become two, three or four and then it would seem like a good idea to go out for a drive. We would take a bottle of something with us and on one famous occasion we found ourselves on Herne Bay Beach, watching the sun come up. Dan then said that he felt a bit peckish and, crazily, I suggested that it would be a good idea to drive into London and have something to eat there. We ended up going to the Dorchester and a couple of my old mates, who were still working there, saw that we were in need of a full English breakfast and proceeded to cook it for us. Naturally, we ate it in the potato room.

We eventually got back to Kent just in time to see Eva getting Sam up. "You boys are up early," she said, completely unaware of the fact that we had been out all night. Rona knew, of course – one of my Dorchester buddies had phoned her to see if we had got back OK – and she was understandably horrified by what we'd been up to. Why are young men so stupid? Fortunately, it was a quiet day at Read's.

Towards the end of his time with us, things began to get Dan down quite a lot. It can be mind-numbingly boring to sit and listen to the drivel some people talk while drinking at that time in the morning. I'm no exception, and he walked out on me on several occasions. However, after a spell in his caravan or a chat on the phone to his mum in Paris he would always come back. But one day he didn't come back and it seemed to me at the time like the end of the world.

Dan had become so closely involved right from the start in helping to get Read's up-and-running that we had begun to think of him almost as family. But at the same time we knew he was far too bright to work for us forever and it came as no surprise when he went on to enjoy enormous success with his own computer software business. He had always been very IT-savvy and in that respect he left us with what turned out to be a very valuable legacy, persuading me to buy outright ownership of the Internet domain names Reads.com and Reads.co.uk in the days long before most people realised that domain names had the potential to become as valuable as the most sought-after personalised car registration numbers. I only paid a few pounds in total for the two of them, but have already been offered £100,000 for Reads.com alone. Dan himself did even better, as the name of his company – Naples Software Enterprises – has the same initials as the National Stock Exchange of India, who offered him £250,000 for nse.com

For a while, after he left, I wondered how I would ever be able to replace him – but not for too long, as it turned out. Among our regular customers at the time were brothers Harry and Jim Bacon, who ran a family-owned soft drinks company, Mr Bacon's Lemonade, and operated a fleet of lorries that sold their product door-to-door all around Kent. Harry and Jim and their families used to spend a lot of money on enjoying themselves, often at Read's, thankfully. Harry had a son called Martin who had worked for a time as a waiter at Marchesi, a good restaurant in Broadstairs, and then as a steward aboard a cruise liner, and who was now looking for something else to do. He came to work for us and slotted into Dan's job just perfectly. He was a smashing chap and everyone loved him. He was also quite happy to live in the caravan that Dan had just vacated.

At the same time, there was an Italian family living just opposite Read's in Painters Forstal who had a nephew, Tony, who was a professional waiter back in Italy and wanted to come to England to learn English. We took him on as well and all of a sudden we had two really good people out front with Rona, just as we'd had with Dan and Sherry. We were lucky in the kitchen, too, with a lovely little girl called Sara, who joined us straight from college. An incredibly hard worker, she was with us for about three years, and although I haven't seen her since she left, I wish I could meet up with her again now, just so that I could say thank you properly for all her hard graft. I don't think that I appreciated her as much as I should have done at the time.

Martin and I were both very keen to learn all we could about wine. We had come to realise that we were out of our depth in this respect with some of the more knowledgeable customers who frequented Read's, in spite of what I had learned from Jimmy, back at the Dorchester. So we both signed up with The Wine and Spirit Education Trust, which was based in London, first attaining the Certificate and then following that up by going for the more advanced Diploma.

It was there that I first met the sort of ex-public schoolboys who are everywhere in the wine trade. They phone us up, usually in the middle of the lunchtime service when we are rushed off our feet, to tell us about a particular wine that we must buy because it is "stunning". Then they want to tell us about another wine, which we shouldn't miss because it is also "stunning". Finally, they save the best till last and wax lyrical about a wine that is not just "stunning" but "absolutely stunning". As it happens, expensive wines don't seem to sell quite as well as these days as they once did – at least, not at Read's. Suffice it to say that we never buy "stunning" wines from anyone.

The wine courses, enjoyable though they were, involved Martin and me in going up to London very early on the morning of our only day off, so as to be there by 9.00am, in time for the start of the class. This lasted for four hours every Monday morning and we did it for two years. When the class ended we would always go for lunch at Sweetings, the long established fish restaurant in the City of London. Martin was an employer's dream, one of those people you generally only get when there is a background of having been part of a family-owned business. It's something to do with the extra commitment, I guess. Nothing is ever too much trouble for them and they work hard without ever looking at the clock. Because of that, Martin and I got on very well and became really close.

Among the more amusing aspects of working in a restaurant are the funny things that happen because of the poor command of English displayed by some of the many foreign employees. Shortly after our Italian waiter Tony had joined us I happened to pop out of the kitchen into the restaurant just as he was in the act of pouring some wine for a customer who was animatedly protesting that it was not his wine, pointing out that he had already finished his bottle. Tony, however, didn't understand what he was saying and, a bit like Manuel in Fawlty Towers, just smiled sweetly and carried on pouring. And, like Basil Fawlty, I had to drag him aside and explain that the bottle actually belonged to the party on a neighbouring table.

A few weeks later, when his English was beginning to improve a little, he was overheard to say something rather inappropriate to a young lady customer who had just arrived. What he was trying to say was: "Would you like me to take your coat, madam"? What he actually said, in his lovely Italian accent, was: "I take your clothes off, yes?"

December and Christmas of 1978 was much better than the previous year, apart from the obvious sadness of it being the first at Read's without Bert. Generally, business was improving and we had certainly learned from some of the mistakes of the previous year. We started taking bookings for Christmas Day much earlier, were soon inundated and thought it best to stop taking any more bookings when we reached a manageable seventy-five covers. In fact, we could have filled the restaurant ten times over, which was obviously frustrating in some ways. At weekends, also, we could have filled the place many times over were it not for the fact that everybody wanted to sit down precisely at eight o'clock on a Saturday evening.

Christmas Day that year fell on a Monday and I got up at 5.00am to put two huge 35lb turkeys in the oven before going back to bed for another couple of hours. On my way back upstairs the phone rang and I went back into the kitchen to answer it. Believe it or not, it was an older-sounding gentleman wanting to know if, by any chance, he had left his hat with us the previous lunchtime. That was just one of the more extreme examples among the many hundreds of phone calls we would often get at ridiculous times of the night, invariably about trivia. What is it about people that they can be so inconsiderate, if not downright stupid? OK, so, as it happened, I wasn't actually in bed asleep when the hatless one called, but he didn't know that when he rang at quarter past five on Christmas Day morning. To receive a call at two or three o'clock in the morning from someone wanting to make a booking way in the future was a regular occurrence that used to drive us mad in the days before answer machines allowed us to turn off the phone and pick up any messages later.

Although the first major UK recession is usually referred to as being in the early 1980's, it actually started in the August of 1979. And it was the one that nearly brought us to our knees, as Read's was not in quite such a strong financial position then as it was later, when the downturns of 1990 and 2008 hit. Company earnings generally declined 35% in 1979 and unemployment more than doubled, from 5.3% to 11.9%. And this was followed by one of the slowest recoveries on record, taking eighteen quarters to get back to the previous levels. We learned that when the economy takes a dip – or a dive, as it was in 1980 – the first thing that people cut out is fine dining.

To compensate for this, we launched a cheap and cheerful three-course menu at lunchtime and billed it as 'Lunch for a Fiver'. The local press got hold of this and as a result it really took off and unquestionably made the difference between us surviving and going under. Its popularity meant that we could keep food turning over. Virtually all our evening business died, except for 8.00pm on a Saturday, but throughout the rest of the week any evening's unused mise en place could be used for lunch the following day, meaning that waste was kept to a minimum.

The cheap and cheerful lunch concept led to us winning the 'Best Lunch in Britain' award some years later in 1988, although by that time it had become 'Lunch for a Tenner'. Two years after that, the good value lunch menu again came to our rescue when the economy went into recession in the early 1990's. Indeed, that 'Best Lunch in Britain' accolade, resulting from a competition organised by The Caterer and Hotelkeeper in conjunction with Luncheon Vouchers, proved to be very good indeed for us for quite some time afterwards.

1980 was the year that our second son, Alex, was born. On Rona's final trip to the doctor for a check-up a couple of weeks before she was due to give birth, they discovered that the baby was in the wrong position and she had to go into hospital for a few days. As I was pushing her down a corridor at the Kent and Canterbury Hospital in a wheelchair we experienced a great example of traditional British reserve. Coming in the opposite direction, also in a wheelchair, was a gentleman being pushed by his wife. Rona recognised them as regular customers of ours and asked how they were? They replied politely that they were "fine, thank you" and added: "How are you?" Rona said that she was fine also and after a moment's slightly awkward silence we each continued on our respective journeys along the corridor without another word being spoken.

The day Ali was born was a bizarre one in many ways. I was still playing the occasional round of golf at the time and had entered an annual competition at Faversham Golf Club known as the Midsummer Cup. This was sponsored by half-a-dozen wealthy local rogues, all of whom were good customers of Read's, so I was expected to play in it. It was a 36-hole competition – 18 in the morning and 18 in the afternoon, with the stableford points from each round being totalled up to decide the overall winner. The unusual thing about this particular event was that five drinks tents were strategically placed around the course, meaning that the players had to pass every one of them twice during each round. The rules of the competition stipulated that you had to have a drink at each one, served by a bevy of scantily clad wenches, before being allowed onto the next tee.

At lunchtime after the first round I returned to Read's to make sure that Rona, who was due to give birth the following week, was OK. I was accompanied by my playing partner, showbiz and fashion photographer Brian Aris, who had become a good personal friend as well as a Read's regular. The restaurant was moderately busy for lunch, but Rona said she was fine and was insistent that I should return for the second round, as I was well in contention with 36 points. And when I came in at the end of the afternoon round with another 38 points I was duly declared the winner. A few minutes later Derek Place, the Faversham pro, came into the clubhouse to say that he had just received a call from Eva to say that I had to return to Read's as soon as possible because Rona had suddenly gone into labour. I jumped into the car straightaway, but by the time I got back to the restaurant she had already gone to hospital and I had to take over in the kitchen.

By about 9.30pm all the main courses had gone out and I was anxious to finish up and get down to the hospital. But then, just as I was about to leave, about twenty of the sponsors arrived, along with some of the scantily clad ladies who had been serving the drinks, plus Derek Place, my partner Brian Aris and the players who had finished second and third, all wanting to eat. By this time I was getting ready to close down for the evening, desperate to get away to the hospital, but there was no way I could do that. I was called out of the kitchen to be presented with £300, my prize as the winner, each of the 150 players taking part having paid £2 into a sweepstake. Although I had sobered up by this time, the rest of them had not, and they were insistent on having something to eat – and drink! It would have been very poor form to refuse them and could have done Read's a lot of damage, as they were all regular customers, so I reluctantly stayed on and cooked for them.

I eventually arrived at the hospital at about half past midnight, just in time to see Alex being placed in something that resembled an eye level grill in order to keep him warm. I had missed his birth by just a few minutes. Rona was shaking violently as some sort of reaction to giving birth, but was otherwise surprisingly calm and very happy. I was assured that she was OK and I was also very pleased to find out that this time there had been no need for the huge pair of glinting shears. We talked for an hour or so and unbelievably she wanted to hear all about my day. I remember telling her not to be so silly, that I'd tell her all about that later. Totally exhausted, she then fell asleep and I left after holding my new son in my arms for a few minutes in order to have my first chat with him, albeit a rather one-sided conversation!

Not knowing in advance whether we were going to have a boy or a girl and thinking about possible alternative names, we had already decided that if it was boy he would be Alex and if we got a girl she would be Ella, partly because we were both great fans of Ella Fitzgerald. It's probably just as well that we ended up with another son because, as somebody pointed out much later, if we'd had a daughter our two children together would have been known as Sam 'n' Ella – not great for a family involved in the food industry!

I arrived back at Read's just before 3.00am to find Eva waiting up for me at the bar. We had a glass of champagne together and I gave her a full report about everything that had gone on at the hospital. I felt guilty about not actually being with Rona for the birth, but Eva tried to make me feel better by explaining that the golfing party, who had only just left about fifteen minutes earlier, had ended up spending well over a £1,000, a huge sum of money for us in those days; not only that, but they had left a £250 tip on top. So, things are not always too bad in a restaurant when your customers are drunk!

Looking back, it gives me great pleasure and a good deal of amusement to recall that what was by far the most glorious triumph of my entire golfing career was only the second best thing that happened to me on that extraordinary day!

7 : We're Not Keeping You Up, Are We?

It is well past midnight, you've been cooking in the kitchen or catching up with paperwork in the office since at least 8.00am and maybe even earlier, slaving away through another long and busy day during which the restaurant has been fully booked for both lunch and dinner. And finally, after a full-on evening service, you've turned off the ovens, got all the washing-up done, cleaned and tidied the work surfaces, completed whatever advance prepping tasks are necessary for the following day and compiled your meat, fish and fruit and vegetable orders to be sent to suppliers overnight for delivery the next morning. You're exhausted and more than ready for bed, but you can't get away just yet because, long after all the other diners have left, one table of four is lingering on. They've enjoyed a very good and highly convivial meal, washed down with three or four bottles of wine, not to mention aperitifs and liqueurs, and by now they are in loud, chatty, high-spirited party mode. They seem totally oblivious to the fact that the restaurant is now almost completely deserted, the last remaining waiter having packed up and gone home after pointedly relaying the tables around them. Apart from them, the only other person now left in the place is me, hovering in the background and making a show of closing up for the night; and yet they completely ignore the hint and call for yet another round of liqueurs and coffees, with a cheery cry of: "We're not keeping you up, are we?"

This kind of inconvenience is just one of the many minor occupational hazards that you have to accept as the chef/proprietor of a successful restaurant. As anyone whose business involves direct, face-to-face interaction with individual members of the general public very soon finds out – it takes all sorts. We've certainly had more than our fair share of awkward customers over the years, ranging from fussy food faddists to self-styled connoisseurs who mistakenly think they know it all and try to show off by acting like Masterchef judges, picking on tiny perceived faults and imperfections, usually out of total ignorance about how things should really be done. To use yet another pun, I could dine out every day for a year on stories about the many extraordinary and often bizarre incidents we have had to deal with over the years – occasionally dramatic, sometimes outrageous, mostly quite comical, often highly entertaining, but frequently just plain irritating.

Never mind the many variations on that old joke that starts: "Waiter, there's a fly in my soup!" – one lady who came to lunch at Read's insisted that her starter of cherry tomatoes, fresh basil and Parmesan crisp, with a shallot and sherry vinaigrette dressing, was covered in broken glass! Even when we showed her the carton of Maldon sea salt with which the dish had been very lightly sprinkled and actually ate a mouthful in front of her to prove the point, she still wouldn't have it, making a big fuss and threatening to call the police and report us to the local Food Standards authority. We did eventually manage to calm her down and she was persuaded to try a different starter on the house, but you could tell that she still wasn't convinced and we certainly never saw her again.

And then there was the woman who was apparently enjoying her meal until the coffee was served, at which point she suddenly leapt up from the table and ran, screaming, into the car park. It turned out that this melodramatic reaction was all because Rona had put a plate of tangerines and mince pies down in front of her, along with her coffee. This was meant to be a little extra seasonal touch, it being around Christmas time, but it then turned out that this woman had a phobia about citrus fruit – not just tangerines, but also oranges, satsumas, mandarins and clementines. Not sure about grapefruit! We were left wondering what an earth could have happened to her in her early life to leave such a deep psychological scar!

Having to cater for the ever-increasing number and range of food faddists has become an extra headache for us. Any one of you who has held a dinner party at home, only to discover at the last moment that one of your guests can't eat whatever you had intended to serve, will know how awkward and troublesome that can be – and in a restaurant situation you can multiply that inconvenience a hundred times over. Not only do we have to allow for the dreaded vegetarians and vegans, but also for people claiming to suffer from allergies, some genuine but others self-diagnosed and often imaginary.

A classic example of the latter is a lady who has been coming to eat at Read's for nearly thirty years now. Let's call her Pauline. Whenever there is Dover Sole Veronique on the menu, Pauline will always choose it and she tells us that it is her favourite dish in the whole world. Now, there are various ways of preparing Dover Sole Veronique, but we do it in the old traditional way, which involves the cooking liquor in which the sole fillets are poached being reduced to a syrupy glaze, at which point we shake in about three ounces of ice cold butter, which forms an emulsion as it slowly melts. We then finish the sauce with a couple of teaspoons of lightly whipped cream before napping it over the cooked fish and glazing it under a fierce salamander. Finally, the dish is accompanied by a timbale of chilled and pipped white Muscat grapes and served with some Jersey Royals if they are available.

We would normal roll the potatoes in a little butter, but from her very first visit Pauline asked for hers to be served plain. However, it was only after several months and many further visits that she explained that she had a serious butter allergy and would have a violent reaction if she had even the tiniest amount. We didn't like to tell her that on each of the several occasions that she'd eaten Sole Veronique she had actually consumed around 75g of butter, which, remaining in blissful ignorance, she has continued to do ever since without the slightest ill effect – and yet she still believes that she has an allergy. If a customer warns us in advance they are sensitive to any one of the fourteen listed allergens we obviously make absolutely sure that they don't eat anything that includes that particular allergen and that there has been no cross-contamination with other ingredients. I don't know for sure, but with so many fussy eaters about these days I rather suspect there are many who, like Pauline, may have become slightly self-delusional.

At the same time, I'm only too well aware that some people do suffer from life-threatening allergies and that you can't be too careful. This was brought home to us at Read's when a woman who was coeliac – allergic to the glutens found in bread, pasta, cereals and biscuits – dined with us one evening as one of a table of six people. She had warned us about her allergy when she booked and we took all the necessary precautions, right down to preparing her own separate gluten-free petit-fours to have with her coffee. However, in a moment's apparent aberration she then reached over to a fellow diner's plate and pinched a brandy snap tuile that did contain flour. Within thirty seconds she had thrown up violently all over her end of the table before keeling over onto the floor in a state of anaphylactic shock. Luckily, there happened to be a doctor or paramedic of some sort in the restaurant at the time and he reacted very swiftly. Having placed her in the recovery position, he took her wrist while looking at his watch and after two breathless minutes announced, much to everyone's relief, that she had a pulse. While we were completely innocent of any wrongdoing, we still had to suffer the consequences of a projectile vomit in a packed restaurant, something which I can assure you is definitely not good for repeat business!

For some years now we have been licensed for marriage ceremonies as well as wedding receptions at Read's and most of the more dramatic incidents we have witnessed have been acted out during the course of the weekend wedding parties that have been held there. They have a whole chapter to themselves later in the book.

On a more light-hearted level, there have been many memorably amusing moments over the years, mostly provided by the extended cast of colourful characters among our regular customers, people like John Butcher and George Freeman – both, very sadly, no longer with us – Stuart Ross, Colin Strickland and Brian Aris. And the high jinks have usually taken place towards the end of a particularly long lunch, or a dinner party that has lasted until well into the early hours of the morning, long after the rest of the clientele have gone home and only a few hardcore regulars are left. That's when things can occasionally start to spiral out of control and get a bit silly. When it came to those late night sessions, I have to say that there have been many times in the past when I would have been a willing participant as well as a mere observer, having finished work in the kitchen before going out to sit down for a drink with people who had become good friends as well as loyal customers, only too happy to mix business and pleasure in that way. On one never-to-be forgotten occasion I enthusiastically led an after-hours wine-tasting session with a select group of the usual suspects that went on until dawn, despite the fact that I and my golf-mad son were due to fly to Augusta for The Masters later that very same morning. Amazingly, as I recall, that proved to be no great problem. But, of course, I was a lot younger then!

In terms of pushing the boat out, Stuart Ross, a local solicitor whom we have used professionally on the odd occasions when we have needed any legal work done, along with his friend Colin Strickland, a successful property developer who has been coming to us since the day we first opened, could be a dangerous duo in their heyday. As well as frequently coming to us for dinner with their wives, Janice Ross and Rose Strickland, they also regularly used to enjoy business lunches together as they sorted out Colin's numerous property deals, and those lunchtime sessions could often last until 7.30 in the evening, just as other customers were beginning to arrive for dinner, and would sometimes go on even later. Stuart and Colin proudly hold the record for the lengthiest lunchtime stay – having arrived at 12 noon they were still in the restaurant at midnight – and also for the most alcohol consumed in one session – aperitifs, followed by seven and a half bottles of wine, plus one or two items from the now defunct liqueur trolley.

The only problem on such occasions was that Colin, in particular, tended to become increasingly expansive as the day and the evening wore on, his stories becoming ever more risqué and his language decidedly fruity towards the end of these marathons. Rona once literally had to box his ears to get him to quieten down and after that he was always very obedient when told to behave himself. Not that anybody on neighbouring tables seemed to mind that much, even when he was in full flow, as he was always so entertaining. He is one of the few people with whom Rona and I will very happily sit down with for a drink and a chat once service has finished, simply because he is such good company. By that time in the evening he will have certainly have had a bottle of wine or two, while we are still stone cold sober, so the conversation will be a bit one-sided. But that doesn't matter because we know that he will always keep us amused with some great stories, all of which make us chuckle even though we will have heard some of them countless times before.

When lunching together, Colin and Stuart would always gamble in some way or other to decide who would actually pay the bill – or, more correctly, to whose account the bill would be added, since they both ran a tab with us. Initially, they would arm wrestle – not at the table, but lying opposite each other full length on the floor, sunny side down. Colin quickly discovered, to his cost, that nobody ever beat Stuart at arm wrestling, so he preferred to 'spoof' for the bill instead, each of them holding out a fist with anything from one to three coins concealed in it and then trying to guess how many they were holding in total, between them.

They would also play another rather curious game that involved taking banknotes out of their wallets and guessing whether the last digit of the serial number was odd or even. To their great credit, they would always leave a substantial tip for the poor waiter or waitress who would miss out on a couple of hours off in the afternoon in order to wait on them during their more extended sessions Most people assume that restaurant staff get paid for attending to people who stay very late either in the afternoon or after midnight, which, of course, they don't, or at least they didn't back in those days.

Even on those occasions when Colin and Stuart's lunches went on until dinner time, Stuart would often get a second wind and would want to carry on to pastures new, his favoured onward destination being the casino at Ramsgate, getting Rona to summon his driver back to Read's to collect him. Whilst waiting for his transport to arrive, he would be likely to request a loan of any cash we happened to have in the till and with anything from £500 to £1000 of our money in his pocket he would then happily depart for the casino.

The following morning either Rona or I would call in to his offices in Preston Street, Faversham, ostensibly in order to see how he had got on at the casino, but primarily to retrieve our money, just in case he might have forgotten about it. The first time this happened, he did indeed claim to have absolutely no recollection of our £500 interest free monetary advance the night before. However, he was a true gentleman and unhesitatingly accepted our word that the transaction had taken place. From then on we made sure that any cash handover was witnessed by at least one of our mutual acquaintances, and Rona would occasionally take the precaution of 'doctoring' the till when Stuart was in, hiding some of the cash and making it look as if we'd taken mostly cheques or credit card transactions, just so that we wouldn't be left too short of ready cash. Sometimes he won at the casino, and sometimes he came out a loser, but we always got our money back.

Stuart was also responsible for introducing me and another long-time friend, John Butcher, to Freemasonry. Despite its name, West Lancashire Lodge 3088 was actually London based. The explanation for this oddity was that it had been founded a hundred years or so earlier by a group of West Lancashire businessmen who used to come down to London four times a year for a bit of a jolly to coincide with the Epsom Derby, the Lord's Test, the Chelsea Flower Show and the Wimbledon tennis. They justified this by holding a Masonic meeting away from home, as it were. For a dozen or so years John, Stuart and I regularly went up to London for meetings held in the Masonic temple located in the basement of the Cafe Royal in Regent Street. And John and I both went on to hold office, our Masonic careers culminating in each becoming Worshipful Master of the Lodge in consecutive years (and in my case on two separate occasions). John, who died suddenly just weeks before this book was published, also became Secretary of the Lodge, a most exalted position.

It was on one of these trips that Stuart and I purchased a racing greyhound, which seemed a really good idea at the time, after a bottle-and-a-half of champagne. My problem on returning to Kent was how to persuade Rona that it was a good investment, especially now that the school fees for our two boys at St. Edmund's in Canterbury were proving a considerable drain on our resources. I mistakenly decided that attack was the best form of defence and told Rona that I had bought a racehorse for £12,000, which was exactly ten times the actual cost of my half share of the dog. The hope was that she would then be relieved when I told her that I was only joking, that actually it was greyhound not a horse and that it was £1,200 not £12,000. It worked to a degree, but as women often do, she then confounded me by saying that she would have preferred a racehorse.

I suffered the silent treatment, well understood by every man in the world, for some considerable time as I insisted that I could not go back on my word as my Lodge was mostly made up of chaps from the insurance business in the City, whose motto was 'My Word is My Bond'. Come on Hawk, as our dog was named, first ran at the unclassified dog track at Canterbury and Stuart and I were reliably informed by our very well respected trainer that it genuinely had a realistic chance of winning a six-bend race. He was 7-2 third favourite with each of the four bookies at the track, but I decided to go with the Tote and take my chance with the odds, betting £200 to win. Stuart had the same bet with one of the bookies.

As the hare came speeding past, Come on Hawk came out of Trap 3 fairly well and was on the shoulder of the leading dog at the first bend. But then the leader ran wide and impeded Hawk, who was seriously baulked and, as a result of the collision, the two of them were overtaken by the rest of the field. Hawk was now trailing the new leader by at least eight lengths, but after composing himself he rallied to make a little headway back through the field. Coming out of the fourth bend he powered down the back straight, absolutely eating up the ground, and was in third place going into the fifth bend. He then ran pretty much the perfect final stretch to get his nose in front about three yards from the line.

Hawk had won the most exciting greyhound race that I had ever seen, and that included all those that I'd witnessed with Jim Harris at Monmore Green in Wolverhampton all those years ago, back in the mid-sixties; and this despite the fact that he had performed a virtual somersault at the first bend. Stuart and I were jumping around and I said that I was off to collect my winnings. Stuart said bollocks to that, that we could do that later and that we first had to go and collect the trophy. In all the excitement I had totally forgotten that we were now owners! We arrived at the finish line in order to cross the track to where the presentation ceremony was to take place on the infield, only to find that the stewards wouldn't let us through as we didn't have an owner's pass. Try as we might they would not let us through and so we never did get to be presented with the trophy.

Our disappointment was tempered by the thought of collecting our winnings. We went back first to Stuart's bookie, who handed over £900, which went a long way towards making Come on Hawk a free dog for Stuart. A couple of minutes later at the Tote I handed over my winning ticket and was presented with £204, which included my £200 stake! I queried this several times before an official explained to me that my "substantial" £200 win bet had wrecked the Tote pool and had reduced the odds on our dog to 50-1 on. To this day Stuart thinks that I also collected £900 for my bet – and so did Rona; I was too ashamed to tell either of them how silly I had been.

If not quite the Usain Bolt of the dog-racing world, Come on Hawk certainly proved to be the Linford Christie and won several races at various venues in and around London and the South East. His prize money more than paid for his kennel fees, on top of which my winnings at the various tracks ensured that I was well up on the £1,200 I had paid for him, despite my silly first bet. Sadly, all did not end well, because Come on Hawk was eventually discovered running under a different name at Catford racetrack in London, a practice that is understandably frowned upon very heavily in racing circles. Stuart and I had no idea about what had gone on, but were nevertheless warned off having any further involvement with him. We accepted our fate, consoling ourselves with the thought that we'd had such a good time with him along the way. I'm afraid to say I have no idea what happened to Hawk after that.

While the likes of Stuart, Colin and some of our other favourite regulars can be a fairly uproarious presence in the restaurant when they are in full flight with a few drinks inside them, they are always welcome because they are invariably good for a laugh and never that much of a problem, except on those occasions when they conspire to lead me astray! This was especially true of George Freeman. One of the first customers through our doors when we opened in 1977 and a regular thereafter until his death forty years later, George was a very successful local businessman who owned a string of menswear shops in the Medway towns before actually going on to run a restaurant of his own for a time. Openly gay, he would arrive at Read's with his partner in his vintage Bentley and the first occasion that I vividly remember was when he celebrated his birthday by pre-ordering a very expensive bottle of Burgundy of the exact same vintage as himself – 1937. Rona had gone through the elaborate and painstaking process of carefully removing the crumbly cork, which you often get with wines of such an age, before decanting it. Later in the evening, Brian Aris and his then partner, Anna, pitched up, as they often did after a long day working together in his photographic studio at Old Street in London, and Rona seated them at the table next to George. Little did we know that this chance placement would lead to a life-long friendship between Brian and Anna, George, Rona and me.

One of things I loved about George was his wickedly dry sense of humour and his sometimes brutally camp repartee. He and his boyfriend at the time were well into their main courses and also their very fine wine when Brian and Anna arrived that evening. The four of them already knew each other slightly by sight and by reputation, both Brian and George fancying themselves as wine connoisseurs, so when George overheard Brian ordering a 1955 claret he couldn't resist mocking him gently for choosing something so relatively young. The remark was made with tongue very much in cheek and accepted with great good humour by Brian and they proceeded to offer each other a taste of their respective wines. Rona and I joined them later in the evening, and so it was that the lasting friendship between all of us began.

It was not long afterwards that George got together with Massoud, the handsome, charming and educated young Iranian who became his partner for many years. George and 'Mash' were an endlessly entertaining couple and evenings at Read's were never dull when they were in, especially if other members of 'the gang' also happened to be present. On such occasions things could often get extremely lively, but always enjoyably so, simply because of the essentially decent, fun-loving nature of the characters involved.

Unfortunately, not everybody is always quite so much fun and the need to be able to deal calmly, efficiently and diplomatically with awkward, fussy, badly-behaved and sometimes objectionably drunken customers is just one of many reasons why, in any restaurant, the quality of the staff – especially those working front-of-house – is all-important. Even on a more everyday level, most of us who eat out regularly will, at some time or another, have experienced the disappointment of having an otherwise great meal ruined by poor service. That is why Rona and I invested so much time and effort in wining and dining our inexperienced young waiters, waitresses and kitchen boys at some of the country's top restaurants, so that they could see how things should be done.

In the age of the modern celebrity chef, waiters, sommeliers and restaurant managers have increasingly become the unsung heroes of our industry, getting very little if any credit at all compared to chefs who, quite undeservedly in my opinion, get all the recognition from both customers and media for the success of a restaurant. Many prominent chefs tend to think that everything revolves around them and are so totally focused on the food they produce that they care little about what happens after it leaves the kitchen. Their attitude is that waiters don't create anything, they just dish out what someone else has prepared – and how difficult can that be? Extremely difficult, is the answer to that.

As a chef/patron in my own small family-run restaurant I have often found myself having to help out in the dining room, particularly in the early days when short staffed, and as a result I have a much better understanding of the difficulties a waiter encounters every day. Though dramatically different, the level of commitment, skill and knowledge required of a waiter in a high-end restaurant is equivalent in many ways to that demanded of a chef. And it is the combination of their respective talents that enhances the customer's overall dining experience and makes for a truly great restaurant.

However, finding the right people is not always easy, especially when you are trying to build a reputation for fine dining while located out in the country, well away from the nearest town or city centre, which is where the more experienced staff usually want to live and work. Over the forty years since Read's first opened we have employed literally hundreds of different people and, interestingly, it hasn't always been the most professionally skilled or competent ones who turned out to be the most valued employees. We've had waiters who were technically brilliant craftsmen but who, when they eventually left, were hardly missed at all by the regular customers. On the other hand, there have been one or two colourful characters who were pretty hopeless in many respects but who, largely because of their personalities, were hugely popular with the customers, who would still ask about them years after they had left us.

One great example of the latter was Sarah 'Windy' Miller, a complete maniac who was nevertheless absolutely brilliant, both with the customers and with our children. Sarah, a local girl who lived just down the road from the restaurant, joined Rona, Martin and Tony front-of-house. I couldn't even begin to tell you all the stories about Sarah, as she is now a respectable married woman and also a great friend. Her father, a lovely individual and a gentleman in the true sense of the word – the sort of chap who would wear a cravat when he was out doing the gardening – had spent a large amount of money on Sarah's education, sadly to little academic avail. However, she was, and still remains, one of the most irresistibly likeable personalities that Rona and I have ever employed.

A big hit with the customers, Sarah was an undoubted asset to the restaurant, but it took us a while to find out that she was not too good with figures, by which time I hate to think how much she had already cost us. I don't know what the numerical equivalent of dyslexia is, but whatever it is, Sarah suffered from it. She would serve drinks at the bar and charge the customer the first figure that came into her head, which often bore absolutely no resemblance to the value of what had actually been ordered. Sometimes the price she named would be well over the top, at others it would be ridiculously low, but rarely was it even close to what it should have been. Once we realised what had been happening we had to insist, as tactfully as possible, that she should leave the billing to someone else while she got on with what she was absolutely brilliant at, which was interacting with customers.

This she did in her own inimitable style. I recall coming out of the kitchen one lunchtime to see her serving a table of four rather stern local businessmen with desserts from the sweet trolley, which was a feature of most restaurants in those days. One of the four had chosen a local Kentish confection known as 'gypsy tart' and she placed it in front of him with the cheery comment that it was "made by a real gypsy and served by a real tart"! I winced, wondering how this might go down, but I needn't have worried – they loved it.

On another occasion she was serving a mango, which was quite an unusual item at the time, to a gentleman who rather mischievously enquired whether it was an aphrodisiac? "Oh no", came her reply. "I don't think they are from Africa – we get them from London". And then there was the time that she recommended my individual sherry trifles to two elderly and very genteel ladies as being "absolutely orgasmic – you'll love them". Again, I froze momentarily, but somehow she always got away with it. She was just so much fun that everybody couldn't help but warm to her. Whenever she had a day off, she would be missed by regular customers who would be quite disappointed, wanting to know where she was. And when she eventually left us to get married, people were still asking after her months and even years later. We have never lost touch with her. In fact, she still comes back to look after Read's when the restaurant closes for the annual staff holidays and we are away – living in, answering the phone, taking advance bookings and generally keeping an eye on things for us. She even has little drinks parties in the bar for old friends among former staff and customers.

By the early eighties, Martin and Tony were sadly coming towards the end of their time with us, as they were keen to go to Italy together so that Martin could learn Italian. One of the problems of employing two good friends, or a couple, is that they naturally tend to leave at the same time, causing double disruption. However, Stephanie Wheatley had joined us in the meantime and she was also a great girl – very efficient, and a perfect foil for Sarah.

This period in the eighties was probably the worst for customers staying late, three o'clock in the morning being quite common and 4.00am or even 5.00am by no means unheard of. Among the worst offenders in this respect were Carl Thompsett and his friend Arthur, a lorry driver whose surname I can't now recall, along with their wives. I admit that I was partly responsible for this as I found Carl and his wife, in particular, to be great and very amusing company and I used to enjoy sitting down with them for a drink once I had finished cooking for the evening. This same period was also the worst (or the best depending upon your point of view) for customers giving the liqueur trolley and the vintage port a serious bashingduring the afternoons, something that hardly ever happens these days for some reason, possibly to do with the more stringent drink-driving laws.

Recalling Carl and Arthur reminds me of the time Rona and I took the children off to France for a couple of days. All we ever used to do in those days was work and Eva told us off for not spending more time with the kids during their school holidays. She was quite right, of course, and we took her words to heart, deciding on the spur of the moment to take an impromptu two-day break across the Channel. We loaded up the car and drove off to Dover and across to France on the hovercraft and all seemed to be going well until we started to look for somewhere to stay the night. Unknown to us, it was a national holiday in France and it proved impossible to find a hotel with any vacant rooms. At about nine o'clock in the evening we decided to give up on the accommodation and made our way back to Calais to catch the last hovercraft back to Dover, only to discover that this had been cancelled, as often used to be the case when there were not enough people booked to make it worthwhile.

The only option open to us was to sleep in the car in the hovercraft car park, which is what we did. We were awoken at about 5.30 the next morning by a combination of the cold and the very noisy gulls. I decided to go on a recce to see where we might be able to freshen up and found that there was a special toilet block mostly used by truck drivers. It was very clean and tidy and well equipped, with lovely showers and fresh towels provided. Sadly, it seemed to be a men-only facility, with no female equivalent, but as there seemed to be no-one around I persuaded Rona that if I and the kids stood guard on the main entrance while she was in there, she could nip in and use it without fear of embarrassment. Having rather nervously taken a hurried shower she emerged from the cubicle, completely starkers, to grab her towel, which was hanging on a peg outside. And right at that very same moment a guy emerged from one of the other cubicles three doors down and called out casually: "Hello Rona. What are you doing here?" before bursting into fits of laughter. It was Arthur, the lorry driver, who must have slipped in unnoticed when I had gone back to collect Rona and the children from the car.

Alex was the one who seemed to be most affected by the lack of sleep on this abortive trip, remaining grufty for a few days afterwards. His stars must have been against him that weekend because when we got back home he suffered what could easily have been a catastrophic accident. While we were away there had been a leak from a pipe in his bedroom that resulted in water running down into the kitchen and dining room below. Eva had called in a plumber, who had rectified the problem but had left the carpet rolled back and the floorboards up so that the room could dry out. Unknown to all of us, Alex had climbed into the exposed space and was busy vroom-vrooming his Dinky Toy cars along the gap in between the joists. This was fine while he continued to sit on the joists, but as soon as he stood up his whole weight was on the flimsy plasterboard.

We were all sitting downstairs in the kitchen having a cup of tea when Alex came crashing through the ceiling, a fall of easily twelve feet. Had it not been so potentially disastrous it would have been quite funny to witness his sudden and unexpected arrival in our midst amid a flurry of dust and debris. Initially, he just blinked, with a pained expression of bewilderment on his little face as if to say: "How did I end up down here?" It was a full thirty seconds before he burst into tears.

Rona and I used to view what thereafter became quite regular trips to France as some sort of brief respite from the non-stop pressure of our busy daily routine, and yet they inevitably turned into busman's holidays as all we ever did was eat in restaurants. Living where we do, it was quite easy to nip down to Dover and get on a ferry and we could be across the water in about an hour and a half. Apart from the previously mentioned Hotel du Centre in Wimereux, our other favourite places included the Chateau de Montreuil, down beyond Boulogne in the little country town of Montreuil-sur-Mer, where you will also find La Grenouillière. All three were excellent in their way.

The cooking at the Hotel du Centre was fairly basic and very honest, while the Chateau de Montreuil was very much at the top end of the scale, being run by a couple of Roux Brothers' prodigies – French chef Christian Germaine and his English wife Lyndsey – who had previously been head chef and front-of-house respectively at the Waterside Inn at Bray, which had three Michelin stars. La Grenouillière was gastronomically somewhere between the other two and has recently been awarded a second Michelin star. We used to return from these French trips with a sackful of ideas for new dishes to be served at Read's, the simpler ones for lunch and the more accomplished to be added to the dinner menu. We never did a straight copy of any of the dishes, simply adapting them to our own style of doing things.

La Grenouillière ('The Froggery') enjoys an idyllic riverside location, with a little bridge nearby where, over the years, it became a ritual part of every trip for Rona to take a picture of me posing with our two ever-growing and ever-heavier sons in my arms. In the more recent pictures it is they, as fully-grown men, who are pictured carrying me between them! Sadly, at the time of writing, we haven't visited as a family for a while, as it gets more and more difficult to arrange such trips now that the boys are busy doing their own thing. Interestingly, all three restaurants still exist pretty much unchanged and are still in the ownership of the same families, which is remarkable, given that it is well over thirty years since we first started going to them.

Back at Read's the early eighties passed relatively uneventfully. We managed to survive the recession, which was the main objective, and the evening trade began to recover. And whereas we had done virtually everything ourselves in the very early days, working with just a skeleton staff, we were now approaching a situation where the business was growing to such an extent that we needed to expand. Up until that time Eva often used to come down and help with the washing-up once she had got Sam off to bed, but that was no longer necessary as we employed a full-time pot washer. Prior to that we had got local village casuals in on busy nights and had done it ourselves at quieter times. We used to dream that once we got more staff, life would become easier, but, of course, as every small business owner knows, that never actually happens; the more staff you have, the more problems they create.

As a small business, you take bookings according to the amount of staff you have available, so when any one of them simply doesn't bother to turn up for whatever reason then you are stymied and there is very little that you can do about it. Over the years, I have had many lectures from customers who, uninvited, have offered a variety of different opinions as to why we are not doing our job properly. These are invariably people who have only ever worked as employees and have never actually employed anyone themselves. The reason that we don't employ a waiter who speaks perfect English, understands the nuances of the language and does his or her job perfectly all the time is that there simply aren't any such people to be had – or, at least, not enough to go around. And this has a lot to do with the way that waiters, and the job they do, are perceived by the general public in this country. We have to find and train up young people ourselves, and they are often from abroad because British people, generally, either aren't up to it, or are unwilling to work the unsociable hours, usually both. The same is true of kitchen staff. There has been a huge explosion of restaurants and food outlets in this country in recent years and there are just not enough trained people to go around.

We have had a few funny characters on washing-up duty over the years, as well as some who have shown a real aptitude for cooking and have gone on to become very good chefs. We had one guy who was a surprisingly bright individual and could hold a seriously intelligent conversation on any subject you cared to mention. His name was John and, once again, I'm ashamed to say that I can't now remember his surname. He lived in a caravan, parked not on our property but about half a mile away, and this was broken into and his portable television stolen so many times that he ended up putting the set in a black bin bag and burying it in the woods under a pile of leaves on his way into work and then digging it up again every evening on his way home. He was always amazed by the quantity of washing-up that chefs and customers manage to generate in a top quality restaurant and suggested that dealing with it ought to be made an Olympic event.

The reason I have difficulty recalling the surnames of some of the people we have employed over the years is simply that there have been so many of them. And given the menial nature of some of the work, there were one or two dodgy characters that I'd rather forget altogether. One of these was a man sent along in the early eighties by staff at the Sittingbourne Job Centre. He seemed at first too good to be true. He was hardworking, punctual, respectful, clean and apparently honest. But shortly after he'd started working for us we began to get strange, anonymous phone calls warning us not to take him at face value. Although he had given us a plausible story about his background and history there were certain things that didn't quite fit into place. Slightly concerned about this, I decided to follow him home one night to where he said he lived, only to see him turn off the road into some heavy undergrowth in a nearby cherry orchard, where he'd got a tent pitched! I then did a little bit of research and discovered, to my horror, that he was a convicted paedophile.

I went straight round to the job centre and demanded to know what on earth they were doing sending us a convicted paedophile, especially as there were two young children on the premises. I was further astonished when they then gave me a form to fill in on which I could request not to be sent any 'repats', which was how they categorised people convicted of crimes, including rape, murder, drug addiction and the like. I was horrified, and still am, although I suspect that the system has been tightened up in recent years as a result of the seemingly endless revelations about child abuse.

I wasn't so easily taken in when a Dutch chap arrived on our kitchen doorstep one day wanting to know if we had any jobs going. I asked him whether he meant front-of-house or in the kitchen and he said that he didn't mind which. I asked him what experience he had, to which he replied: "None, but how difficult can it be?" I couldn't resist saying that actually, if you did the job properly, it could be very difficult indeed, at which point he gave me a withering look. I didn't like him or his attitude and although we could have done with taking someone on in the kitchen at the time I told him that we didn't have any vacancies. However, I remembered that Harry Bacon, Martin's dad, had been looking for draymen for his lorries, so I gave him Harry's number and sent him on his way. And that was the end of it, or so I thought.

Unfortunately, as it turned out, Harry did take him on. And only a matter of weeks later he actually murdered someone who was out walking his dog. The dog was also killed and strung up in a tree next to the dead body of its owner. It then emerged that the Dutchman was also wanted for murder back in Holland. A kitchen can be a volatile place, so I thank God that I didn't take him on. Harry was very understanding about it, but whenever I saw him after that he would always ask: "Got any more murderers for me, David?"

We once had another kitchen porter who was so tall that he used to kneel down with his elbows on the kitchen sink to do the washing-up. But without doubt, the two best plongeurs we have ever had were Les Palmer and Alison, two very different characters. Les was an incredibly hard worker who would often be in the kitchen until the early hours of the morning, long after he'd finished his regular duties, busying himself by polishing the copper pans and cleaning the silver. Endlessly willing, he was happy to turn his hand to anything that needed doing. In addition to the washing-up, he would also help to prepare vegetables and cold starters as well as offering to mow the lawns, look after the bins, wash the cars and even play with the kids.

He did, however, have an Achilles heel. He was a staunch socialist and even though he loved us, he hated all Tories on principle. Unfortunately, he perceived all of our customers to be Tories as, in his mind, no socialist would be able to afford our prices! Diners would sometimes have to walk past the kitchen back door when leaving the restaurant in order to get to the rear car park, in which case they were likely to be accosted by Les who would enquire in a jokey but casually menacing way if they were "goin' 'ome to see if you've bin burgled?"

I forgave him such minor indiscretions because, as far as I was concerned, he was loyal and hardworking, way beyond the call of duty. In 1985 and 1986 I was to do quite a bit of important competition and demonstration work and on every occasion it would be Les who was there all through the night beforehand, helping me get ready.

Alison was a mature lady with a grown-up family and, both in age and temperament, was not at all the type of person we normally tended to employ. She first started working for us on an occasional basis back in the early Painters Forstal days, coming in from time to time on busy evenings to help with the washing-up, and ended up becoming a regular in the kitchen, staying with us for about twenty years. She would cheerfully grind her way through the daily slog of dealing with the mountains of washing-up; I say cheerfully, but there were inevitably times when her generally good-natured disposition would be sorely tested, usually between midnight and 1.00am at the end of a busy Saturday evening service when the pastry chef would finally get round to clearing up his station after the last desserts and been served, appearing with another huge pile of dirty equipment. At that point, she would get as near as she ever got to delivering a torrent of abuse, with a despairing cry of: "Crikey me!"

In a trade where, behind the scenes – and especially in the heat of a busy kitchen – crude and disgusting language is often the norm, Alison would preside over our team of all-too-often foul-mouthed young misfits in a totally motherly way and was respected by all of them. Every Mother's Day Sunday morning she would prepare two trays of sausage rolls at home before coming in to work early to cook them for all of the staff to eat while they were busy getting ready for the lunchtime service. And she was the sort who would never make a cup of tea for herself without making one for everyone else as well.

Whenever she came to the end of her tether in the kitchen late at night and would have a 'Crikey Me' moment, I would leave it a few moments before going over to her with yet a little more washing-up and say with mock impatience: "Come on Alison, stop farting around". She would always then lean forward with her elbows on the sink and we would both collapse in fits of laughter.

I was on my way back from Shrewsbury after a football match in March 2013 when her son called me on my mobile with the news that Alison had died unexpectedly. It was a great shock and I had to pull over in order to compose myself before resuming my drive home. Alison hadn't always been dealt a good hand in life's game of poker, but she always gave her all and worked tremendously hard for Rona and me. Read's was a better restaurant and a better place for the part that she played in it. I loved and respected her enormously and I will always miss her.

8 : Chef of the Year

In 1983 I received an entry form from the Craft Guild of Chefs inviting me to enter the Chef of the Year competition that in those days was held every other year, with the finals staged at the Hotelympia event at Olympia. Rona and I realised that the publicity surrounding the competition might do us a bit of good and so we decided to have a go and managed to get through to the London area semi-finals, held at what is now Thames Valley University in Slough. Having been fortunate enough to win our heats there, we found ourselves alongside eleven other national finalists at Olympia in the January of 1984. To cut a long story short, I had chosen a dessert that wasn't really strong enough for a competition of that stature and, as a result, finished outside the top three.

However, several of the judges took me to one side after the final and encouraged me to have another attempt in 1986, explaining that it was only my choice of dessert that had let me down. The publicity surrounding the final had indeed made it worthwhile and we decided that we would definitely enter again in two years' time. The entry form actually arrived at the end of 1984 and had to be submitted by January 1st, 1985 and during a quiet week or two around November I worked hard on formulating a menu that I thought might be strong enough. But then, because we were short-staffed at Read's and very busy during December, I forgot all about it and didn't actually get around to filling in the form.

New Year's Eve 1984 was again very busy in the restaurant and in the early hours of what was now January 1st, 1985, having said goodbye to the last of our customers, I poured myself a large glass of white wine and went to watch something on TV. I had just sat myself down when Rona came upstairs, replaced my glass of wine with a large mug of coffee and put the Chef of the Year entry form in front of me. I protested strongly, as I knew from experience that it takes at least three hours to fill in the form properly. We were due to fly to Madeira for our family holiday with the boys at 9.00am that morning and we hadn't even started packing yet. Rona replied that she would pack when she had finished downstairs and that I should shut up and just get on with it. I further explained that the entry had to be in at the Craft Guild offices by the end of the day that had already started and she replied that we could go to the airport via London and drop the form off on the way.

By way of explanation, the entry form consisted of the formulation of a menu that had to include as many high level culinary skills as possible, with recipes for each of four courses along with the costing of all the raw materials, every item having to be individually priced to prove that the total cost fell within the £30 limit specified by the rules of the competition. Sitting there, shattered after a long New Year's Eve at the end of a very busy December and with only a few hours to go before flying off on holiday, it seemed to me like a monumental task.

There were no word processors back then – or, if there were, we didn't have one – and the entry form had to be typed. I somehow managed to complete it by about 5.00am. By then, Rona was already up, getting the kids ready after only a couple of hours' sleep herself, while Eva and my mum, who was down for Christmas, were also up and about and said that they would take the entry form in to the Craft Guild offices so that we didn't have to divert to London on our way to Heathrow. If ever there was a real team effort, this was it. As it turned out, filling in that form proved to be the best three and a half hours' work I would ever do in the whole of my life, but as with everything else it wouldn't have been possible without Rona and our respective mums.

It was during February that we received the letter to say that we had once again made it to the London regional semi-finals, which this time were to be held at the BBC kitchens, then in Tottenham Court Road. The experience that Rona and I had gained in the previous campaign stood us in good stead, as we knew exactly what was required of us, and also how nervous we would feel. 'Windy' Miller came with us to help with transport and the loading and unloading of all our gear and I vividly remember her squeal of delight as we were announced as the winners of the London area heat – not that that had done us any good in the previous campaign. I remember it was Budget Day and the press photographers had me standing on a traffic bollard in the middle of Tottenham Court Road, dressed in my whites and holding up a red Gladstone dispatch box, like the one the Chancellor of the Exchequer traditionally waves about outside Number Ten on his way to the Commons to make his Budget speech.

I'd had a good attempt at the competition the first time around, and Rona and I were now determined to give it our very best shot. We practiced the dishes I had chosen to do for the final over and over again and even though they weren't real money-makers, we put also them on the menu at Read's, just so that I could rehearse them even more. We had learned the previous time how to get the press and television involved and in terms of the publicity we received our involvement had already paid off even before the finals came around.

The night before the finals I went to bed early, which was a big mistake because, as a result, I found I couldn't sleep. I should have done what I always normally used to do, which was to have a couple of glasses of wine with my supper once I had closed the restaurant, and go to bed quite late. My mind was whirring at a hundred miles an hour as I lay in bed and I kept getting up and making more notes to remind me about things that I had already got sorted. Isn't it strange the games that your mind plays on you in the early hours of the morning? It felt like I didn't finally fall asleep until about half an hour before my alarm went off at 4.00am, although I'm sure I had probably dozed quite a bit more than that. Competitors have to provide all the food and equipment for the competition themselves and Les arrived a few minutes later to help me get all of the ingredients out of the cold room and all the equipment loaded into the car.

As we drove into London, a track from Steve Winwood's album *Arc oof a Diver* was playing on the radio. The title of the song was *While You See a Chance (Take It)* and in a way it inspired me. It's still the first track on my iPod all these years later. On the way through town we dropped in at Hyam and Cockerton, a specialist vegetable and fruit supplier in Covent Garden and got some of the best produce I've ever seen in my entire working life. We arrived at Olympia in plenty of time and unloaded, and with everything going according to plan I was beginning to feel that it might be my day. However, experience has taught me over the years that in our business nothing goes completely according to plan and I wondered what would be the first thing to go wrong.

The second competitor to arrive was Bruce Sangster from Scotland, a strong contender whom I knew well. He spotted my perfect tiny mangetout and said he wished he had been able to get some quite as good. I rather stupidly invited him to "take some if you want – I've got plenty." He replied: "Oh no, I couldn't possibly." But his wife grabbed two handfuls from the box, saying: "Oh yes, you can". I think the girls are sometimes more cutthroat than the boys! But at the end of the day everybody understood that this was not just a cooking competition – we were all fighting for our families and our businesses. And as it happened, Bruce himself was to win Chef of the Year some years later.

I didn't enter that many competitions, but when I did Rona would always commis for me and on this occasion we had worked together incredibly hard on many little things that were nothing to do directly with the actual cooking. For instance, we had a large cupboard specially made that was similar to a chest of drawers, with four huge compartments and also with castors, so that it could easily be moved around. Each drawer contained the component parts of each individual dish, first course in the top, fish course in the second and so on. We had actually adapted the idea from Brian Price, who had done something similar when he had won Chef of the Year twelve years earlier.

All of the equipment pertaining to each dish was also kept in the same drawer. This helped to streamline every part of the preparation process, saving a great deal of time and trouble. Whilst I was busy working away on the front table, under the watchful eye of the judges, the audience and the TV cameras, Rona would be getting everything ready for the next task at the back of my small kitchen area, with all the appropriate equipment readily to hand. She would immediately spot when I was about to complete a dish and would be ready and waiting to whisk it away, together with the associated equipment, before bringing along everything needed for the next task.

Our experience of knowing how to demonstrate, learned during our teaching days, was an advantage. After an hour or so our work area was perfectly clean, organised and tidy. I recall looking across at the competitor next to us and noticing that his section resembled an explosion in a mattress factory. Rona and I were of the opinion that to a certain extent you can persuade the judges that you are a major contender before you put any food down in front of them simply by being well-organised. Of course, the food you give to them has got to be great, but it helps if you have already impressed them with the way you go about your work. The judges actually told us later that we displayed the best teamwork ever seen in the competition.

Remembering how nervous I had been the last time round, when my hands were shaking so much early on that I found myself struggling to do some of the more intricate work involving the creation of delicate sugar flowers, I decided in advance that my first job this time would be the preparation of the Savarin paste from which to make the Marignons for my dessert. This simply required beating the hell out of a sort of bread-like dough in order to develop the gluten, a basic task that helped to settle my nerves. As it happens, making Savarin paste is actually quite a difficult thing to do well under competition conditions, but the recipe was one of Sid Halsey's, so I was very confident about it.

Everything was going well until about an hour before the end when my expected blunder occurred. I had always been used to working on solid top stoves and when I somewhat carelessly placed my Sauteuse (a slope-sided copper pan, narrower at the bottom than at the top) on the open-top burners we were using, it toppled over and the contents were lost. This was the lamb stock needed for the rosemary sauce that was to go with my main course and it had taken me two hours to prepare and reduce earlier in the competition.

Luckily, the accident happened in front of several of the judges who were watching me closely at the time. You may wonder why I say 'luckily', but when you are judging a chef and something goes wrong, as it is always likely to do in a high-pressure situation, you want to see how the chef will overcome the problem. If they had not witnessed the accident they would have assumed when they tasted my sauce and found it wanting that it was the best I could do and would have marked me down. As it was, they were aware of how potentially disastrous the spill had been and obviously appreciated the fact that I had managed to rescue the situation by getting some lamb fat and trimming from the butchery task I had performed earlier, quickly making a new stock and with the addition of a little cream and fresh rosemary, plus some juice that had seeped from the saddle of lamb joint whilst it was resting, achieving a pretty good result.

Believe it or not, you can sometimes end up with higher marks after you have shown that you can overcome a serious problem than you would have done had the accident not occurred in the first place. Rona was now more aware than I was that I was running behind schedule because I was concentrating too much on rectifying my mistake. I had temporarily lost the plot and had it not been for the fact that Rona knew exactly what was going on, all might well have gone down the pan right there and then.

Cooking is all about timing, and the service slots were now approaching. You are given a ten-minute service window for each course that you MUST stick to. Most people in a competition tend to run a little late because they are working in a strange environment, with equipment they are not used to. Coupled with that there are the added pressures of being in front of TV cameras and an audience, as well as knowing that the next half an hour could possibly change your life forever.

It is obviously better to serve spot-on at the start of your service window, as the judges will all be there waiting for your particular dish and will therefore see it at its very best. A dish will cool, form a skin and deteriorate in all sorts of different ways if it is not judged immediately. God forbid you should miss your service window altogether, because the judges will then quite rightly move straight on to the next chef who serves up in the allotted time. If you are outside your allotted window you will not only automatically lose a lot of marks, but your dish will be judged after everyone else's, when it is probably way past its best.

If you are playing golf and you hit three really ugly shots up the fairway but then manage to chip in from off the green for a par 4, that score is all that will register on your card, and to all intents and purposes you will have ended up with the same result as someone who played the same hole with four textbook shots. But if you mess up in the kitchen you will end up with an ugly mess on the plate at the end of it all, and there's no way you can get away with that.

I was putting together all the component parts of the Marignon dish, my final course, and the chairman of the judges had signalled the two-minute warning to the end of the competition, at which point all the competitors have to stand back from their stations, irrespective of whether they have finished or not. I was having trouble assembling the sugar flowers and trellis that I had made to finish the dish off in style, unable to get them to stand up quite right.

I looked up and saw that I was the only one still performing and all of the judges AND my fellow competitors were standing around watching us. Rona was repeatedly asking me to plate the sweet and push it on to the front of the table so that at least it could be judged, even though it was not quite as it should have been. The master of ceremonies was starting to count down the last 10 seconds and I finally got it right as he got to 6-5-4… So, it actually looked as if I had planned everything perfectly, right down to the last couple of seconds, which, of course, was not the case at all.

Eva, my mother, Sam and Alex had arrived sometime during the competition, along with the entire restaurant staff from Read's. When it was all over our two boys ran in to our kitchen area to give their mum and dad a hug and a kiss. Rona and I were squatting down on our heels so that we could be at the same height as the kids and just as we looked at each other to say well done, we both burst into tears as the pressure began to seep away.

That little family huddle we were in was, after all, the reason we were taking part in the competition. I suppose that I should really have stayed and watched the judges tasting my dishes, but somehow I was glad it was over and I just wanted to get us all out of there for a minute or two. Irrespective of the judges' findings, and leaving aside the lamb sauce incident, it was just about as good as we could have done and we were generally happy with our performance. And when it comes to a competition of that stature, this is all you can ever hope for.

As we walked away from our allotted kitchen (number 6 of twelve) I remember looking back at the total mess that all the other competitors' kitchens were in, with dirty pots and pans everywhere, discarded food waste and rubbish. The only things on our section were the four dishes that we had just placed on the judges' table and the chest of drawers that contained all of our stuff. Our station positively sparkled; Rona had done an incredible job.

Someone thrust a pint of lager into my hand. It was Pat Grigsby who, unknown to me, had been watching from the audience. Earlier that morning he had returned from France, where he was on holiday, in order to give me a box of live crayfish. He knew that I had been having difficulties getting some really good ones and had come back from his holiday especially to get them to me. As it happened, I hadn't needed them as I had eventually managed to find a supplier at the last minute, but he didn't know that and I could well have been desperate for them. That was something only a real mate would have done.

I can't really remember what happened next, but about an hour after the end of the competition the announcement was made. Bruce Sangster had come third, David Fellows had come second (for a split second, when I heard the word "David", I thought it was going to be me in second place) and then, finally, came the announcement that Rona and I had won. As well as medals and various other things, we got a prize of £1,000; just two competitions later the prize money had gone up to £10,000!

Rona and I were told that we had to attend a presentation ceremony at one of the big London Hotels and that we were also expected to stay overnight at The Royal Garden Hotel for another special event of some kind. I can't remember now quite what it was. As usual, Eva and Daphne rallied round to organise the children for us and also set about getting all the equipment back to Faversham.

The following morning, there were television appearances and various radio interviews to be undertaken and we didn't eventually get back home until that evening. Speaking on television and radio is an art that needs to be learned, just like anything else, I suppose. Like most people I was pretty poor at it to begin with and regretted saying some of the things that I said (or didn't say!). I quickly realised that I needed to go into an interview situation with a clear idea of what I wanted to say and plan how to manipulate the interviewer's questions so that I could make the points I wanted to make. I still continue to learn, even though I am rarely interviewed these days. Mostly, I just try my best to be amusing wherever possible.

As a result of winning Chef of The Year we had a huge amount of local publicity in newspapers and on both radio and television. Whenever the local media wanted an opinion or a sound bite on anything to do with food it was always us they came to. Sometimes it would all be a bit silly. On pancake day, for instance, we would be invited to appear on TV to demonstrate how to make and toss a pancake, and at Christmas it would be suggestions about what to do with turkey leftovers on Boxing Day. The difficulty then was to avoid trivialising what we were trying to do at the restaurant.

Looking back, there were plenty of opportunities at around this time for Rona and I to get involved in the sort of television cookery that was then in it's infancy, but we had our own business to run and, rightly or wrongly, we chose to concentrate on that. Had we been employees at one of the major hotels or restaurants we might have gone for the TV thing big time.

Rona and I were the first winners of the Chef of the Year competition to be self-employed and as a result we didn't have the backing of a big company to promote us in any way. Our success in the competition put us well and truly on the culinary map, although, on reflection, I have to say that we could really have done with some professional advice on how best to handle some of the situations that arose. For instance, one of the sponsoring companies of the competition asked me to endorse some of their products, which I didn't feel that I was able to do, and this unfortunately caused all sorts of problems with The Craft Guild of Chefs, whose competition it was and who wanted to get as much publicity as possible. As a result, I felt obliged to discontinue my membership of the Guild, something that I now wish that I had not done, although at the time I didn't feel that I had a great deal of choice.

On the plus side, I was invited shortly afterwards to become a member of what is now The Royal Academy of Culinary Arts, the organisation of which I am now, more than thirty years later, Vice Chairman. The Royal Academy could be seen by some to be in direct competition with the Craft Guild, but in many ways its goals are the same.

I was also asked to do some product development work for various major international companies such as Mars, as well as one or two very well known high street chains and supermarkets. I would sometimes have to visit the Mars factory in Slough and our children used to think it was very funny when Rona, asked where I was, would reply: "Daddy's gone to Mars today."

Soon after our Chef of the Year triumph, I was brought crashing down to earth by a young employee at Currys in Canterbury. I had gone there to buy a replacement microwave oven for the one that our schoolboy washer-up had ruined by totally immersing it in a sink full of water in order to give it a "bit of a clean"! He thought that it would be a good idea to leave it submerged for twenty minutes of so in order to give it a really good soak! Anyway, I entered Currys to be approached by a 17-year-old salesman, who proceeded to give me the full extent of his recently acquired knowledge regarding microwave ovens.

"These ones ere 'ave got turntables, mate", he told me, moving briskly along the display: "These other ones 'ere have got yer defrosting, pulsing ability and then you've got these ones what have got combination ovens that can brown yer chickens as well as cookin' 'em." Finally, saving the best until last, he introduced what was clearly the Rolls Royce of microwave ovens, one that could be set on a timer so that one's feast would be ready and waiting for you when you got home, four or even twelve hours later. At this stage I thought it appropriate to call a halt to his sales spiel and explain to him that I only wanted the simplest piece of apparatus; the oven I was after would need only two controls – an on/off switch and a timer dial.

He looked puzzled for a moment and then, obviously quite hurt that all his efforts at salesmanship had apparently fallen on deaf ears, he took one step closer to me and actually put a consoling arm around my shoulder. "Now look 'ere, mate," he said patiently. "You obviously don't know nuffink about cookin'".

Another of my old Dorchester buddies was a chap called John Hornsby. He was from Norfolk and was a bit of a rogue, but also great fun, and I loved spending time with him. His father had been an engineer with lift manufacturers Otis and John had worked with him before coming to London intent on forging a career as a chef. Anton Mosimann had taken over at the Dorchester and was making friends all over the country, but also some enemies in the kitchen because of all the dramatic changes he was introducing. John became the blue-eyed boy; not only was he a great cook, but he was also tough when he needed to be with the rebellious types. He was a great ally for Mosimann during those early years and was very quickly promoted to become one of the senior sous chefs.

John could have stayed at the Dorchester for as long as he wanted, but after a few years with Mosimann he decided that he wanted to run his own kitchen and left London to go to The Castle Hotel in Taunton as head chef. The Castle was owned and run by the Chapman family and was a really well organised establishment, although some might say a little old fashioned, not that there's necessarily anything wrong with that. However, John was responsible for dragging the kitchen into the 20th century, something for which his successor at The Castle, Gary Rhodes, got a lot of the credit. Please don't misunderstand me – I'm a great admirer of Gary and he did a tremendous job down there and really made a name for himself, but it was John who laid the foundations.

John had a hankering to go to work in the USA, having travelled there many times with Mosimann, doing various promotions for either the Dorchester or for Mosimann's books, and so when the job as head chef at The Four Seasons Hotel restaurant in Washington DC was advertised, he applied. Arriving there for his interview, he was greeted by a lady who introduced herself as the assistant manageress and explained to him that because the elevator wasn't working they would need to use the stairs to get up to her office. John enquired as to what the problem was with the lift and was told that an engineer was expected later that morning, whereupon he asked if he could have a quick look. He entered the elevator, removed one of the tiles in the ceiling of the lift so that he could access the machinery and promptly repaired it. He then simply turned to the manageress and asked if there was somewhere he could wash his hand before proceeding with the interview that by then, of course, was little more than a mere formality. There was little doubt that with his experience at the Dorchester, a glowing recommendation from Mosimann and his repair of the elevator, no one else stood a chance of getting the job and he was promptly appointed.

John heard of our success in the Chef of the Year back in the UK via the trade press in America and invited me to go to Washington and put our winning menu on at the Four Seasons for a week-long promotion. At the same time, purely by coincidence, a couple who ran a British government sponsored organisation in the US called Food from Britain also heard that we were going over and said that they would pay for our flights if we would stay on and do a week of promotions for them as well – an offer too good to refuse.

The week included guest spots at various hotels and food shops. For instance, in New York we did promotions in what was then the Barbizon Hotel and also at Bloomingdales, which was the nearest equivalent over there to Harrods, Selfridges or Fortnum & Mason. In Chicago it was the Ritz Carleton and in Atlanta it was the Waverley Hotel. In Washington and Florida we went on radio and television to promote British companies such as soup makers Baxter's. The whole tour was repeated again in 1988.

Meanwhile, I was also being asked to go and speak at various conventions such as The World Congress of Chefs, which was being held in South Africa. Rona and I would have liked to have been able to accept all the invitations that came our way, but because we were in the unique position of having our own business to run we could not accept everything that was offered. The trip to South Africa in 1987, which included visits to both Johannesburg and Cape Town, was not only the first time that both Rona and I had left the restaurant together while it remained open, but was also the first time we had both gone away and left the children at home. We wouldn't have been able to do any of these things without Eva to look after everything in our absence.

We travelled over to South Africa with the likes of Paul Bocuse and Anton Mosimann, the only difference being that they were in first class and we were in steerage. Also, Paul Bocuse had a bodyguard assigned to him when he went diamond shopping and we didn't. Not that Rona and I ever got to go diamond shopping, you understand. But if we had, I doubt whether we would have rated a personal minder!

One of my outstanding memories of the Congress was being seated at a table with heart surgeon Dr Christian Barnard on one side of me and Paul Bocuse on the other. Paul Bocuse, of course, was one of the all-time great French chefs. His main restaurant was L'Auberge du Pont de Collonges in Collonges-au-Mont-d'Or, the village where he was born in 1926 and where he died in 2018 at the age of ninety-two. It had three Michelin stars and Bocuse was named Chef of the Century in 2012 by the Culinary Institute of America, so it was a wonderful privilege for me to be able to sit and chat to such a legendary figure.

Towards the end of the event I plucked up the courage to ask if he would allow me to have a photograph taken of us together, but much to my disappointment, and slight embarrassment, he was rather dismissive, saying something like: "We'll see. Perhaps." He then got up and disappeared and I thought that would be that until he suddenly reappeared, having changed into his full whites especially for the photograph! So I ended up with a wonderful memento of our meeting, even if I do look a bit of a scruff standing next to him in my casual blue-and-white hooped polo shirt, while the great man is immaculate in his whites.

Our contact in South Africa was a lovely chap called Bill Gallagher, who was from Newcastle and an avid Sunderland supporter. I had worked with Bill at the Dorchester on several sections and he had become a good friend. He was also a good footballer and a solid member of the Dorchester team's midfield. He and his wife-to-be Linda, and I and my then girlfriend, used to spend time together at their flat in Turnham Green, eating, drinking and talking about our ambitions for the future. He left to go to South Africa, where he worked for Southern Sun Hotels, starting off as a chef before rising over the years to become a director of the company. He was already a household name in South Africa by the time we visited.

Tragically, Bill was shot through the window of his car one night in 1998 while driving home from work in Johannesburg by someone intent on trying to hijack his Mercedes. The bullet entered his lower spine and, as a result, he became a patient at Stoke Mandeville Hospital for about six months, but remained paralysed from the neck downwards for the remainder of his life. I met up with him on many occasions in various places around the world and we would always reminisce about those early days at the Dorchester and Turnham Green. He did recover some limited use of one of his hands, but that was all. Sadly, he died in 2016 at the age of 67. I have very fond memories of Bill and Linda.

Speaking in public was not something that came naturally to me, so I was nervous about going to the conference in South Africa. I had already spoken at the Chefs Conference in London and, to be honest, had made a hash of it and realised that it was something I would have to work on if I was going to get involved in promotional work. Happily, speaking at the Jo'burg conference was the first time I felt really happy with my performance and that did my confidence a power of good.

When the conference was over we were given the choice of either going on safari for three days or going to Cape Town. Rona and I chose the latter, visiting some great hotels and restaurants as well the winelands of the Western Cape, including Stellenbosch and Franschhoek, as doing all the touristy stuff such as going up Table Mountain.

Although all this may make it seem like I was away from Read's a lot, in actual fact I mostly accepted and organised only those trips that coincided with our periods of closure for annual staff holidays, generally around early January and early September. And whenever possible, Rona and the children came too. I can only remember doing a handful of trips on my own while we were open for business back at Read's.

Anyone who has done a guest spot abroad will know that it is tremendously hard work if you do it properly, both from the point of view of organising it all before you go and working all the hours God sends whilst you are actually there. Looking back, one of the most enjoyable trips I did was when I was invited by Her Majesty's Government of the day to represent Great Britain at the Azalea Festival celebrations in Norfolk, Virginia, in an event organised by NATO in conjunction with Food from Britain.

One of the most memorable events of my working life, this included being transported wherever I went in an official motorcade. Having an escort, complete with four police outriders on motorbikes stopping the traffic and overruling the robots (traffic lights) is a real experience. My only regret is that on this occasion I was on my own and didn't have anyone with whom to share the experience. There were moments when I felt like bursting into song, with a chorus of: "If they could see me now". There's no doubt that the Americans are the greatest bullshitters on earth when it comes to making visitors feel important.

On one of my earliest promotional trips there, aware that the schedule was tight and that I would have very little time to get things ready for my first demonstration, I decided to take some prepared items with me, such as reduced stock, which would cut down the prepping time of some of my sauces from twenty-four hours to little more than one hour. I also took some black pudding and Jersey Royal potatoes, knowing full well that such items were banned from entering the country under the strict food import rules, but unwisely deciding to take a chance.

Once I had arrived at JFK airport, I declared the knives and general cooking equipment that I had in my luggage, but did not mention the illegal food that I was trying to bring in. I must have looked guilty because they decided to search me and packed me off to a room accompanied by an enormous black customs officer, whose shirt was sweat-stained at the armpits and who was packing a handgun, plus another guy equipped with a machine gun, who stood in the corner just watching. I was absolutely terrified and wished that I had never brought the stuff with me. I thought about coming clean there and then, but for some reason decided against it.

I knew that if I was caught the best I could hope for was that I would be immediately deported, and that things could actually get a lot worse than that. The customs officer asked to see my passport, but this had been confiscated earlier and it seemed like an age while I waited for it to arrive. I was now the most scared that I had ever been in my life. The passport eventually arrived and was handed to the customs officer who again seemed to peruse it for an extraordinarily long time. Then he looked up at me over the top of his rimmed spectacles and said: "Hey, Dave, I see you gotta a birthday comin' up soon." And at that point he handed me back my passport with a cheery: "Have a good trip."

It took me a good four hours to calm down. I was a complete wreck and vowed never to take a chance like that ever again. And yet, amazingly, I briefly found myself in a similar and potentially even more difficult situation on a later demonstration trip. On this occasion the problem arose as I was leaving the US to come home, and I certainly wasn't guilty of trying to smuggle anything illegal. It was a set of six Le Creuset ramekins that I had been using in one of my demonstrations that set security alarm bells ringing. When my luggage was scanned they looked on the screen a bit like half-a-dozen grenades! I was pulled out of the line and once again marched off by armed security officers, while my luggage was taken away to be searched.

In view of these experiences, I was understandably very nervous when, at the end of one of my demonstrations in New York, a table of four men asked to see me, saying that they were from the CIA. My first reaction was – what have I done now? I was pretty sure all my papers, including my work permits, were in order. And whilst the meal I had prepared might not have been the best that they had ever eaten, it surely wasn't so bad as to attract investigation by the Central Intelligence Agency! Anyway, it turned out that they were from another CIA – the Culinary Institute of America – so, thankfully, all was well. In fact, they were extremely complimentary about my cooking.

9 : Michelin Man

The Good Food Guide was the first restaurant guide to discover Read's, back in 1986, introducing us to a lot of new customers. The GFG, Egon Ronay, the AA and the Michelin guides are always aware of what each other is doing and the others all followed suit shortly afterwards.

It was in 1990 that Rona and I became aware that Michelin were paying us a lot of attention and as a result I requested a meeting with Derek Bulmer, their chief inspector for thirty years and also editor of the highly respected guide. At the time, we had an inclusion entry only and obviously wanted a coveted star. Mr Bulmer, a personnel manager at Brown's Hotel in Mayfair before joining Michelin, paid us a visit and we had a nice chat at the end of which he asked how we would feel about having a Red M, a symbol that in those days was awarded to restaurants that were considered to be on the way up and which was regarded as being like half a Michelin star. Rona had already started saying how nice that would be when I rather rudely interrupted to say that we were not interested in a Red M – that as far as I was concerned it was a matter of all or nothing. I didn't want to be seen in any way as being second best, not quite up to the highest standard, as it were; I'd rather not be mentioned at all. After Derek had left, Rona gave me a severe telling off for taking such a bold stand and appearing ungrateful for his offer, but it turned out that I had been right to hold out for the main chance, because when the 1991 guide was published it revealed that we had indeed been awarded a full Michelin star.

We got nearly as much publicity from the award of the star as we had for winning the Chef of the Year title. Now, most people could be forgiven for assuming that the accolade of achieving such a highly prestigious rating would result in the whole world beating a path to your door, but that's not actually the case – quite the opposite, because in those days many people automatically assumed that a Michelin star meant that the restaurant would be expensive and the food over-elaborate and they would therefore avoid it. At the same time, it does attract some extremely demanding, over-fussy diners of the sort who are under the often mistaken impression that they are true gourmets and God's gift to restaurateurs.

Where it does make a significantly positive difference is in attracting capable young chefs to come and work for you. Of course, they are only there to pinch your ideas, so you mustn't feed them too much information too quickly or you won't get any benefit from them before they are off to pinch someone else's ideas – just as I myself have done from time to time over the years

I see a lot of chefs, particularly the younger ones, who are obsessed with gaining a Michelin star, to the exclusion of almost everything else. They don't care about making money for their employers and they don't even really care that much about their customers. The only time they come alive is when they think they might have an inspector in the restaurant. They often go to the lengths of making sure that they have a list of all of the inspectors from each individual guide and also the heavyweight food journalists – sometimes complete with photographs, so that the restaurant staff will be able to recognise them. These are invariably the same chefs who take youngsters from the catering colleges and work them into the ground, with the result that after six months they are so totally burnt out and so disillusioned with the industry that they leave to do something else.

Despite such minor quibbles, I recognise the fact that every industry needs its 'Oscars', standards of excellence to which all those involved can aspire, even if I do take issue with what I see as a tendency for Michelin to award stars to those restaurants that specialise in producing the sort of ridiculously complicated, ostentatious and artificially concocted dishes that have to be assembled with tweezers. One has to have had a Michelin star in order to slag off the system, otherwise it will be seen as sour grapes. We retained a star for twenty-one years, from 1990-2011, and I will always be immensely proud of that.

I was obviously disappointed when I eventually lost that star, but if I'm honest, it was probably justified. For one thing, its withdrawal coincided with a time when, having reached my early sixties, I was starting to step back a little in the kitchen and to delegate more, and to a degree I perhaps took my eye off the ball. Apart from that, Michelin tend to put quite an emphasis on innovation, and yet we had come to find ourselves catering mostly for the kind of regular customers who didn't take kindly to too much change and didn't want to see old favourites among our dishes disappearing from the menu, so it was becoming increasingly difficult to strike the right balance.

I have no great hankering to regain the star – and I certainly never had the slightest ambition to have more than one. At the two or three-star level the costs involved in producing the expected range of truly exceptional dishes means that even at the high prices charged it is difficult to make a significant profit purely on the food. Where chefs at that exalted level make their money is through all the various merchandising spin-offs, such as books, television appearances and so on.

As already mentioned, even having one star can bring a few negatives in terms of frightening some people off, while simultaneously attracting all those self-styled gourmets and wine buffs with their wine diaries and vintage charts and their opinionated and often mistaken views about how everything should be cooked and presented, forcing us to choose between giving customers what they want and what the likes of Michelin think they should have.

The truth is that we are so well established after more than forty years that having or not having a star doesn't make that much difference any more. We still currently have a score of 6 out of 10 in The Good Food Guide, and that is still pretty high by their standards. The best we ever achieved was 7 out of 10, which, for about ten years, put us among the top restaurants in the country. The GFG is a much more interesting read than the Michelin Guide, but doesn't carry quite the same clout, certainly as far as a chef's kudos is concerned. The AA guide is, in our opinion, a bit of a non-entity and of little significance when compared with the other two. Egon Ronay was a good guide before its demise and there are one or two others that are definitely on the way up, such as Harden's and Sawday's.

Younger chefs who came to work with me in the days when I had the Michelin star often used to ask me what they would have to do to earn one. The best advice I could give them was to say that one shouldn't pander to the food guides. Winning an accolade from a guide should be a by-product of doing a good job, not a goal in itself. That has always been my attitude

Long before we were awarded our star we were already becoming conscious of having outgrown our little converted mini-market and had begun to accept that if we really wanted to progress and improve then we would have find new premises with a bit more character; also, possibly, somewhere with the potential for conversion to include letting rooms. We were constantly being asked if there was anywhere decent to stay locally by people who were coming quite a distance to eat at the restaurant and didn't want to drive all the way home afterwards, and it seemed a pity to be turning all that potential business away for the benefit of local hotels and guesthouses.

We started to look at country houses in the area that we thought could be converted and actually got as far as making tentative offers on one or two properties. The nearest we came to finding anywhere really suitable at this time was a place in Sheldwich, a little village just a couple of miles away. However, this presented us with a problem when it came to selling our existing premises. Who in their right mind would buy Read's as a going concern if we were then going to open up a couple of miles down the road and take all our customers with us? The absolute minimum requirement for someone purchasing Read's at Painters Forstal would be to impose a 25-mile exclusion zone, prohibiting us from opening another restaurant within that radius. This meant that Sheldwich, and anywhere else in the near vicinity, would be out of the question – unless, that is, we could find a way of selling Read's as something other than a restaurant.

Over the years we had been approached several times by people interested in buying the strip of land on the side of our property, and making very good offers for it. As mentioned earlier, the original plan had been for Bert and Eva to build their own house or bungalow there, but they had never got round to doing that, partly because we found that we were all quite happy living together in the main house, but mainly because the decline in Bert's health then meant he could no longer contemplate getting involved in such a big project. We now started thinking that if people were prepared to pay so much for just that little strip of land down the side, then what would the entire plot be worth if one could get planning permission to demolish Read's and sell the whole one-acre site for development? Our negotiations for the house at Sheldwich were moving along nicely and we had reached a verbal agreement with the owners that they would sell it to us; we even had the gas supply to the property upgraded to industrial-sized pipes that were laid to where the new restaurant kitchen would eventually be. Meanwhile, we began looking seriously at the possibilities for developing the Painters Forstal site.

However, we soon discovered that the property development world is full of people who would happily sell not just their grandmothers but their mothers, wives and children as well if they thought they could make a few quid by doing so. As we approached the exchange of contracts for the house at Sheldwich, the owner, a property developer himself, took me to one side and explained that during the previous couple of years he had obtained a government grant for the renovation of the central part of the property and that if he were to sell within a five-year period then he would have to repay the grant. I seem to remember that the figure that we were talking about was around £30,000. He went on to suggest that he would only sell to us on condition that he could retain ownership of the central part of the property long enough to avoid the repayment. At the end of the five-year period he would then sell us the remainder of the property. I could not agree to this for obvious reasons and threatened to withdraw from the agreement if a solution could not be found. It couldn't, and so we duly opted out.

That the whole deal had collapsed in this way was disappointing, but, on the plus side, Rona and I had learned a great deal from the experience, the main advantage here being that we had begun to appreciate the true potential value of the property we were sitting on at Painters Forstal. We had got as far as consulting our local planning officer and without saying as much, or putting anything in writing, he had intimated that he would look favourably on our restaurant and the adjoining house being demolished in order to make way for a development of up to six three and four-bedroom houses. He further suggested that he would look even more favourably at the project if we were to be setting up in business somewhere else nearby with a restaurant that included letting rooms, thus providing employment for even more local people. Rona and I were learning fast and beginning to get the idea; in the restaurant business you tell people what they want to hear, and it seemed that in certain circumstances things were no different when it came to the local planning authorities.

For various reasons, however, we shelved the idea of moving for the next few years – mainly because we had become so busy at Painters Forstal following the award of the Michelin star. From the early to the mid-nineties the food at Read's was probably the best we had ever cooked up to that point – or since, for that matter – and we were winning most of the awards that were available to us at that time, including County Restaurant of the Year in the Good Food Guide.

Meanwhile, although deliveries down to our part of Kent were improving they were still pretty poor, and consequently I still had to go to London two or three times a week to get supplies. Very occasionally I would get waylaid and treat myself to a late bite to eat somewhere nice, taking the opportunity to keep up with what was going on and pinching the odd idea here and there. On these occasions I would sometimes have a little more wine than was good for me and my homing instinct for Langan's would then kick in.

Co-owner Richard Shepherd was the consummate professional and would always be there, still chatting to his customers even late at night, after finishing in the kitchen,and he would invariably welcome me in. It was quite likely that he would have had one or two drinks himself by then and would be in the mood to carry on, in which case he would suggest that we went on somewhere else. I would protest that I really couldn't, as I had a car full of meat, game, fish and whatever else it was that I'd bought that day and that I needed to get home with it. But he wouldn't take no for an answer and would simply call someone over and tell them to take my car keys and put my 'shopping' in one of his cold rooms or fridges while we popped out. The trouble was that when Richard decided that the night was still young, you never just popped out; you really went out on the town! He was a superstar in those days and wherever we went we were treated like royalty and never ever paid for anything. The session was likely to go on until dawn and I would arrive back in Painters Forstal just in time for breakfast! At that point, I always swore to myself that I would never again turn up late on Richard's doorstep – but, of course, I always did.

In 1996 our two boys were invited by Dan Jenkins to travel over to see the Olympics in Atlanta Georgia, where he was living by then, and Rona and I decided to travel over after the games had finished to join them for a family holiday. We met up with Sam and Alex at Los Angeles Airport and whilst we were having a drink together in the bar there and catching up, Rona was thumbing through an American foodie magazine and drew our attention to an article, saying: "Look at that – wouldn't it be wonderful to go there?" What had caught her eye was a piece about The Beverly Hills Hotel, which included a photograph of the Executive Chef de Cuisine, Gary Clauson, whom I instantly recognised as an old Dorchester kitchen colleague from twenty-five years earlier. Gary had been a star member of the Dorchester's football team – and one of my flatmates at Cathcart Road in Earl's Court whom I had accidentally come close to gassing! He had joined the Dorchester kitchen as an apprentice straight from school but, even so, had proved himself to be one of the best young cooks in the kitchen. The last I had heard of him was when he went off to South Africa with my other old Dorchester mate Billy Gallagher, only to stop off en route in Bermuda. And now here he was, Chef de Cuisine at one of the best hotels, if not THE best hotel, in the whole world.

We duly booked a table in the renowned Terrace Restaurant there on the day that Sam was rather nervously expecting his A-level results, hoping we'd have something to celebrate. When I made the booking, I mentioned that I was and old friend of the chef and that it would be great if he could spare a few minutes to say hello at the end of our meal. The receptionist explained that, sadly, it was Gary's day off, but our message would be passed on to him the following day when he returned to work.

On a day of perfect California weather, the four of us arrived at the incredibly beautiful venue, the entrance to which was surrounded by a spectacular display of bougainvillea, and were escorted to what was unquestionably the best table in the restaurant. No sooner had we been seated than we were promptly presented with a stratospherically expensive bottle of vintage Louis Roederer Crystal champagne, on the house. Whilst we took our first sips of the delicious bubbly, a selection of the most exquisite canapes that I had ever seen arrived, including Royal Beluga caviar, lobster and foie gras.

The maitre d' suggested that if the boys might like to choose whatever they wanted for their lunch from the á la carte menu, a special tasting menu had been arranged for Rona and me. I was beginning to get a little worried about what the bill might amount to, even allowing for the fact that we would not be charged for the champagne. I remember asking the sommelier for the wine list, intending to choose something fairly modestly priced, only for him to explain that an appropriate wine had been selected for us with each of the seven courses.

We all enjoyed every morsel of what we ate and it remains one of the top three dining experiences of our lives – you may remember that Richard Shepherd's meal at the Capitol was one of the other two. And it was certainly the most memorable setting. We were wallowing in the joy of it all over coffee when Gary suddenly emerged from the kitchen to make a surprise appearance and joined us to chat about old times. He had a house nearby in Beverly Hills and after I had booked our table the maitre d' had phoned him to pass on my message and he had come in on his day off specially to treat us so royally. He stayed and chatted for an hour or so and we both got a bit emotional when we thought how far the pair of us had come, both literally and metaphorically, since the days when we were kitchen boys, sharing that doss house in Cathcart Road!

After Gary left, I asked the maitre d' for the bill, but he explained that anyone with whom chef Clauson sat for over an hour did not pay. I tried to leave a substantial tip, not wanting the dining room staff to be deprived as a result of Gary's generosity, but I was not allowed to leave anything at all, despite my best efforts to do so.

That particular family treat was equalled, if not surpassed, by another visit to the States some six years later, this time to the East Coast. And the story of how what turned out to be the trip of a lifetime came about is quite extraordinary in itself. It all began one evening back at my flat in Forest Hill in 1972, some time before Rona and I got together. There was a knock at the door and as soon as I opened it a man pushed into the corridor and, without further ado, launched into a sales pitch for a life insurance policy. Back where I came from that sort of unsolicited hard sell was considered well out of order and as the salesman wasn't very big, I informed him in no uncertain terms and not so many words that unless he promptly got himself out of my flat, there was likely to be violence.

Well, I obviously don't have what it takes to be a really threatening hard man because, to cut a long story short, within ten minutes he had got me to sign on the dotted line of this policy that, in return for a few shillings a week, would result in me receiving a lump sum of about £25,000+ in thirty years' time. Or so he assured me. It was, he explained, a with-profits life policy that upon maturity would allow me to live a life of luxury for the remainder of my days – and he was so convincing that for some reason I believed him, to the extent that a couple of years later he managed to sell a second policy to Rona and me together.

The years went by and the direct debits were routinely taken on the 1st of each month, becoming increasingly insignificant over time to the point where we had almost forgotten all about the policies. So when that first one reached maturity it came as a very pleasant surprise when I received a cheque for £32,000 out of the blue. Its arrival sparked a family debate as to how we were going to spend this unexpected windfall. By coincidence, Rona and I had been involved in a conversation a few days before and had come to the conclusion that family experiences were infinitely more valuable than material possessions or cash in the bank.

And so it was that Rona booked all four of us onto Concorde for a five-day family round trip to New York. She also informed me that 'slumming it' whilst we were there wasn't an option, so a suite at the New York Plaza was chosen as the place to rest our weary heads. We queued up for Letterman, went to see the best shows on Broadway and ate in the best restaurants. That five-day trip, and especially the flight on Concorde, remains one of the great experiences of our lives. And although it was extravagant hedonism in the extreme, I have absolutely no regrets about it at all. Sadly, when the second policy matured Concorde was no longer available for a repeat performance, having finally been taken out of service in 2003; and neither was the Plaza, for that matter, the hotel having been converted into ridiculously expensive luxury apartments overlooking Central Park. One of my outstanding memories of the whole trip (and there were many) was of the moment on the outward Concorde flight when Rona and the boys each gave me their individual pots of caviar that came with lunch. I hadn't had that much caviar in one go even back in the Dorchester days. I suppose it was their way of saying: "Well done, Dad, you did OK taking out that policy."

Meanwhile, back home in Painters Forstal in the late 1990s, a couple of years before the Concorde trip, Rona had been behind the bar at Read's when Basil Neame, a member of the local Shepherd-Neame brewing family and someone who had supported us very well over the years, was in with his extended family and came up to the bar in order to pay his bill. Rona had always loved Macknade Manor, the

18th century house where he lived and which she remembered going to for somebody's twenty-first birthday party when she herself was sixteen years old. Basil had had a couple of drinks and was in a jovial mood, so Rona took the opportunity to mention casually that if he ever decided to sell, would he please give us first refusal? To her surprise, he replied that he didn't actually own the property, that he was only a tenant, adding that the house, along with the farm to which it was attached, was owned by the Prudential insurance company and so would probably never come onto the open market.

Quite by co-incidence, we then heard not that long afterwards that Prince Charles was involved in purchasing an organic farm somewhere in Herefordshire that was apparently the best of its kind in the world and which, co-incidentally, also happened to be owned by the Prudential. More significantly, word had it that the Prudential had insisted that they would only sell it to the Duchy of Cornwall as part of their entire portfolio of farm properties. If true, this could mean that His Royal Highness would end up with a whole load of farms and estates that were surplus to requirements and might want to sell some of them on, including, possibly, Macknade Manor. We decided to write to the Pru, to inquire about the situation.

They responded very promptly, confirming that Macknade Manor was no longer owned by them, but had indeed been acquired by The Duchy of Cornwall. We then very quickly wrote to the Duchy expressing interest in acquiring the property and they responded equally quickly to suggest a meeting. This was duly arranged and we made a verbal offer for Macknade that was accepted. The deal was completed very quickly, the title deeds showing, much to my amusement, that the sale had been agreed between, on the one hand, His Royal Highness Charles Philip Arthur George, Prince of Wales, Duke of Cornwall and Rothesay, Earl of Chester and Carrick, Baron of Renfrew, Lord of the Isles and Great Steward of Scotland, and on the other hand by … David and Rona Pitchford!

All we had to do now was to sell Painters Forstal. We wanted to let people know that we were up for sale without formally putting it on the market, in the hope of being able to do a deal without going through an agent. This wasn't difficult to achieve. In any restaurant there are always plenty of well-connected, gossipy regulars who like to think that they know everybody's business and everything else that is going on. We knew one or two customers, in particular, who, if we told them something important and swore them to secrecy, would promise not to tell a soul, only for the news to be out all over Kent within a matter of days. Sure enough, no sooner had we divulged our 'secret' to the right blabbermouths than we were inundated with enquiries from property developers interested in buying a site for which, by this time, we had secured extended planning permission for eight three and four bedroom houses

We were so sure of being able to sell quickly that we did something that virtually everyone will tell you never to do; we took what we thought to be a calculated riskand secured a bridging loan for the huge sum of £450,000, with Painters Forstal as security for the loan. For those of you unfamiliar with bridging loans, the daily interest rates are eye-watering, so we couldn't afford to waste any time in unloading Painters Forstal.

It was now that those two highly and sometimes outrageously colourful characters among our most loyal regular customers and friends – property developer Colin Strickland and solicitor Stuart Ross – proved to be a great help.

Colin first used his contacts to bring our property to the attention of Sunley Estates, a development company owned by the late Lord Sunley, who, as it happened, was also a frequent visitor to Read's. Rona and I had hoped to get around £630,000 for our piece of land, this being about the going rate at the time, but we decided to start the ball rolling by inviting offers around £700,000, which in catering parlance represents 'a serious lot of soup'.

Yet another of our customers, David Parry, whom we employed as our selling agent, insisted that this was far too much and would frighten some people off, but we did it anyway. And to Parry's and our amazement, Sunley offered the full £700,000, on condition that we settled quickly. Of course, we wasted no time in accepting their offer, after which things continued to proceed, although a little slower than we had hoped, as is often the case. For some reason, unknown to Rona and me, Sunley Estates started to drag their feet and no matter how much pressure we applied, we could not get them to complete the deal. Several weeks passed by and we were accruing huge amounts of interest on our bridging loan and were starting to get desperate.

At this point I decided to concoct a story in order to try and force their hand. I phoned Stuart Ross, who was acting for us, and spun him the little white lie that we had just received a great offer from a private individual keen to buy Macknade Manor from us as a private house. I explained that this person had offered us a quarter of a million pounds more than we had just paid the Duchy for it, and that we were inclined to accept the offer, pay the capital gains tax, take the profit and stay where we were at Painters Forstal.

I really had no idea what might have happened if the bluff hadn't worked, but at least we would know where we stood. Thankfully it did work. Stuart duly passed the message on to Sunley and by 4.00pm of the same day everything had been sorted and the money had been handed over. We found out later that, behind the scenes, Colin Strickland had also been quietly bringing pressure to bear on Lord Sunley on our behalf, which undoubtedly helped. Relief wasn't the word for it. It transpired after the deal had been completed that the reason for the delay was that Sunley's moneyman had miscalculated the value of the development potential of our land by about £70,000 and they were busy trying to get planning permission for an extra house on the site by way of compensating for this. Apparently, the man who had been responsible for the mistake was 'let go' immediately it was discovered.

The idea of having paid over the odds obviously rankled with Lord Sunley, whom we had got to know quite well through his visits to Read's. Among other interests, he owned a string of racehorses and whenever I happened to bump into him at a racecourse or at Royal St. George's golf club, where he was a member and where I also played from time to time, he would take great sarcastic delight, when introducing me to his friends, in describing himself as my "benefactor". Not that he lost out in the end through his financial adviser's mistake, as he did manage to get planning permission for an extra house on the site, one over the eight for which we'd got permission. And when Rona and I sat down on completion of the deal to work how much the venture had cost us in legal fees and the interest on the mighty bridging loan that we'd had to service while he had delayed, we discovered that it added up to about £75,000; the Lord giveth and the Lord taketh away!

Another local aristocrat among our regular customers was Earl Sondes, a colourful individual who had inherited about £30 million back in the early 1960's and proceeded to try and drink it all away – quite often, thankfully, at Read's. Henry Sondes had his estate nearby and each autumn he would invite parties of Americans over to shoot pheasants and partridges, charging the Yanks huge amounts of money for the privilege. These shooting parties would usually consist of about fifty people when you included wives and girlfriends, and after a weekend's sport they would all come to Read's for supper on the Sunday evening. We are normally closed after lunch on Sundays, but Henry would arrange to book the whole restaurant for a private function.

This would be a seriously posh do, with all the American women in their jewels and finery and, rather amusingly, the sort of ankle length mink coats that had long gone out of fashion over here by then. Lady Sondes, Henry's long-suffering fifth wife, used to try valiantly to curtail his drinking by telling our waiters and sommelier that under no circumstances was he to be served any alcohol other than the wine that he would consume at the table during the meal. He, in the meantime, would have bribed the same staff, with fairly considerable amounts of money, to supply him with four shots of whisky in each of the diet cokes that he would order before and after

At the end of the main course we would allow twenty minutes or so for some speeches and prize giving and on one occasion I was in the kitchen, just preparing the hot raspberry soufflé for dessert, when the swing door leading to the restaurant flew violently open and four female members of staff, including Rona, came running in with their heads in their hands, one or two of them screaming. They explained that Henry had got his willy out and had plonked it on a side plate, apparently in an effort to encourage all the other chaps present to do the same in order to establish how many Jewish gentlemen were present. Of course, he was the only one to expose himself, but an amusing aside to the story is that Sarah 'Windy' Miller, who had been in the kitchen helping me to arrange the petits fours on the side plates for when coffee was served, was the only one to run into the restaurant to view the proceedings!

Mention of both Sarah and Colin Strickland within the space of a few paragraphs reminds me of another amusing incident involving the two of them together, shortly after Read's had moved to Macknade. I actually hesitate to describe it as "amusing" because it could have been disastrous but for the good-natured humour and understanding of the gentleman concerned. A regular customer, he was a double amputee, confined to a wheelchair, and so whenever he made a booking we made sure in advance that our special wheelchair ramp was in place on the steps into the restaurant so that he could come in and go straight to his table without any fuss. However, on this particular occasion he and his companion decided that they would prefer to sit outside on the terrace

Colin and his wife Rose nearly always choose to eat lunch on the terrace if the weather is decent, and sometimes even if it isn't, due mainly to the fact that Rosie is a smoker. On this occasion they were already on the terrace and well into their second bottle of wine by the time the disabled gentleman arrived. In the meantime, Sarah had already moved the ramp around from the front door to the terrace entrance at the side of the restaurant. She would normally have gone to find one of the male members of staff in order to manhandle the chair down the ramp, but for some reason, known only to herself, decided to do it on her own.

As most sensible people will know, it is not generally a good idea to push a wheelchair and its occupant forwards down a steep gradient – much better to turn around and go down backwards so that you are in complete control. But this did not occur to Sarah. At this stage in the story you will not need me to tell you that she managed to tip him out onto the terrace floor, where he rolled over twice before coming to rest against the legs of Colin and Rose's table.

While Sarah panicked and ran away in tears to hide in the linen cupboard, hugely embarrassed by what she'd done and fearful that she may have caused a major injury, Colin rose to the occasion, picked the poor chap up off the floor and put him back in his chair. However, once he had established that no serious injury had been suffered and having been thanked profusely for his kindness, he risked spoiling it all by exclaiming loudly, and in characteristically jocular fashion, that over the years he'd seen plenty of people legless in Read's –but never, as far as he could remember, *before* they'd had a drink!

Not many people would have seen fit to make a joke out of such a potentially serious incident, but Colin did, and somehow got away with it. Fortunately, the accident victim saw the funny side and laughed it off, whereupon all twenty or so people who were eating on the terrace broke into a round of applause. Sarah eventually emerged from the linen cupboard, distraught and in tears, but hugely relieved to find that no serious damage had been done. And Colin, as incorrigible as ever, then rounded things off by seeking her out when he left so that he could hand over a "tip for the tipper".

10 : Same Name, New Location

The purchase of Macknade was completed towards the end of 1999 and part of the deal with Lord Sunley was that we could continue operating rent-free at Painters Forstal until Valentine's Day of 2000. In the interval we made a start on applying for change of use at Macknade, from private house to restaurant/hotel, and on planning and preparing for the huge renovation project ahead of us.

I don't know that we had ever thought in much detail about what converting and renovating a 220-year-old Grade II listed Georgian manor house was going to be like, but let's just say we were ill-prepared for the full extent of what was eventually to be involved, both inside and out.

Structurally, the main change was the re-organisation of the first floor, where nine bedrooms, three bathrooms and two staircases were to be replaced by six en-suite letting rooms, with one main staircase. Elsewhere, almost everything had to be renovated. The roof had to come off and the whole house had to be re-plumbed and re-wired. All the pipework was very ancient and had to be replaced, at a cost of £80,000, and complete re-wiring cost about the same, while the bill for the fire-proofing required to meet hotel and restaurant regulations was even higher at over £100,000.

The extra work involved in installing the safety features needed in order to qualify for a fire certificate included demolishing all the ceilings (some of them beautifully ornate) in the cellars and on the ground and first floors and sandwiching a layer of fire-retardant material between the new ceilings and the floors above. And every door in the building had to be treated with fire-retardants and fitted with intumescent strips. Conforming with regularly up-dated health and safety regulations has been an on-ongoing, expensive and occasionally counter-productive headache. For instance, after one of his regular annual inspections the local fire officer insisted that we had to install a newly invented piece of sound sensitive apparatus that automatically closes the door between the kitchen and the restaurant if the fire alarm goes off. This is all well and good in theory, but in practice the sensor is so sensitive that a spider only has to fart in the pastry section on the other side of the kitchen for the door to close. And if a waiter should happen to be passing through at the time with four carefully prepared main courses there is the potential for a costly accidental collision, with a hundred and twenty quid's worth of Wedgwood crockery lying smashed on the floor and four main courses to be prepared all over again.

To a degree, one can usually negotiate with the listed building people, planning officers and building regulations officials in order to find some sensible and mutually acceptable compromises, but with fire officers you can't do that; what they say goes and there is no arguing. If you do not do exactly what they tell you to do, you don't get a certificate. No fire certificate, no business. Sadly, because of the huge expense and disruption involved in carrying out the extensive alterations needed to bring them up to the required safety standards, we still have three potentially beautiful attic rooms on the second floor that we are unable to use – not as guest rooms, staff accommodation or even as storage rooms.

Outside, the original main gate and driveway to the house had not been used for decades and as a result the drive was very overgrown, while the area destined to become the customer car park was like a jungle, so dense that the architecturally outstanding Georgian building itself could not be seen from the main road. We set about re-instating the gates and driveway, making both a little larger than before. And because there was no mains drainage on our side of the A2 we had to go to the considerable added expense of building our own sewage system – and I don't mean a septic tank; I'm talking about a fully independent sewage treatment system.

Although Rona had had some experience of employing plumbers, builders, bricklayers, electricians, plasterers, painters and decorators both at Alrona and Painters Forstal, it quickly became obvious to us early on that we were going to need someone to manage the project for us. I remember thinking at the time how much a healthy Bert would have enjoyed taking on the job. We eventually employed the services of a chap called Bill Brown, who had renovated many properties locally, and although his previous ventures had only been on a relatively small domestic scale, it appeared to us that he at least looked as if he knew what he was doing.

There were many disagreements with various building contractors along the way, as one should have expected, I suppose. But the biggest bone of contention was the vast difference that existed between the work ethic of our two trades. Whereas we catering types are programmed to work all the hours God sends, trying to meet several deadlines a day, the building mentality seems to be quite the opposite. You are lucky if you get five solid hours work a day out of a builder, and if nothing gets done at all it is no great surprise. Some of the contractors I listed earlier seemed to think that they worked hard, but they didn't really. Among the few exceptions were a team of three plasterers who used to work for us during the day, but all of whom also had full-time night shift jobs at the Post Office. Now, plastering is genuinely hard graft – I know that because they once let me have a go at it. I asked them how they managed to combine such a tough day job with working all night as well and they explained that the Post Office night shift was a doddle and that they all took it in turns to sleep.

Looking back, Bill Brown did a very good job in getting us where we wanted to go, even if it did take a little longer than anticipated. Altogether, around ten months elapsed between the time we bought Macknade and the time that we opened for business. But given the magnitude of the task and the many frustrations we endured, what we achieved in that time was actually quite remarkable. By the time we finished, the place had been almost totally rebuilt, apart from the outside walls.

The last couple of months at Painters Forstal were manic in the true sense of the word. We had traded on that site for the best part of twenty-five years and some of our customers had regularly spent whole afternoons and evenings there, had held their wedding receptions there, had clinched major deals there and had generally enjoyed many downright good times there. As a result, there were literally thousands of people who wanted to come for one last nostalgic visit and we were booked solid for every single session.

All this coincided with the numerous decisions that had to be made at the new place, mostly by poor Rona. Painters and decorators, roofers and tilers, planning officers, fire officers, environmental health officers, kitchen designers, engineers of all kinds, carpet layers, curtain makers, kitchen equipment suppliers and gardeners... the list of people who had to be dealt with and supervised went on forever. Those two months were probably the busiest time of our lives and, even though I say it myself, it is amazing, looking back, the amount of work that we got through. I'm afraid that I have to confess to having a little giggle when some of our customers tell us about how shattered they are after a hard day's work at the office, complaining that they couldn't get away until 5.30pm!

In addition to everything else that she was doing, Rona had also taken on the creative task of overseeing the furnishing and décor of the bedrooms, albeit rather reluctantly. She wanted to employ an interior designer, but I was very confident that she could do an equally good job without the enormous expense of one of these supposed professionals. And what would happen, I argued, if we spent all that money and then didn't like what they came up with? In the end, our two sons and I, between us, persuaded her to have a go at two of the rooms and see how they turned out if she simply followed her instincts. We had decided to name each of the six rooms after one of the substantial trees that could be seen from its window. Rona did the designs for the two front rooms, Willow and Chestnut, and everyone agreed that she had done a brilliant job. This gave her the confidence to tackle the remaining four, which she also did beautifully.

The only mistake she made was to furnish them a bit *too* beautifully, with genuine antiques and top quality carpets and curtains that we might have bought for our own home. Sadly, this turned out to be wasted on some guests, who took it all for granted and treated it without any respect. People would think nothing of putting a dripping bottle of champagne straight from the ice bucket on to a beautiful walnut table, ignoring the coasters that we provided, while red wine and a variety of other drinks regularly got spilled over rugs and carpets that had cost many thousands of pounds.

The relentless, mindless damage that was done was heartbreaking and was frequently caused by people who, quite frankly, one might have expected to know better. Sometimes they just didn't think. Take, for example, the bridegroom who arranged for someone to go up to the bridal suite after the bride had left for the ceremony and scatter red rose petals all over the bed for when they returned to the room. A lovely romantic gesture, but unfortunately the £800 counterpane on the bed was stained and ruined forever – and they'd only paid £185 for the room. This wasn't wilful or mindless behaviour in the same way as some of the other stuff that went on, but it was still soul destroying for us.

Then there are the people who leave the bath taps running, intending to return a few minutes later only to then doze off, flooding the bathroom and causing severe water damage in the restaurant rooms downstairs. Apart from the obvious problems of stained wallpaper and ceilings, there are the electrical complications that cause chaos for all our staff and other customers. We have insurance, of course, but those sorts of incidents are why our premiums are sky high – and it takes a huge amount of time and effort to put things back as they were.

We always try to help everyone carry their luggage upstairs when they check-in. That is easy enough, but it is a little harder to anticipate when they are going to bring it downstairs upon their departure. A lot of damage is done to wallpaper by the sharp edges of heavy suitcases, not to mention the occasional splintering of the delicate spindles on the beautiful old Georgian staircase. And then there are the gentlemen who, for some reason, hang their bulging washbags from the light fittings in the bathroom, literally tearing them off the wall. You would be surprised how often that happens.

You have to bear in mind that we are supposed to be a fairly up-market establishment and could therefore be forgiven for expecting a reasonable standard of behaviour from our guests, but I'm afraid to say that in my experience a lot of people are either thoughtless, careless or simply carry on like "semi-house-trained polecats" to coin the phrase used by the then Labour leader Michael Foot in an attack on Tory Norman Tebbit. Even in the bear pit of political debate, that was a bit over the top, but I'm sad to say that it could be much more fairly applied to some of the people we have had staying at Read's. Believe me, some of the behaviour that we see on a regular basis is truly jaw-dropping.

I could carry on grumbling for the next ten pages about the sort of things some people get up to, but I'll make this the last one. It's more of an observation really, rather than a grumble. I wouldn't consider myself a prude by any stretch of the imagination, but going up to a bedroom in the early evening in order to turn down the covers, only to find a condom that has been opened and carefully placed in the centre of the pillow on the perfectly made-up bed is somewhat unusual, to say the least. In front of the other pillow was a rotating rabbit. Now, I'm not sure whether this should have been regarded as shocking or hilarious. But surely whoever was responsible must have known that a member of staff would be going into the room to turn down the coverlet and refresh the room? And although I may not be the most truly romantic soul, I find it hard to imagine a situation in which anyone would want to open a condom four hours before it was needed and leave it lovingly placed on the pillow next to a rotating rabbit. I'm afraid this is another occasion when I drifted into full Basil Fawlty fantasy mode and pictured myself going down into the packed restaurant with the rabbit in one hand and the condom in the other, to inquire: "Do these belong to anyone here?"

Throughout the three months between finally closing down at Painters Forstal and opening up again at Macknade we kept all of our staff on the payroll. For many of them it was the first time in their working lives that they were able to have evenings and weekends off and they were like kids let loose in a sweet factory to begin with, partying every night. But the money ran out very quickly and after a while they drifted back into a more routine way of life, volunteering to help us out in any way they could, even if it was just a matter of preparing surfaces for the professionals to paint. Others dug holes or trenches, just as Dan and I had done all those years earlier. One or two became as good as the professionals at using mechanical diggers and various other power tools and bits of machinery, although I suspect that the Health & Safety people would have something to say about that sort of thing these days. They also helped us to start work on clearing the three-and-a-half acres of gardens surrounding the house that were in a very poor state, having been badly neglected for so long.

With the renovation of the main building completed and the new Read's open for business, work started on converting the coach house, which was to become our family home. As with the main house, the roof had to come off and the building was totally re-wired and re-plumbed, and while all that was going on we lived for nearly two years in one of the guest bedrooms. That was probably the worst time of all, because most of our stuff was still in storage all over the place and we often didn't know where things were. I remember going to London for an Academy meeting wearing one brown and one black shoe, although no one seemed to notice. It was a chaotic time in our lives, but, in hindsight, it was nonetheless enjoyable because of the satisfaction and sense of achievement that we got from what we had accomplished.

We eventually moved into the coach house in February 2002, but our dog Mo – pedigree name Moët et Chandon of Painters Forstal, her predecessor having been Dom, or Dom Perignon of Painters Forstal – wasn't so keen to transfer from our temporary living quarters in the guest bedroom. For the best part of six months after we moved we would still find her, at the end of evening service, lying outside that same bedroom door, waiting patiently for us to come up. The upside of the move was that we now had an extra bedroom to let out, although I must admit that prior to us moving we had let all six rooms on many occasions, meaning that we had to move out temporarily and sleep on the two sofas down in the bar.

Rona's insatiable enthusiasm for anything to do with Macknade, was just the same as her father's had been for the old Read's at Painters Forstal and once one project was completed she would immediately move on to the next. Her work ethic was - and still is – incredible and comes mainly from having that small family business mentality that she inherited from her parents.

The next task at Macknade was to work on the walled kitchen garden. In some ways, this reminded me of the children's book *The Secret Garden*, because although it had once obviously been very splendid it had then been very badly neglected for many decades prior to our arrival and was in a really dreadful state, completely overgrown to the point where it had almost disappeared. We grubbed out all the dead and diseased fruit trees and reinstated all the old pathways. Once it had been cleared of all the rubbish it looked a bit like a prison exercise yard and Rona set about commissioning the Brogdale Trust to re-instate all of the espaliers on the walls, replanting fruit trees of the same variety that would have been around in 1778 when the house was first built. As a result, it's like a little museum of our local fruit heritage and another typical example of the way in which Rona always goes the extra mile to make sure that everything she does is done properly.

We also planted new beech hedges that were in keeping with the many other established hedges on the property, dividing the kitchen garden into two halves. One half was to be open to our customers, who would be free to wander around and see for themselves what we were growing. The other half was for the sole purpose of giving us a little privacy between our living space and the public areas. It's quite amazing what nosey parkers people are, particularly when they are residents. They will think it perfectly OK to wander into any private area, open every cupboard, check behind each door and peer through every window in order to see what is behind or beyond. This included the Coach House where we were living at the time.

Anna Zeville, a great friend of ours who had been wonderfully supportive in the early years, helping out in all sorts of ways, put us on to a farmhand, Melvyn, who lived just down the road from her cottage, had recently been made redundant and was looking for employment. We took him on as a gardener and within a year we had really started to get things underway. Although keen to feature home-grown produce on our menu, we had no experience of creating a proper kitchen garden and travelled all over the place looking at examples at stately homes and hotel restaurants with similar set-ups to ours, in order to get ideas.

One of those we visited was at Le Manoir aux Quat Saisons, but that was really on a far grander scale than anything we could even begin to think about. Raymond Blanc (or Ray White as he's known in the trade!) has created a vast and truly magnificent garden in Le Manoir's extensive grounds and can often be seen polishing his aubergines for the cameras. Rather than a showpiece like that, we wanted more of a working garden. We didn't get things quite right at first – for instance, in the first couple of years we ended up with such a glut of tomatoes that we could have supplied every restaurant in the area and still have had some left over, while at the same time we grossly under-planted other produce. It was only after about four years and a great deal of hard graft from Melvyn that we eventually began to get things properly organised. Melvyn was later succeeded by Glen Scott, whom we took on after discovering that he had swept the board two years running at the local Faversham flower and vegetable show, winning prizes with both the flowers and vegetables that he produced on his two allotments. Thanks to Glen's exceptionally green fingers, the restaurant is now self-sufficient in fresh home-grown vegetables, herbs and some fruit throughout the summer months.

Having duly moved out of Painters Forstal on February 15th, 2000, we were aiming to get the work at Macknade completed and all the final arrangements made in time to open for business there in the first week of May. Because of our close proximity to our previous location – we were less than three miles away from Painters Forstal – we were lucky enough to be able to take our old telephone number with us to the new venture, a big advantage. From the moment that it was reconnected by the exchange it rang incessantly and we were soon fully booked for several months ahead, long before we actually re-opened.

In my experience, many newly opened restaurants seem to think that just because they are inundated with calls in the first few months, this means they have cracked it. They then make the mistake of adopting a rather superior attitude to people ringing up to book a table, apparently taking great delight in announcing that they are fully booked in a slightly dismissive manner – as if to say: "What makes you think that you might be able to get a table here when you must know we've got people queuing round the block to get in?" They often learn the hard way that it's whether or not the phone is ringing a year after the opening that is the key to whether or not a restaurant is going to be a long-term success. We have always made a point of making it clear when we have to turn people away that we hate having to do so and hope that they will try again.

Whilst we were still deep in the final throes of the renovation process at Macknade and the place literally resembled a building site, a very brave English couple, who were living and working in America at the time, approached us to see if we could possibly cater for their wedding reception on the May 6th, 2000. That was around the time we were hoping to be ready and we explained over a chat and a cup of coffee that certain teething problems might be beyond our control, but if they were happy to take the risk, then so were we. They seemed like reasonable people and loved the idea of being the first customers at the new Read's – and, if we could get the licence details sorted out in time, the first to be married there. We spoke to the council authorities responsible for licensing premises for weddings and it all looked possible, so we agreed.

From our point of view, it seemed a good idea to set ourselves a hard deadline for opening, as we knew from past experience that deadlines tend to make things happen. It also seemed the ideal way to get started because, as any restaurateur will tell you, it is much more straightforward to provide a set menu for seventy people, complete with pre-ordered wines, than it is to cater for forty individuals ordering from a full á la carte menu. There was also a further plus point in that the couple wanted to book all six guest bedrooms for the night of Friday 5th, as well as for the night of the wedding. The only problem that we could foresee was that Rona and I would have to give up our bedroom and would have nowhere to sleep – but we decided to cross that bridge when we came to it.

As the date approached we were all working flat-out in order to finish everything off in time and tempers became very frayed indeed. On the night of Thursday, May 4th, we still had thirty-four men working here at 9.30 in the evening, including painters, decorators, carpet fitters, electricians, plumbers and curtain makers. Earlier in the day I had taken delivery of thirty-six guinea fowl that were to be the main course at the wedding reception. When I had finished mowing the lawns I came in and whipped the legs off them and made a sort of Coq-au-Vin, with an enormous pot full of braised Puy lentils on the side. At 10.30pm about forty of us then sat down in one of the newly decorated restaurant rooms and devoured a hearty feast, with loads of crusty bread, all washed down with about twenty bottles of Côte du Rhone. It would have been forty bottles if I hadn't called a halt to the proceedings after about an hour. We still had a tremendous amount to do and the workforce, including a team of electricians working for Rona's brother, Alan, got up from the table and got on with the jobs they were doing.

Although we were becoming extremely tired by this time it was one of the best days I can ever remember at Read's, simply because we were all beginning to feel that we were finally getting somewhere and were enjoying the sense of achievement. Sadly, it was followed by one of the worst days that I can ever remember, not just at Read's, but in my whole life.

The wedding party, or at least the twelve members of the immediate family who were due to occupy our six rooms, were due to arrive on the Friday afternoon and the arrangement agreed with the bride and groom was that they would then go out to eat somewhere locally, which meant that we could carry on and fine-tune everything.

Of the outside jobs, the driveway and car park still had to be finished off before their arrival. The hard standing had been completed some days earlier and all that remained to be done, we were reliably informed, was the application of the tar and the gravel, which would then be rolled flat with a road-roller. The gang of men arrived as planned at 6.30am and commenced work.

Three hours later there was a very loud bang on the front door, which was opened to reveal two wedding guests from America, who had just arrived direct from Heathrow. Complaining that they'd had to knock three times before anyone answered – the sound had been drowned out by the noise of all the work that was going on – they stated that they would like to be shown to their room so that they could get a few hours' sleep.

SLEEP! There were still twenty-five men working furiously to get everything finished on time, all hammering, drilling, sawing, banging, singing, farting and cursing – not to mention the navvies outside with the road-rolling equipment. I have done that flight into Heathrow many times and I know they must have been exhausted, but so were we. I tried hard to explain that things were beyond our control and guests were not due to arrive until mid-afternoon, but they were totally unreasonable and demanded to be able to rest. At that point I, in my tired state, also became totally unreasonable, lost my patience and told them in no uncertain terms to "p*** off". I had a bigger picture to consider at that moment, but almost immediately felt ashamed of my behaviour. It was too late. It had happened and, very unfortunately, I could not now undo it. It was my big Basil Fawlty moment!

When the bride and groom arrived at the allotted time later that afternoon they had already heard about the altercation and were understandably upset for their friends. I apologised and tried to explain things from my point of view, but had to concede that I had been well out of order and that it was unforgiveable to have spoken to guests in such a manner, however stressed I had been and however difficult and demanding they were being.

To my relief, the bride and groom were very understanding and said that they would put it all to one side, explaining that their friends had now been booked into a local Holiday Inn Express a few miles down the road, so would not be requiring the room that had been allocated to them and would therefore not expect to be charged for it. The upside of this, of course, was that Rona and I now had somewhere to sleep.

At about 10.00pm that evening someone suddenly asked: "Has anyone seen Kevin"? It seemed that Kevin, the carpenter, had gone missing – in fact, no-one had seen him all day. A little bit of investigation then revealed that there were no doors on any of the en-suite toilets in the guest bedrooms. They all looked OK because they were leaning against the wall in what looked like the open position. It sounds ridiculous now, but it is amazing what you don't notice when you are busy and under extreme pressure.

I don't know if you have ever tried to hang a door, but it is not quite as easy as one might imagine and we had to fit six before the party returned from the restaurant nearby where they had been having dinner. I have spent a great deal of my life waiting for guests to return to the hotel from a night out and normally grumble at their lateness when they eventually materialise. But on this occasion I was grateful that our wedding party were delayed, as it gave us time to complete the job. We later noticed that some of the doors on the downstairs toilets were also not fitted, but at least we had all night to do something about that. I wondered whether or not during that frantic hour and a half whether Kevin's ears were burning; they should have been ablaze!

Thankfully the big day got off to a good start. The new boiler room, which looked a bit like the engine room of the Titanic, seemed to be coping well with all the guests showering and bathing at the same time, as well as providing hot water for the kitchen with its industrial laundry machines and dishwashers. As the morning progressed, we appeared to have everything under control and it was all going smoothly until about fifteen minutes before the ceremony. At that point, for some unknown reason, the fire alarm decided to go off and no matter how many times I punched in the code to re-set the system it was to no avail. I phoned the alarm monitoring company who helpfully explained that there was only emergency cover at the weekend, but that they could have someone with us in about three hours.

There are four sirens strategically placed throughout the ground floor of the building as well as one in each of the guest bedrooms. The only solution to the problem, with the wedding ceremony imminent, was for me to get my claw-hammer from the tool box and smash all the ground floor sirens off the wall, which is what I had to do. Luckily, the wedding guests seemed to be enjoying the calamity. The likelihood of some teething troubles had obviously been explained to them all beforehand and in a strange way it all seemed to contribute to the fun element of the occasion, though some of it was proving expensive for us.

Miraculously all of the kitchen equipment was working OK and everything was going to plan as the guests were filing out of the room where the ceremony had taken place. I had positioned myself at the kitchen door as all the guests walked by on their way to get a glass of champagne with which to toast the happy couple. I was trying to catch a glimpse of the bride's dress, which Rona had told me was exceptional.

It was then that I caught sight of my American friends, whom I had not seen since the previous morning. I offered a faint smile in the hope there might be a slim chance that after twenty-four hours to reflect on what happened the two of them might have been able to see my point of view and we could at least call a truce. But with a contorted face that was full of loathing, the wife hissed: "Don't you dare smile at me!" My reply was out before I knew it: "It's a professional smile, madam, it means absolutely nothing." We hated each other and there was nothing that could be done about it.

The wedding passed without further incident and when everybody finally left on the Sunday afternoon they seemed, to all intents and purposes, perfectly happy. No mention was made of my faux pas of the Friday morning. But just to put things into perspective, we got to hear just over a year later that the groom, tragically, had been one of those killed in the 9/11 terrorist attack on the twin towers in New York. Suddenly, all the troubles we'd experienced that weekend paled into insignificance.

11 : White Weddings and Blue Movies

By the time I get to the end of this manuscript – or perhaps I should say, IF I get to the end – I wouldn't mind betting that the weddings that we have catered over the last forty years will have provided me with more material than any other subject.

At the first meeting with the bride and groom-to-be it is usually all sweetness and light, everything seems wonderful and it's difficult to imagine how anything could possibly go wrong. We don't normally meet the respective families until the day itself, and that is when the trouble tends to start. In fact, things have so often got out of control from that moment on, and especially once the booze begins to flow, that we are now very picky about doing any weddings at all.

It doesn't matter how well-bred a wedding party like to think they are, there is always someone who will drink too much and cause ructions of one sort or another. During our first eleven years at Macknade, Rona and I continued to live in the adjoining Coach House, just twenty yards away from the back door of the kitchen. When there are just a few resident guests sitting in the bar at, say, 1.30am, we are generally quite happy to explain to them that we have to be up early the next morning, that we would like to get to bed and that we will lock up, set the perimeter alarm and leave them to help themselves to another drink, should they want one, with the request to keep a tab.

It goes without saying that there are some people that we would never dream of leaving alone and unsupervised with access to the bar. But most people are fairly reasonable human beings and although they might pour themselves slightly larger measures than we would have served to them, losing the odd whisky is better than the alternative, which is to have an already overworked member of staff staying on until 3.30am listening to a load of drunken drivel. Anyway, the member of staff would probably pinch a couple of drinks for themselves if they were anything like me, so what's the difference?

To guard against those who decide to betray our trust we have a tiny CCTV camera installed in the corner of the bar – and as well as allowing us to catch up with those who are seriously dishonest this has also occasionally provided some jaw-dropping Candid Camera-style entertainment.

One example of the latter that sticks in my mind concerns a wedding reception that had passed uneventfully until, at about 2.00am, there were fourteen people left in the bar – twelve of whom were booked in for the night. The two non-residents were eventually persuaded to leave when Rona explained that we were going to switch on the alarms before retiring for the night, and at that point seven of the remaining twelve also decided it was time to call it a day. Despite having been drinking all day, everyone seemed lucid and in control so, as usual, we invited the last five diehards to help themselves if they wanted more to drink and then left them to it.

In the morning, I came in to clear the bar area of what the customers had left the night before, light up the stoves, cook the croissant and pan au chocolat and generally get everything ready whilst Rona was preparing for what would be a table of twelve for breakfast. For some reason, I was a little suspicious that the very expensive Cognacs on the top shelf had been interfered with and went back into the office to play the CCTV tape back to see if anybody had been at it. Well, two of them certainly had, but not in the way I had suspected.

When I fast-forwarded the tape, it showed that within half an hour of Rona and I having left them, three of the five had also gone to bed, leaving just one man and a woman. I thought that it must have been them who had helped themselves to the £60-a-shot cognac, so continued to watch the recording. When left completely to themselves, the couple became very touchy feely and it was quite obvious that they liked each other a lot. When the chap realised that he was on to a winner he got up off the settee, wedged the back of a chair under the door handle to prevent anyone entering the room and proceeded to have his wicked way with the lady on the sofa (rather clumsily, I thought) After a suitable little rest, they also decided to call it a day and went upstairs to bed.

When the whole party emerged at about 9.30 on the Sunday morning it became obvious that the two main protagonists in my unintentional blue movie were not in fact a couple at all. They had each returned to their own partners in separate rooms upstairs following their passionate impromptu liaison in the bar downstairs. (As it turned out, my reason for checking the tape in the first place proved unjustified as the top shelf drinks had been left untouched).

We had developed quite a good rapport with the newly married couple and asked, whilst they were eating their breakfast, whether there was anything to be added to the previous night's bar bill. Of course, I knew full well that there wasn't, but it did give me the opportunity, which I couldn't resist, to inquire jokingly in front of everyone else in the party: "Can I trust you, or should I maybe go and check the camera in the bar?" At that moment, the expression on the faces of my two blue movie film stars was a joy to behold.

Rona and I and various members of our staff all have memories, fond or otherwise, of certain bizarre, dramatic or entertaining incidents that have enlivened receptions held at Read's. It is often the best man who sets the tone and in this respect there was one, in particular, who stole the show in no uncertain manner. This chap was without doubt the most unforgettable best man who has ever got up to make a speech at a Read's wedding reception; in fact, he ranks high among the Top Ten list of the most colourful and interesting characters who have ever visited the restaurant.

I first became aware of him towards the end of the evening when he asked one of our Romanian waiters for a runcible spoon in order that he could start his speech. When our waiter came in to the kitchen and asked for said spoon we assumed that it was just another language problem and Rona went out to the top table to clarify the situation. But sure enough, it was indeed a runcible spoon that had been requested.

Apart from reading about one in Edward Lear's poem *The Owl and the Pussycat*, I must confess that – like most people, I rather suspect – I really have no idea what, exactly, a runcible spoon is. While we were still discussing what we should send out to him he arrived in the kitchen and started to look around. He eventually found a container full of what I would call ladles and proceeded to rifle through our considerable collection, looking for one of exactly the right size and shape for his purposes.

Having already consumed large amounts of alcohol during the reception, he had continued to drink throughout the meal, so that by the time he got up to speak he was obviously a little tipsy, although by no means as drunk as one might have expected him to be, given his substantial intake. We have heard many best man speeches over the years, some highly amusing and others toe-curlingly embarrassing; either kind can be equally entertaining from our dispassionate standpoint, able to listen to them in a detached way without the emotional attachment of being a guest or family member. Our man with the runcible spoon was the best ever, by a long way. He was absolutely hilarious and had everyone present, including the staff, in fits of laughter. Unfortunately, I can't even begin to describe it to you here in any way that would do him justice. He was clearly well known to the assembled throng and the laughter rang out throughout the half an hour that he was on his feet, followed by rapturous applause and a standing ovation. This guy could easily have made a decent living as a professional after-dinner speaker had he been so inclined. The evening passed without further incident and I think we finally left them to it at about 1.30am.

Rona and I were then awoken at about 6.15 by the alarm going off in the main house and I quickly put on my dressing gown and went over to investigate. I disabled the alarm at the kitchen entrance and made my way to the front door of the main house, which I found to be wide open. This, most irritatingly, was a regular occurrence and was usually caused by inconsiderate smokers who couldn't wait any longer for a drag and who disregarded the sign on the inside of the front door, written in large capital letters, which read:

> FOR YOUR SAFETY A PERIMETER ALARM IS SET. OPENING THIS DOOR OR ANY DOWNSTAIRS WINDOW WILL TRIGGER THE ALARM. IF FOR ANY REASON YOU FIND YOURSELVES IN DIFFICULTIES DURING THE NIGHT PLEASE ENTER THE OFFICE, LIFT THE TELEPHONE RECIEVER AND RONA OR DAVID WILL BE WITH YOU PROMPTLY.

Over the years, we have come to the conclusion that there is not a lot else that can be done about this and despite the occasional disturbance of being called on to open up, it is at least preferable to having people smoking in the bedrooms, which renders the room unusable for at least forty-eight hours because of the lingering stench, (at least, it's a stench if you are a non-smoker).

(Above) Read's in its new location at a completely renovated and refurbished Macknade Manor. After more than a year, workmen were still on site doing last minute jobs as the first guests arrived.

The 18th century walled kitchen garden that means we are self-sufficient in vegetables throughout the summer months.

One of the guest rooms, interior designed by Rona.

Four past winners of the Chef of the Year competition over two decades – (from the left) our own Mark Sargeant, Gordon Ramsay, internationally renowned German chef Eyck Zimmer and me.

Brian Turner up on deck as the cruise liner on which we worked together goes through a lock on the Panama Canal.

Richard Shepherd, legendary founder of Langan's and for many years President of the Royal Academy of Culinary Arts pictured with Rona and me after presenting Rona with her prize after she had won the ladies' section at the Royal Academy's annual golf day at Turnberry, now known as Trump Turnberry.

We're not keeping you up, are we? Late night shenanigans involving regular customers John Butcher (on the right, with John Hill, a fellow restaurateur) and photographer Brian Aris, with mutual friend Elaine Read sporting a Darth Vader look!

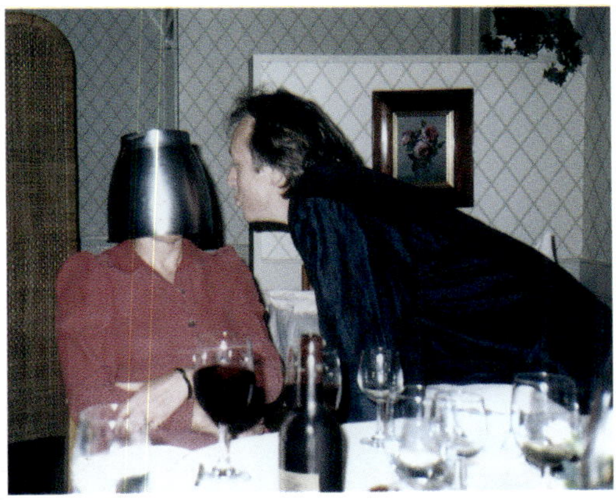

(Below, left) George Freeman, camping it up in my son Sam's Cub Scout cap; and Colin Strickland, for whom lunch often lasted until after dinner!

The drawing, featured on the menu at Read's, that was done specially for Rona and me by legendary artist and cartoonist Ronald Searle, a customer who went on to become a great personal friend.

(Left) Me with Ronald and (below) Rona with Ronald's wife, Monica.

(Above) As captain of the British international hotel and restaurant soccer team (front row, with the ball) and (right), some fifty years later, as a director of Shrewsbury Town FC, pictured with club president Mal Starkey (centre) and chairman Roland Wycherley.

In relaxed mood at a wedding at which my son Alex served as best man.

Proud young dad with Sam (left) and Alex.

(Above and right) Role reversal with Sam and Alex, a few years apart, on the bridge at Hotel La Grenouillère, Montreuil-sur-Mer.

(Clockwise from top left) My mother with me and with Rona's mother, Eva; Rona's brother Alan, in his regalia as Mayor of Swale, with his wife, Heather, and children Benjamin, Simon, Charlotte and Hannah; and me recently reunited with boyhood friend John Maw.

Pater familias: Myself and Rona flanked by Sam and his partner Mel (on the left) and Alex and his wife Sarah, who is holding their baby daughter Margot, the latest addition to the family. On the bottom step are (l to r) Alex and Sarah's elder daughter Millie and son Wilfred and Sam and Mel's younger daughter Evie, with elder daughter Lola out in front.

I shut the front door and went back over to the Coach House to have another half an hour in bed, or so I thought. But just after 7.00am we were awoken by a telephone call from the duty officer at our local police station, informing us that in response to a call from the public a man had been apprehended at the petrol station a little way down the road from us and wanting to know if it would be possible to confirm that he was a resident guest at Read's? We asked for a brief description, to which the officer replied that he was wearing a dressing gown and was claiming to have been the best man at a wedding reception at the restaurant the previous day.

We realised immediately who it must be and, when we asked why he had been apprehended, we were told that he had been seen standing in the middle of the road outside the petrol station performing a traffic calming exercise, as, in his opinion, passing cars were all travelling too fast along the A2. He had then proceeded to the petrol station forecourt, where the patrol car officers found him distributing flowers, that it later turned out had been part of the decorations at the wedding reception, to anyone who stopped for petrol.

Once we had confirmed that he was indeed a guest at Read's, the patrol officers bundled him into their panda car and brought him back to us, explaining that as no damage had been done and no crime committed there would be no charges. We said we would take him back upstairs to his room, but the two young officers, one male and one female, insisted that they had to return him to his wife in person. We all dutifully plodded upstairs to his room and knocked on the door.

His wife answered our knock and confronted by the sight of her husband standing rather unsteadily before her in his dressing gown and accompanied by two police officers, immediately burst into fits of laughter. This was not really the reaction any of us had expected and the two young officers didn't seem at all amused by her reaction, clearly seeing it as showing a lack of respect, and duly threatened to formally arrest our man. (Let's call him James, to save any possible embarrassment.) Far from encouraging a modicum of respect, the threat of arrest seemed to provoke James, who announced airily that he had just decided to embark on a life of crime and that he intended to concentrate his criminal activities in the Faversham area.

There was a brief moment of stunned silence and then, before we could caution him to shut up before he got himself into real trouble, he went on to declare that as there was an obvious lack of bona-fide policemen and policewomen in Kent, and given that the "children" who were at present employed by the local constabulary were apparently too busy occupying themselves with trivial matters to get on with the serious task of catching real criminals, he might as well take advantage of the situation to pursue an uninterrupted life of crime.

I could see where James was coming from, because the two young PCs did indeed look far too young to be police officers, but I suppose that said more about us, and our age, than it did about them! However, it was true that their tender years had somewhat diminished the authority that their uniform was designed to invest in them. On reflection, I suspect they may have been in their very early twenties. And to their credit, they did permit themselves an involuntary smile as they slowly came to the realisation that James was harmless enough. They departed with a friendly warning to keep him under control, whereupon his wife led him into their room, saying: "Come on, you silly sausage."

On our way back down the corridor to the kitchen Rona noticed that one of the numerous framed pictures on the wall was upside down and in correcting it noticed that one next to it was also upside down. Further investigation revealed that every single piece of artwork on the whole of the ground floor was the same. There were about sixty of them in all and they had all been perfectly re-hung but the wrong way up, including a collection of six Japanese rice paper paintings that had taken me an hour to hang correctly when I had first put them up.

I suggested that perhaps we should go the office and fast-forward the CCTV footage in order to assess what else James had been up to during his nocturnal adventures. Not every room in the place has a camera, so it was not possible for us to track all his activities, but his picture re-hanging exercise had taken him most of the night, punctuated only by numerous trips to the bar, where he had helped himself to huge quantities of alcohol of various different types. How he had managed to remain upright, vaguely lucid and coherent, after such an intake, was a total mystery.

Later that morning he sat down to eat a hearty breakfast, looking none the worse for wear, and ordered champagne all round for the rest of those wedding guests who had stayed with us overnight. Meanwhile, his wife took great delight in recounting the events of earlier that morning to one and all. Before the party finally checked out James came into the kitchen, where Rona and I were clearing up after breakfast, and apologised profusely for the fact that sometime during the previous twelve hours he had mislaid our 'runcible spoon'. He then presented me with a cheque for £3 million, saying, deadpan, that he thought that should amply cover the cost.

I would love to have known more about James. According to one of his fellow guests, he was a highly respected and very important captain of industry, although we never found out exactly who he was or what he did. His friends were all very discreet about that. Anyway, despite all his drunken antics he left us with the genuine feeling that we were all the better for having met him. Very sadly, I seem to have mislaid the £3 million cheque, but maybe it will turn up somewhere one day. I had intended to have it framed and hung on the wall next to the rice paper paintings – upside down, of course!

The wedding receptions that go smoothly and without incident tend to fade into history and are soon forgotten; the ones that stick in the memory are always those at which the proceedings don't quite go according to plan for some reason. In that respect, there have thankfully been only very few occasions when things have actually gone badly wrong.

Sometimes it is the best-laid plans that go awry. One unfortunate couple, who were not regular customers, had left nothing to chance, first coming for a 'test' dinner to make sure that we would be a suitable venue for their nuptials. We obviously passed the test because at the end of the meal they asked us to join them for a drink and announced that they would like to hold their special day at Read's. They made a second visit a few weeks later and again asked if Rona and I would join them for a drink before then going through every minute detail. They paid extra to book exclusive use of the restaurant and all our six bedrooms for the entire weekend, both the Friday evening before the wedding and the whole of Saturday, through to Sunday morning. They also asked if they could bring their golden retriever, Gordon, to join in the festivities, which was unusual but absolutely fine with us.

It goes without saying that we and all the staff at Read's try our very best to make sure that a wedding, or any other celebration for that matter, runs as smoothly as possible. With the best of intentions, I am sure, this couple tried to include us in all the arrangements, as if we were guests ourselves, but whilst we appreciated the gesture, this wasn't really possible. People often have the mistaken perception that part of the attraction of running a pub or a restaurant must be the opportunity to socialise with your customers, whereas the truth is that it has to remain strictly business. As many people who follow their dream of running a pretty country pub soon find out, the idea that you can be on both sides of the bar is one you can forget. Even if you could find the time and energy, mixing business and pleasure in that way simply doesn't work. However, on this occasion we did make a small concession, joining the eve-of-wedding party on the Friday for a while, in between sorting everything else out.

On the morning of the ceremony all was going well and, as usual, I positioned myself at the kitchen door so that I could catch a glimpse of the bride as she came downstairs for the ceremony. She was quite the most beautiful bride that I had ever seen – apart from my own, of course! – and I remember waxing uncharacteristically lyrical as she walked by, commenting that she reminded me of a Botticelli Angel, only for her to give me a puzzled look, as if she wasn't sure whether it was actually meant as a compliment.

Everything continued to proceed nicely until the groom's speech, which gave us an early indication of what was to come. It was OK, except that he swore rather more that he perhaps should have done – nothing really nasty, but not quite appropriate. It was a beautiful early evening and virtually all the guests were outside on the terrace or in the bar, enjoying the occasion. But then it gradually became apparent that the groom, encouraged by his best man, was drinking too much and was completely ignoring his new wife. Like the rest of us, she could see what was happening and made one or two unsuccessful attempts to slow the drinking down. The best man started ordering trays of shots and it began to look more like a rugby club do than a wedding reception. The bride tried again to rescue the situation, but without success and then asked me if I would have a quiet word in her husband's ear. I did so, as diplomatically as I could, only to be left in no doubt that my involvement was not welcome, being told in no uncertain terms to "lighten up".

Rona and I now found ourselves in a difficult situation, one that every licensee knows only too well. On one hand, we wanted to sell drinks, but at the same time we didn't want the occasion to be ruined.

The bride became quite upset and in a final desperate attempt to save what had otherwise been a lovely day, ordered Rona and me to close the bar, which we did.

There were now a group of seven or eight hefty lads who, egged on by the best man, as well as a few dozy girls, decided that if they could not drink in the bar then they would retire to one of the guest rooms upstairs. Obviously we had not anticipated this and had not taken the precaution of removing the alcohol from the guest pantry upstairs, which continued to fuel them. Believe it or not, they chose the bride and groom's room in which to have their party. This was where the dog Gordon had recently been sleeping and he found his way downstairs to us. It was now approaching 1.00am and everyone was either at the party upstairs or had left out of sheer embarrassment.

Rona decided that enough was enough and decided to go to bed and I was left with the dog and a sobbing bride, who had refused to join the party upstairs. The three of us sat on the sofa in the bar and the only idea that I could come up with was to suggest a cup of tea, to which she replied: "Oh yes, please". She followed me into the kitchen and asked if we had any marmite, which we did. She said that some hot toast and marmite would make her feel a lot better. So, toast and marmite for two it was, then – or three, actually, because Gordon had some too.

It got to about two o'clock and she decided to go upstairs and find somewhere to sleep. I don't know what happened after that. Just to be safe, I didn't set the perimeter alarm as I could foresee all sorts of things happening during what remained of the night. Rather surprisingly, it proved uneventful.

The following morning was a very sombre affair, with very little conversation going on over breakfast, except for the best man, who helpfully suggested: "Well, if you can't have drink on your wedding day, when can you?" I can't remember ever feeling more sorry for someone than I did for the young bride that morning; it was quite heartbreaking.

When the somewhat less-than-happy couple eventually departed, I helped carry their bags out to the car park, shook the husband's hand and wished him good luck; that was something he was certainly going to need for the next day or so. I extended the same hand to his wife, but she ignored it, stepping forward instead to give me a huge hug and whispering "Thank you, thank you" several times over. As they drove away she turned and gave me a look that was haunting. We often see a couple returning many times for wedding anniversaries in the future, but we never saw those two again.

Sad though it was to see a bride's Big Day end in such early disillusion, it was nothing compared to the tragedy suffered by another of our brides, whose father went home immediately after the reception and committed suicide, shooting himself with a 12-bore shotgun. The newlyweds had stayed with us overnight and Rona and I were awoken the next morning at 5.30am by the arrival of the police, who had the unenviable task of having to break the terrible news of what had happened to the daughter. The awful wailing noise she made as she was told will remain with me forever.

I have to confess that it has not always been the fault of the guests when things have gone embarrassingly wrong. On one occasion it was we who were accidentally to blame for ruining a couple's big day – and it proved to be a very costly mistake. As hotel owners, you obviously don't want to lock anyone out of your establishment when they have paid good money to stay with you – especially not a newly married couple on their wedding night! This, sadly, is exactly what Rona and I inadvertently managed to do one summer's night back in 2002.

In this instance, the wedding and reception had not been held at Read's but at a popular local wedding venue about five miles away. The couple had simply booked to stay with us overnight, before going off on their honeymoon the next day. They had dropped their bags off with us earlier that morning and had warned us in advance that they would probably not be returning until well after midnight and possibly not until 2.00am. As we were clearing up just after midnight, following a particularly busy Saturday evening in the restaurant, Vanessa, our main front of house girl at the time, said she would wait up for them, only for one of the French waiters to assure us that he had seen them coming in about thirty minutes earlier. Unfortunately, we all took his word for this, although in hindsight we should probably have checked more carefully that he was right. However, had we actually done so and had they been in residence, I am not sure how welcome a knock on their door half an hour after they had retired on the first night of their honeymoon would have been!

The first we knew that anything was amiss was when we were half way through serving breakfast to other guests on the Sunday morning. The phone rang and Rona's cheery "Good morning. Read's. How can I help you?" was greeted with a torrent of abuse from the very unhappy bride that lasted at least a minute before Rona could get another word in. It emerged that the couple had duly arrived outside our front door in the early hours of the morning, having been delayed a little longer than expected at their reception, only to find the place locked and bolted. There were no signs of life and they had been unable to rouse anyone to let them in. Fortunately, they had not dismissed the taxi that had brought them over, otherwise things might have been even worse. As it was, they were driven back to the bride's family home, where they had to sleep on a makeshift bed, all the bedrooms being occupied by close relatives among the wedding guests who were staying there.

As things slowly began to calm down Rona apologized profusely and, by way of compensation, offered the couple complimentary overnight stay in the future, with dinner and drinks on us. By the time they took us up on the offer a few months later they had somewhat mellowed and had to admit that there was a funny side to the event, the story of which they had dined out on many times in the intervening period. It wasn't so funny for us. When we totted up the total cost of two nights' lost room revenue, dinner for two, plus a very expensive bottle of champagne and an even more expensive bottle of claret it came to the thick end of £1,000. At the same time, it was just as well that the couple were reasonable people, because otherwise I think they could have made things much worse for us.

At this point I should stress again that most of the weddings we have hosted have been extremely happy and successful occasions and have passed off without a hitch – other, that is, than the marital 'hitching' that these occasions are all about! But they, of course, are the ones that don't tend to make for such interesting reading. Before you tire of hearing my disaster stories let me tell you about the wedding, above all others, that we wished we had never done.

I vaguely knew the husband-to-be as he was the brother of a chef I had worked with many years before. The chef was a bit of a wide boy, and so was his brother as it turned out, but I thought them both harmless enough and they could be quite amusing at times. I naturally assumed that the chef would be best man, but as it transpired, he wasn't even included among the guests.

During the first twenty-five years that Read's had operated, I could count on less than the fingers of one hand how many times I had not worked on a Saturday. However, on the occasion of this particular wedding I had managed to get three top-notch tickets for the Monaco Grand Prix, something that our eldest son Sam and his best friend, Paul, had always wanted to go and see. Again, it was an exclusive use wedding, meaning that the restaurant would not be open for lunch on the Saturday. And with just a straightforward set menu in the evening we decided that Rona could manage without me and that I would therefore be able to go and enjoy a really special father-and-son day, the sort you never want to miss out on as a dad.

Staying in the same small hotel as us in Monaco were another British father and son, and on the Saturday evening they and other family members were excitedly celebrating the young son's victory in a junior race on the circuit earlier in the day. I don't remember hearing his name at the time, but a few years later I happened to see Lewis Hamilton being interviewed on television with his father and realised instantly that it had been the Hamilton family that we had seen. One way and another, Sam and I had such a lovely time that weekend that we have returned several times since then as a family.

However, while Sam and I were enjoying ourselves we had no idea of the horrors that Rona was having to deal with back at Read's with what should have been a straightforward wedding party. It was only when we returned on the Monday that Rona sat me down and explained all that had happened on the Saturday night and during the early hours of Sunday morning.

The groom, being a chef, had chosen a foie gras first course, followed by pheasant, whereas, without being snobbish, I suspect from what Rona told me that most of the guests would probably have been happier with a prawn cocktail and a well-done steak and chips – or even a McDonalds. They had already consumed large quantities of drinks prior to sitting down and then got through a good deal more wine during the meal itself than had been pre-ordered.

It was during the dessert course that Rona became aware of one couple who were arguing about some family issue or other. The woman taunted the man relentlessly, but he just ignored her and carried on drinking and joking with his male friends. At the end of the meal, and after two or three speeches, one of which was fairly lewd and disgusting, most of the guests who weren't booked in overnight departed, while the remainder retired to the bar.

The argumentative woman continued to do her best to make her partner's life a misery, taunting him endlessly, apparently to no effect. Eventually, however, at about 1.30am, something in him seemed to snap and he hit her with a left-hook that Henry Cooper would have been proud of and that Cassius Clay, as Muhammad Ali was still known in those days, would certainly not have got up from. The full-blown punch launched the lady over the back of the settee where she lay in a limp, heap, totally unconscious.

After briefly surveying his handiwork with an air of quiet satisfaction, our heroic pugilist simply sat down again and carried on chatting to his numbskull associates, as if nothing had happened. Rona told me that some of the other female guests, along with the bride, attended the stricken woman, who remained out for the count for several minutes. As she slowly regained consciousness, she unbelievably started on him again and he looked as though he was positioning himself to administer another wallop.

It was at this stage that Rona decided to intervene and ordered them both to leave, at which point everyone else came to the conclusion that it was a good moment to call it a day and proceeded to file upstairs – all, that is, except our bickering couple, who continued to threaten each other with violence. Ignoring Rona's order to leave, the man also started to make his way upstairs, whereupon Rona went up to the bride's room and told her that the couple must leave, as she couldn't be responsible for the woman's safety.

The bride explained that our pugilist was, in fact, a publican by trade and that the threat of calling the police would make him come to his senses, as he would be in danger of losing his license if charged with an offence. Rona again confronted him, this time in his room, and the threat of calling the police did indeed seem to work and he reluctantly agreed to leave the premises, calling Rona all the names under the sun as he went. It later transpired that he had indeed been a professional boxer before owning a pub. I can only begin to imagine how difficult that it must have been for Rona, having to handle all that on her own and from that day forth I never again left her alone to look after a wedding party. Mind you, I have found that it is invariably better to leave the females to handle such situations, as male involvement can sometimes only serve to make matters much worse.

On this occasion insult (to us) was added to injury (to the unfortunate woman) when we ended up being paid only about half of what we were due – and it took us over a year to recoup even that much. When a couple book to come and see us for the first time to talk about the arrangements for their big day, we get a pretty good idea of whether or not they are the kind of people we would like to cater for, but we can never be quite sure what all their guests are going to be like. And we can hardly put a sign up saying 'No Chav Weddings', can we? And, contrary to popular belief, wealth doesn't necessarily mean a classier wedding, while on the other side of the coin, some of the nicest ceremonies and receptions that we have laid on have been for people with little to splash out by comparison. So you never can tell. When you agree the contract you can never be quite sure what to expect, but if you want the business I guess you just have to accept that it's really a bit like a line from the old traditional wedding vows – "for better or for worse".

In admitting that women are probably better than men at sorting out difficult and potentially volatile situations before they get out of hand, I have my own failings in this respect very much in mind – well aware of my tendency to slip all too easily into Basil Fawlty mode, losing my rag when provoked by difficult customers. Telling those inconsiderate American wedding guests to p*** off was one example. Much worse was the situation that developed when by far the most awkward customer we have ever had to deal with wound me up to the point where I eventually exploded in fairly spectacular fashion, and with dire consequences. Looking back, elements of what happened were so farcical that I can now see the funny side. But at the time it was certainly no laughing matter.

It all took place around one Christmas in the late 1990s, towards the end of our time at Painters Forstal. The late middle-aged customer concerned had booked a table for two for lunch, but turned up some time before his much younger lady companion and had a couple of glasses of wine before she arrived. I found out later that he had already downed a couple of pints of Guinness at the pub across the road before he came to us, which might help to explain some of his later behaviour.

It seemed he was in the antiques business and the first thing he took exception to was the fact that we had two pieces of furniture from different periods – one Edwardian and one Georgian – in the same area of the restaurant. He pontificated loudly to the effect that under no circumstances should these two pieces be present together in the same building, let alone the same room, complaining that he found their proximity to each other offensive to his gaze. And once he had sat down and ordered, he found fault with virtually everything that was served to him and his partner – although only after the two of them had both cleared their plates.

The pair of them were still there at 6.00pm, by which time they had consumed two bottles of wine with their food and liqueurs with their coffee. Rona, who had been fielding all his complaints and relaying them to me in the kitchen, had already left by this time to attend a carol service at Canterbury cathedral along with Sam and Alex, explaining to me before she went that she had prepared their bill and had left it behind the bar, where I could add anything else they ordered.

They were now the only ones left in the restaurant and I went out to top up their coffee in the hope that they would call for the bill and leave. I was in my whites, whereupon he asked if I was responsible for the awful food they'd been served with, complaining, among other things, that the duck breast he'd ordered had not been crispy – which it was not intended to be – and offering to come into the kitchen and teach me how to cook duck properly. I ignored this insult, turned my back on him and started to make my way back to the bar to get the bill that I was now intent on presenting him with, even though he hadn't asked for it.

He immediately lurched from his chair and followed after me, calling out something like: "Oi! I'm talking to you." At that I spun round pretty sharply to face him, at which point he stepped backwards and fell over a low bar stool. He then staggered to his feet, accusing me of hitting him, which, of course, I hadn't. However, I had now definitely had enough of him and without another word, I went back to the table, got hold of all four corners of the tablecloth and whipped everything off the table – coffee cups, milk jug, sugar bowl, glasses, cutlery, the lot – walked to the kitchen, leaving a trail of coffee, milk and wine on the carpet, and dumped it all in the sink.

I then went back into the restaurant to find that he had disappeared, leaving his partner sitting alone at the bare table. Rather bizarrely, she smiled sweetly and asked if there was any chance of another coffee, instead of which I simply handed her the bill. As she was fumbling in her handbag for a credit card, her partner walked back in from outside accompanied by a female police officer, having apparently called the local station from the telephone box across the road and accused me of stealing his mobile phone. To cut a long story a little shorter, the two of us, along with the policewoman, went into the kitchen where I lifted the submerged tablecloth from the water in the sink to find his phone nestling among the rest of the messy contents. At this point I was arrested.

Although I was never in the end charged with anything, what followed was six months of legal wrangling, which ended up costing both of us a lot of money, time and effort without getting either of us anywhere. That's why, as a rule, I am happy to stay in the kitchen and leave it to Rona to sort things out front-of-house. Like Sibyl Fawlty, she is much better than her husband at dealing calmly and diplomatically with any difficult situations.

Of course, chefs have always had a traditional reputation for being volatile and temperamental types, with stories of daggers drawn – or, more likely, meat cleavers brandished – during heated disputes within the kitchen when things go wrong, as well as angry confrontations with customers who, for instance, make the mistake of asking for salt and pepper in a Marco Pierre White establishment! I can honestly say that I'm not that prickly.

As it happens, one of the worst examples of kitchen rage I ever encountered was at a hotel where the boot was on the other foot, as it were, and I happened to be with the customer who provoked it. I had gone up to the Fylde Coast in Lancashire for a few days' golf with three friends, including one very forceful and well-travelled character who ate out a lot, was extremely demanding and wouldn't hesitate to kick up a fuss if things weren't exactly to his liking. He and one of the other members of our group had driven up together in the other chap's new Ford Sierra and had arrived at the hotel in Southport well before I got there, along with the fourth in the party. By then, our picky friend, nicknamed 'the Ayatollah' on account of his tendency to adopt a rather imperious manner whenever he felt that standards weren't up to scratch, had already complained about the state of his fly-infested room, demanding that he be moved. At dinner, which admittedly wasn't all that great, he then sent back his main course, insisting angrily that it hadn't been cooked properly and was virtually inedible.

The 'Scouse' chef then came out of the kitchen and the two of them had a heated exchange, but things eventually cooled down and we didn't really think too much more about it until after breakfast the next morning when we walked out to the car park to collect our cars and drive to the golf course, only to find that the Sierra in which 'the Ayatollah' had been driven up had been comprehensively vandalised – panels beaten in and windows smashed. Somebody had clearly attacked it with a hammer – and it didn't take Sherlock Holmes to work out that the disgruntled chef was responsible. The hotel management admitted as much and had the car completely repaired and re-sprayed by the time we left a couple of days later.

In a way, I can understand how that chef felt. There have been times when I've wanted to murder certain truly awkward, rude, and sometimes shockingly badly behaved customers, or at least fantasised about grabbing them by the lapels and forcibly ejecting them from the restaurant. But I've learned to take a more rational and subtle approach, even to those who brazenly try to rip us off.

We had a problem at Macknade not so long ago with an outwardly very respectable couple who booked dinner and a room for the night. They arrived quite early, checked into their room and enjoyed a couple of half-bottles of champagne from the mini-bar before coming down to dinner, during which they consumed a couple of bottles of expensive wine. At the same time they expressed mild dissatisfaction with the food, none of it justified and only after clearing their plates.

At the end of the meal they then started getting very aggressive, complaining that the food was rubbish, that they were not going to pay for it and that they would no longer be staying the night, but would be leaving straightaway. And with that they disappeared upstairs to collect their stuff. It was obvious to me that the whole act was a premeditated scam to get a free meal, but, in the circumstances, trying to do anything about it would have been more trouble than it was worth. However, as things turned out, they didn't get away scot-free. As they stormed out of Read's it was obvious that the pair of them had both had way too much to drink and they hadn't got more than a few hundred yards up the road before they were pulled over by the police, who breathalysed the driver and, not surprisingly, found him to be well over the limit. Very satisfying! Had the local police been tipped off by some public-spirited citizen that the couple were about to do a runner from the restaurant and that neither of them was in a fit state to drive? You might possibly think so, but I couldn't possibly comment – except to say that revenge is a dish best served if not cold, then at least lukewarm!

12 : Celebrity Customers

We have had dozens of famous people as customers at Read's over the years. Some, like Jonathan Ross, have played to the crowd, while others, like racing driver Damian Hill, have hidden themselves away in a quiet corner of the dining room. Damian had just been crowned World Champion when he first came in and yet he kept a very low profile, doing his best to avoid attracting any attention.

It is amazing how insensitive the general public can be when it comes to celebrities; they just cannot leave them alone, even when it is perfectly obvious that they wish to have a quiet evening out. We would usually put any VIPs on Table 10, which is in a corner and became known as 'the showbiz table'. This was a tradition that started when my photographer friend, Brian Aris, used to live in Eastling, just a couple of miles along the road from us in Painters Forstal, and would often come in with one or two of the famous pop and rock stars, actors, actresses, models and other well-known people with whom he happened to be working. This gave our other regular customers the impression that we were a favoured haunt of the rich and famous, and although this wasn't strictly true, of course, the punters liked the idea of rubbing shoulders with the stars and so it was generally very good for business.

Jonathan Ross – no shrinking violet, as you might imagine! – came in one evening with Vic Reeves and Bob Mortimer, all of them with their partners. They couldn't decide where each one of them was going to sit and made a big joke of it, arguing playfully for a few minutes in front of a packed restaurant. Jonathan eventually suggested that if no solution could be found than they should all sit on the same chair, which they proceeded to try and do, squabbling over who should be on the top and who should be on the bottom. This silliness lasted quite a while, much to the amusement not just of everyone in the room, but also the chefs and kitchen staff, who were peering around the door, joining in the fun.

At the opposite end of the spectrum, Catherine Zeta Jones, David Jason, Pam Ferris and Phillip Franks came in when *Darling Buds of May* was at the height of its fame back in the early nineties. It was Sod's Law that they were the only table booked that night, so absolutely nobody else was there to see them. At the end of their meal they invited Rona and I to join them for coffee and liqueurs and we spent the next hour or so having a real laugh. They all seemed genuinely to enjoy not being pestered and were really relaxed and friendly.

Susan George and her late husband Simon McCorkindale were fairly regular visitors as was Noel Edmonds, all of them first brought here by Brian Aris. Bob Geldof and Paula Yates were also regulars, especially during the Live Aid years, often ringing us at the last moment on a Saturday evening when we were already fully booked. On one such occasion Bob rang and begged for a table, saying that he was entertaining some Americans who had promised Live Aid a huge amount of money and he needed to feed them. I said that I could fit them in as long as they didn't mind coming early, at 6 o'clock, although this meant that the staff didn't get their usual break and staff meal. I then asked how many would be coming and he replied: "Fourteen"! As we all now know, Bob can be very persuasive. He lives in Faversham and still comes in from time to time.

There are some stars who are instantly recognisable as much for their voices as for their faces – people such as Tom Baker of *Dr Who* fame, Virginia Wade, Sir Alistair Burnett, Honour Blackman and Gyles Brandreth to name but a few. These are personalities that you don't need to see in order to know that they are present. Actresses Natalie Portman and Scarlett Johansson were the focus of much admiring attention when they came in together while co-starring in The Other Boleyn Girl, parts of which were shot at locations around Kent, with Dover Castle standing in for the Tower of London.

Some of the celebrity customers who've eaten at Read's have told us really interesting stories. Actress Mia Farrow informed us over her coffee and petit-fours one evening that her sister Prudence had been the inspiration for the Beatles song *Dear Prudence*, written by John Lennon. Prudence Farrow was deeply into meditation and was out in India practising with Maharishi Mahesh Yogi at the same time as

The Beatles, but was so shy that she would hide away in the caravan in which she was living, refusing to come out. And Lennon, who was intrigued by her, would serenade her from outside, singing: "Dear Prudence, won't you come out to play/ Dear Prudence, greet the brand new day/The sun is up, the sky is blue/ It's beautiful and so are you/ Dear Prudence, won't you come out to play." The song is included on The Beatles (White Album), released in 1968.

John Lodge and Justin Hayward of the Moody Blues and Kenney Jones, the drummer with The Small Faces and The Faces before going on to take over from Keith Moon in The Who, were all regulars. Pop and rock stars could often be pretty rowdy, partly, I suppose, because they felt they had to live up to the image. Our regular customers were divided between the star-struck ones who were thrilled to see them and those who found them highly annoying, so they were the cause of a fair number of complaints.

The Hairy Bikers – David Myers and Simon King – came to Read's to record one of their series of TV shows, which turned out to be a rather humiliating experience for me. There was a competitive element to the show, the Hairy Bikers on one side and me on the other, each preparing a different main course dish for a group of specially-invited guests, who then voted for which they thought was best. The idea was to use regional ingredients and while the Bikers chose to do a Dover sole dish, served with sea purslane, a vegetable plant that you can gather on local estuaries, I went for a celebration of Kentish lamb, including loin, saddle, fillet, kidneys and even a miniature shepherd's pie.

It was all filmed one Monday, when Read's is closed, and for some reason I hadn't realised until everybody started arriving that people were actually going to be sitting down and eating the food we cooked – I thought we would just be cooking for the camera. That's my excuse, anyway, for how it came about that the jury of invited guests ended up voting 9-0 for the Hairy Bikers' sole! The fact that I had actually given them a hand only helped slightly to lessen the embarrassment But, of course, it was all a bit of fun and nobody took it too seriously. In fact, the exposure was very good for us, bringing in a lot of new customers and generally raising our profile.

However, it was not great for my ego when the show was screened some weeks later on prime time national television. Doing some shopping down in Faversham the following day I was serenaded by a group of lads on the opposite side of the street, who recognised me and chanted "nine nil, nine nil, nine nil, nine nil" football-style, to the tune of amazing grace. The upside of all this was that Dave Myers is now a regular customer at Read's, having moved to a house nearby. There was also an amusing postscript some time later when Rona and I were on a trip to France, switched on the television in our hotel and found ourselves watching a dubbed version of the show, with me apparently speaking perfect French!

Some of the older people reading this may remember a diminutive boxer named Terry Spinks. He became a regular customer when, later in life, he ran a pub nearby, and I always enjoyed talking to him at the bar after his meal. He was originally a professional jockey before turning to boxing, going on to win the flyweight gold medal at the Melbourne Olympics in 1956. Having turned professional shortly afterwards he enjoyed a successful career as a featherweight, becoming British Champion in 1960. He was a true Eastender, with a strong cockney accent that somewhat belied his considerable knowledge of food, gained through visiting restaurants all over the world during his fighting career. Once, on a visit to Read's, he was kind enough to bring along the medal he won in Melbourne and I must admit that I was somewhat overawed at actually being able to hold an Olympic gold.

Many stars from the culinary world have visited us over the years and it is always great PR to get that sort of seal of approval from the likes of Gary Rhodes, Ainsley Harriot, Antony Worrell Thompson and, in the early days, Robert Carrier and Graham Kerr, alias The Galloping Gourmet, the two household names who were probably responsible for kicking off the fashion for food and cooking programmes on TV. Our son, Alex, worked for Gordon Ramsay for eight years and, as a result, Gordon used to come down to Read's regularly, usually to do some photography for one or other of his numerous books. He was actually seen here so often that rumours started circulating that he was planning to buy the place from us. This was never the case, but the more we denied it the more people seemed to believe it.

On one occasion, having come down with a photographer to take pictures of the pigs at the back of our property for one of the books, he was enjoying a glass of wine just before leaving when he spotted a raspberry soufflé on its way out of the kitchen to a customer in the restaurant. He stopped the waiter, took the soufflé from him and asked the photographer to take a shot of him posing with it. A couple of weeks later we opened the *Sunday Times* to find the shot included in a feature about Gordon, with the caption 'Gordon Ramsay's Raspberry Soufflé', complete with his own recipe. In those days we used dessert plates with our name, Read's, inscribed on the rim and he had carefully placed his thumb over the name. Could this have been chance? Knowing Gordon as I do, I think probably not. It's no mystery how he has managed to get on in life. Good luck to him, I say.

One Wednesday evening in September 1993 a rather distinguished-looking couple came to eat at the restaurant. It was the first time they had been in and as Rona seated them at Table 4 they got chatting and told her that they were on a visit to Canterbury from their home in France. Rona spoke to them quite a lot during the evening and kept coming into the kitchen to tell me what an absolute delight they were. At the end of their meal they asked if we would both join them for a drink and although I was still a bit too busy in the kitchen, clearing up and preparing food orders for the following few days, Rona did sit down with them. As they left, they booked in again for the following night.

They had introduced themselves as Ronald and Monica Searle, and although the name immediately rang a bell we didn't really make the connection until Rona did some checking and we realised that Ronald was the artist and celebrated satirical cartoonist best known to most people as the creator of the schoolgirls of St Trinian's – an association, incidentally, that in some ways he detested. He once complained to me that for somebody who had done so much other, often more serious satirical artwork, being famed only for his St Trinian's cartoons was rather like "a top chef being known only for knocking up a couple of jam tarts".

He and Monica came back not only the following evening but the evening after that as well, accompanied on the third occasion by Monica's sister, Marion. Rona and I both joined them for drinks on these subsequent visits and we all got on so well that when they finally left and returned to France they invited us to visit them at their home in Tourtour, a little Provencale village in the Var, just north of Draguignan. It was the start of a close friendship that was to last over twenty years, during which time we got to know and love them in the same sort of way that you love your own parents.

Ronald's career as an artist had been interrupted by the Second World War, during which he was captured by the Japanese in Singapore and imprisoned in the notorious Changi prison camp, before being forced to work with other PoWs on the construction of the Burma railway – the so-called 'death railway' – an unimaginably terrible experience that a great many of his fellow prisoners failed to survive. The drawings and sketches that he somehow managed to carry on doing throughout this horrifying ordeal – despite going down with malaria and beri-beri and also being half-starved, as a result of which his weight dropped to just seven stone – later formed the basis of his book *To The Kwai and Back*. He and his fellow PoWs suffered terrible mistreatment at the hands of the Japanese, but he would only very rarely talk about it. And on the odd occasion when he did, Rona and I found ourselves listening in total silence at the end of which we would realise that we had been listening with our mouths literally gaping open.

Our trips to France to see the Searles always involved a great deal of eating out, as Ronald was something of a gourmet. We never stayed at their house, as they only had one bedroom, but each day we would meet at the water fountain in the middle of Tourtour just before midday and drive to one of their many favourite restaurants in the area for lunch. Then, after a bit of a siesta back at their house, we would be ready to go out again to another restaurant for dinner in the evening, usually somewhere nearer-by.

Officially honoured as a Chevalier of the Legion d'Honneur, Ronald was so well known and respected in France, not just locally but throughout the country, that almost everywhere we went with him we would be offered food and wine with the compliments of the house. But because Ronald had an understanding of the tiny profit margins that are made in the restaurant industry, these offers of hospitality were never accepted. We would always take it in turns to pay.

I remember going to eat at a Michelin-starred restaurant called Les Gorges de Pennafort, presided over by one of the Searles' favourite chefs, Philippe de Silva. Because Ronald insisted on paying, Philippe kept sending out smaller courses of virtually every dish on the menu saying: "Well, only eat what you like". Rona and I recall eating fourteen small courses each before having to retire gracefully. On another occasion we visited a likeable rogue called Bruno, who had a reputation as the truffle king of the area, and he, too, continued to send out a procession of dishes, all of which contained truffles in some way, shape or form.

As the years began to take their toll (on all four of us!) we would usually go out to eat only once a day, usually for lunch rather than dinner, after which we would go back to the house for late afternoon champagne. Eventually, when Ronald and Monica were in their late eighties, we would only ever go to their favourite local restaurant, the Cheine Vert in Tourtour. In the early years they would both walk up to the fountain in the centre of the village where we would be waiting to meet them with the car. As they got older the chef/patron Paul Bajard would collect them from their home and drive them to the restaurant and we would meet them there before driving them back to the house afterwards for one more bottle, always champagne.

The walls of the Cheine Vert are full of some of Ronald's funniest and finest illustrations. Some of his original artwork is also on display in a bedroom named in his honour at the Hotel d'Aiglon in Paris, where he and Monica would always stay when they were in the capital. We would meet up with them there once a year and Rona and I still stay there when we make our annual visit for the Prix de L'Arc de Triomphe – and we always ask for that particular room.

Very sadly, and also rather ironically, it was a fall at the Cheine Vert, the restaurant that Ronald and Monica loved most of all and in which they had spent so many happy times, that precipitated Monica's eventual demise. In her forties she had been diagnosed with a particularly virulent type of breast cancer and had been given just six months to live at one point. And yet, having undergone what was then, in 1969, pioneering chemotherapy treatment, she went on to survive for another 42 years. Now, as a result of the fall, she badly injured her spine and never really recovered, dying a little over three months later in July, 2011.

She and Ronald were such a devoted couple that Rona and I had always wondered what would happen to the other, when one of them died. They themselves used to say jokingly that the best thing would be that one day after a long lunch they would drive off the edge of the mountain together on the way home, so that neither of them would have to live without the other. As it was, Ronald himself died just five months after Monica in December 2011 – at least partly, we suspect, from a broken heart.

The letter we received from Ronald after Mo died was certainly heartbreaking and always brings a tear to our eyes whenever we re-read it. The following year, Rona and I travelled to Tourtour once more for our own little pilgrimage and visited the couple's memorial in the village cemetery. It won't be the last time we visit Tourtour.

It was only very rarely that Ronald would ever talk about his years of captivity, and we would never ask him to do so. But when he did open up, the stories were both horrific and fascinating. Explaining how he had managed to complete and salvage around 300 sketches and drawings while in the prison camp, undetected by the guards, he said that the Japanese had an almost superstitious fear of getting too close to people who were dying, so the best place to hide his work was under the beds of the sickest prisoners. He would also tell of one particular Japanese soldier who seemed to appreciate what he was doing and would supply him with horsehair from which he could make his brushes, as well as scraps of paper.

The Imperial War Museum still holds some of the original artwork that Ronald did when he was a prisoner of war at Changi and at the railway camp, and if you make an appointment to visit and ask specifically to see his work, it stands as a lasting memorial to the suffering that took place. Alternatively, you could get hold of a copy of his book *To The Kwai and Back*. Everyone should read it.

We always felt that Ronald had not received the respect that he deserved in the UK. A few years before his death we wrote to Sue Lawley at the time of the VJ Day celebrations marking the 60th anniversary of the Japanese surrender. Sue was still presenting Desert Island Discs at the time and, as a result of our letter, she invited Ronald to become the castaway for the second time in his life, having first featured in the 1950's, when he was at the peak of his fame as a graphic artist and Roy Plomley was still the presenter. Because Ronald, by then in his mid-80s, didn't feel he was up to travelling to London, Sue Lawley and the production team travelled to Tourtour to record the programme, only the third time that this has ever happened. It is also very rare for anyone to appear as a castaway for a second time. Shortly after the show was broadcast, Ronald was made a Commander of the British Empire, but, again, a representative had to go to Tourtour in order to present it to him.

On one of our visits back to the house in Tourtour – which now bears a plaque commemorating his residence there – Ronald took Rona and me to the office where, even in his eighties, he was still working every day, to show us some of his latest drawings. I happened to notice that on the wall above his black leather office chair was a frame containing a wine cork, with a rusty nail banged through it. I asked Ronald about it, as it didn't seem to make a lot of sense to the casual observer, especially the nail.

He then explained that Mo had bought a bottle of Chateau Y'quem 1967 to commemorate the year in which they were married. It is generally accepted that the 1967 vintage was among the greatest that Chateau Y'quem had ever produced. Some years later he had opened the bottle to celebrate a significant wedding anniversary and recalled that it had been one of the gastronomic highlights of his life. The rusty nail was a souvenir from the horror he had experienced on the Burma railway – and, together, they represented what had been the best and worst moments of his life.

Eating good food and drinking good wine was one of the great joys of his life and he was a gourmet in the true sense of the word, always genuinely interested in our lives as restaurateurs. At the table, wherever we were eating, he would always cut off a little of whatever he had ordered for himself and share it with us, while we, in turn, would always offer a sample taste of our dishes.

As I say, we visited Ronald and Monica regularly over a period of about twenty years and every time we went over we would be requested to bring with us a variety of things that they couldn't easily get in their part of France. Among these delicacies were marsh mallows, smoked haddock, parsnips, blackcurrant jam and Cox's Orange Pippins. We, in turn, would arrive home laden with cases of their favourite extra virgin olive oil or local wine. Ronald also gave Rona an original drawing of a Searle cat sitting under a restaurant table. We asked his permission to use the illustration on the cover of our menu at Read's, to which he readily agreed, considering it, amazingly, to be a great honour.

Monica used to refer to us as "the children" when talking to Ronald, even though we were in our fifties and sixties for most of the time that we knew them. She was fiercely protective of Ronald and his work and because she didn't have children of her own she was able to travel with him all over the world, whenever and wherever he was commissioned to work abroad.

Towards the end of their lives the two of them became quite frail and Monica would occasionally grumble about how horrible it was to be getting old, whereupon Ronald would gently reprimand her for disclosing their discomfort to us; a more loving, gentle and devoted couple there has never been. Monica was very accomplished at making jewellery and, over the years, she presented Rona with many gifts that she had made herself, treasured mementoes of a very special friendship.

13 : Mark of Distinction

Any small family-run business is only as good as the staff it employs – and that is especially true of a restaurant, whether it be talented chefs behind the scenes in the kitchen or lively and attractive personalities front-of-house, where waiters, waitresses and bar staff have to be able to engage with the public face-to-face. We have been fortunate over the years to have had people in both areas who were so good that we thought at the time that they were indispensable – until, of course, they got a better offer elsewhere and moved on and we found that, actually, we could get by OK without them, however much they might be missed. Sometimes the real stars come from unexpected quarters and in a very few cases you unearth a talent so outstanding that you actively encourage them to seek career opportunities further up the ladder, which you feel they deserve but that you yourself simply can't offer.

Mark Sargeant was an outstanding example of this, undoubtedly the most naturally talented chef we have ever employed. He arrived on our doorstep in December 1990, asking if we had any jobs going in the kitchen. I told him that we didn't, but that if he would like to leave his CV with me I would contact him next time we needed anyone. He then surprised me by asking me if there was anything at all that he could maybe do whilst he was here.

Anyone who conducts job interviews on a regular basis in our industry will know that you can be inundated with numbskulls and that when someone shows a little spark of something extra in the way of enthusiasm or personality, it can be a good sign. It had been snowing quite heavily overnight and I said that if he really felt inclined to help he could clear away the snow from the car park ready for the evening customers, something that I had been planning to do myself later, during my afternoon break. "Sure thing," he replied, without a moment's hesitation, and proceeded to do a thoroughly good job with the wheelbarrow and shovel that I provided him with.

He then came back again just before we opened for the evening and asked: "Anything else you need doing?" There really was nothing I could offer him, but I was impressed by his attitude, told him to keep in touch and made a mental note to contact him as soon as anything suitable came up. Before that happened he rang me to say that he had managed to get himself a job in the kitchen at Boodles Club in London. The chef at Boodles at the time was Keith Podmore, one of the most highly respected chefs in our industry and a genuinely lovely man, so I knew that he was in very good hands indeed.

Several months later a vacancy did arise in the kitchen and I duly phoned Mark to offer him the job. He said he would love to take it, but would have to talk to Keith first. Keith, being the gentleman that he is, phoned me to say that Mark was keen to come to Read's and could do so with his blessing, even though he did not want to lose him. Characteristically, Mark then insisted that he should give Keith six months notice, as he didn't want to let him down. Keith, however, had a queue of people wanting to come and work at Boodles and was therefore happy to release him after only a month.

Every day, right from the word go, Mark was there on the doorstep several hours earlier than he was asked to be and was always the last one to leave the kitchen. I had never had a young chef like him before. He was like a sponge in the way he absorbed every bit of information and took in everything that was going on around him in the kitchen. This was all wonderfully impressive, but I actually found that satisfying his thirst for knowledge and experience could actually be quite draining. At the same time, furthering his culinary education was both a rewarding and a slightly humbling experience. Bearing in mind that Read's was on the brink of achieving a Michelin star, and that just a few years earlier I had won the industry's top accolade as the National Chef of the Year, it was really quite remarkable for me to be showing a young lad how to do something in the kitchen only for him immediately to do it just as well, if not better himself! It was not long after Mark joined us that we were actually awarded our Michelin star and if you asked him now, he would unquestionably say, jokingly, that it was all down to him; and to a certain extent I would have to agree.

It is absolutely wonderful to have someone like that by your side when you are fighting hard to produce the very best that you can and, sadly, it doesn't happen in our industry as often as one might think that it should. Towards the end of the time that he was with me, I reluctantly began to realise that I couldn't – or at least shouldn't – try to hang on to him any longer. Although it would have been good for Rona and me, and for Read's, too, he needed to be somewhere where he could realise his full potential. I started to write to the top people in the industry at the time, telling then that I had a very talented young man who needed to move on.

One of the people that I wrote to was a young Gordon Ramsay. Gordon had just won the National Chef of the Year title and had a very successful restaurant called Aubergine in London. He wasn't a household name back then, let alone the world famous chef that he has since become, but we in the industry knew that he was destined for great things and that he was assembling a great team of young chefs around himself. I suggested to Gordon that he should have Mark working at Aubergine for a day to see if the two of them would get on well together. The rest is history; Mark went on to become Gordon's trusted right hand man, with him everywhere – on television, helping to write his numerous books and ultimately taking charge as head chef at Gordon Ramsay at Claridge's.

Gordon has always remained very loyal to me and Rona as a result of the introduction to Mark and has included me in many things that he needn't have done, such as judging the Gordon Ramsay Scholarship, while also coming down to Read's regularly and even inviting us to his very exclusive 40th birthday party. The day Mark finally left Read's was a very sad one indeed, one of the few occasions when, alone in the kitchen, I have shed a few tears. At the same time, I am immensely proud of having played a small part in his success. He went on to win the Young Chef of the Year competition in 1996 and the National Chef of the Year title in 2002, just as Gordon and I had done earlier. As well as having built a great career for himself, he has a lovely wife and family. We have remained close friends and see each other regularly, and he is also very loyal to me in many ways. He was the first one to make me realise that if you really love people, you have to know when to let them go.

As well as being an exceptionally talented chef, 'Sarge' was also a great 'money-maker' – able to manage his kitchen in such a way as to maximise the percentage profit made on the basic cost of ingredients. To do that you need to be more than just a good cook – more than just good on the pans, as we say. You also need to be able to plan your menus, buy in supplies at the right price and in the right quantities and manage your fridge efficiently, all in such a way as to ensure that everything is used up and wastage is reduced to an absolute minimum. This is something that is more difficult to achieve than you might suppose and not that many chefs are good at making money out of food. Mark's ability in this respect was reflected by the fact that as the star of the Ramsay empire, he was always top of the kitchen percentages table. And, rather immodestly, I think I can claim some of the credit for that because of the way I trained him. In all the years we've been running Read's we've never strayed more than two percentage points either side of a 71% gross profit. That's the way I worked and what I always aimed to achieve.

During the same period that we had Mark in the kitchen, we were also fortunate to have David Pearce working in the restaurant. The two of them joined us at around the same time, having both been on the same hotel school course at Tonbridge College in Kent. They also lived virtually next door to each other in Maidstone, which was handy as it meant they could travel over to Faversham together. David was another of those people that any business would be pleased to have on board, always cheerful no matter what the circumstances and incredibly hard working. Unlike Mark, who was only ever interested in being in the kitchen, David preferred to be front-of-house and, in particular, concentrated his efforts on learning everything he could about wine. He returned to us three or four times over the next two decades and became the backbone of the service, putting his rapidly expanding wine expertise to very good use as our sommelier. He eventually went on to write several books on the subject, focusing primarily on Australian and Californian wines, and also started his own wine importing business. David is one of life's lovely people and even when he left Read's to do his own thing he would often drop everything and help out if we had a last minute staff crisis; and, as with many of the young staff who worked with us in those earlier years, he became a great friend.

After Mark, the next young chef to arrive on our doorstep was a big friendly giant with green hair. His name was James McLean and we had got to know him through his mum, who worked in the office at St. Edmunds in Canterbury, where both of our boys went to school. She and her husband still come to visit us at the restaurant on a regular basis, sometimes with James himself.

There have always been ambitious young chefs who want to come and work at Read's in order to pinch our ideas, and it has to be said that James was certainly one of those. He was not naturally gifted in the same way that Mark was, but he managed to achieve his ambitions through sheer hard graft and determination. James was with us as the No.1 boy for more than two years and within a few weeks of leaving us to go to the Mandarin Oriental Hotel in Knightsbridge he, too, won the Young Chef of the Year competition. James was really thrilled with his victory and Rona and I were both there with his mum on the day, just as we had been with Mark's mum when he took the title; they were both memorable occasions.

Ben Williams turned up one day looking for a job as a chef when we were fully staffed in the kitchen, but desperate for waiters out front. Incidentally, during the whole of the forty years that we have been operational, we have rarely got the staffing levels worked out perfectly for the kitchen and front-of-house at the same time. Either we have a full complement of chefs and have to keep the numbers down because we don't have enough waiters or vice versa

I told Ben that we didn't have a spot for him as a chef, but that if he would like to help me out by waiting on tables then I would give him the first job that became available in the kitchen. Ben knew of our reputation for doing things properly in the kitchen and although he wasn't interested in front-of-house for the long term, he agreed to fill in there. Actually, I wasn't being totally honest with him, because although he had done a very expensive Pru Leith cookery course in London, that sort of course is more appropriate for domestic rather than professional restaurant cooking, or so I thought at the time. To his great credit he took the bull by the horns and did a great job for us out front. Ben is one of life's lovely people and he got on well with everyone, both customers and staff. So, as soon as a vacancy did arise in the kitchen, I decided to give him his chance there, even though I was not convinced that he'd got what it takes.

He soon proved me wrong, turning out to be one of the finest all-round chefs that we have ever had. He worked for us for two spells, each lasting about four years, and a more valuable employee you could not wish for. In between the two periods of employment with us, he worked in London in some very good places indeed, including The Square, a two-star Michelin restaurant run by the great Phillip Howard.

He had improved enormously by the time he returned to us for the second spell and I got to the stage of relying heavily on him at a time at a time when I was looking to step back and take more of a back seat. He was one of those rarities among chefs, someone who was innovative and had great finesse, but who was also a real grafter and could get through enormous amounts of work on his own. Every chef that I have ever met has an Achilles heel, and Ben's was fridge management, but he even got that right in the end. He initially had ambitions to have his own business one day and I suspect he could have been very successful once he had learned all the ropes at Read's, instead of which, rather sadly to my mind, he opted for the relative security and regular hours of a teaching job.

Over the years we have had a great many bright-eyed, ambitious young chefs pitching up on our doorstep. Some were straight from college and some, especially in the Michelin starred years, had worked elsewhere before coming to us. But if you were to ask any of them what they wanted to achieve in life, they would all answer in exactly the same way: "I want to have my own place". Those that actually managed it were very few and far between. Some were like sponges and would work incredibly hard to the exclusion of everything else: "Chef, will you show me how to do butchery, pork, beef, lamb, veal? Chef, will you show me how to do fishmongery – round fish, flat fish, molluscs, crustaceans? Chef, will you teach me the sauce, fish, roast, garnish and larder sections? Chef, will you teach me all about game, furred and feathered? Chef, will you teach me the pastry section? Chef, will you teach me all about pate, charcuterie and terrines?" And then, finally, when you've done all of that: "Chef, I'm too good for this place – I'm leaving."

In some ways, that was fine – at least they had the confidence to think they were going places. It was the ones with potential who just gave up who really disappointed me. All too often, as they got into their mid-twenties and started serious relationships, it would be a case of the female influences starting to kick in: "Why do you want to work every evening? Why do want to work every weekend? Why do you want to work every bank holiday? Why do you want to work every Christmas?" Family life is certainly very important and has its own rewards, but it was often heartbreaking to see the ambition being drained away from talented young guys, who would eventually come knocking on my office door and uttering the dreaded words that I have heard so many times: "Chef, have you got a minute?" They would then proceed to hand in their notice, saying that they had got themselves a job in a local hospital or old peoples' home where they could work a regular eight-hour day and have their weekends off. The words were coming out of the guy's mouth, but it was the wife or girlfriend talking.

I am genuinely amazed that more of my fellow chefs have not gone on to own their own restaurants. What separates those who have from those that haven't is perseverance, coupled with single-minded determination. Nothing that I know of can take the place of these two attributes. Some talent is required, of course, but not necessarily exceptional talent. I know plenty of highly successful people who are not especially talented and some very talented people who have never done as well as they should have done. Nor is education necessarily that important. I know a good many educated idiots and quite a few who left school at fifteen or sixteen who have made it right to the top. Pushing on and keeping going will usually get you to where you want to go in this life, and you should never let yourself be put off by a few setbacks.

Simon McNamara arrived one evening to help with the washing up and I remember thinking as he walked through the door that he was going to be no use at all. His mum and his sister had each helped us out part-time on various occasions, but for some reason neither of them was available on this particular occasion and so they had volunteered an obviously very reluctant Simon to come in their place. Even with something as simple as washing-up, young people straight from school are often completely useless, as they have never learned how to wash-up properly at home, let alone in a professional kitchen.

To my surprise, Simon turned out to be quite different in that respect; he did every job that we gave him very methodically and conscientiously. At the end of the session, at about 1.00am, everything was clean, tidy and in its place. He hadn't asked for a break at any stage during his seven-hour shift and had been polite and well-mannered throughout. As I paid him off, I had to admit to myself that I'd got him totally wrong and that he would be very welcome if he wanted to come again. From then on he worked for us regularly on a casual basis, each time learning how to do another task in the kitchen and proceeding in his quiet efficient way. Slowly but surely he became a more and more valuable member of staff and we eventually decided to employ him full time. That first evening was back in the late 1990s, in the Painters Forstal days, and he went on to become my head chef, a position that he held for seven years.

In some ways Simon reminded me of myself when I was younger, insofar as he, like me, probably didn't achieve too much at school and people perhaps never expected too much of him as a result, just as I hadn't when he turned up on that first night. But I came to have the greatest respect for him. We had a few minor disagreements during our professional relationship, but no real explosions or violent shouting matches, which in our industry, and over such a long period, is most unusual. As already mentioned, I have employed some exceptional chefs over the years, some of them very innovative, but if I had to choose just one to be beside me in the culinary trenches when I was seriously up against it and the going was getting tough, then it would unquestionably be Simon that I would choose.

Rob Best was the last of my home-grown chefs, youngsters who joined me in their formative years and learned every section at Read's before leaving for what they thought would be greener pastures elsewhere, only to realise that the promise of a kitchen utopia that had tempted them away didn't actually exist. They would then occasionally re-appear with their tails between their legs asking if they could come back, which wasn't always possible as I would usually have employed someone else just as good in their place. But, luckily, I did manage to find a place for Rob when he asked to return a couple of years after leaving. I say luckily because when Simon eventually decided to leave shortly afterwards, it was Rob who stood tall and stepped into his shoes, filling them more than adequately.

Although always talented, Rob was a bit of a rough diamond when he joined us first time around, sometimes finding it difficult to take any criticism, however constructive. He also had a bit of an attitude problem, but I was absolutely sure that underneath it all there was a nice guy trying to get out, and so it eventually proved. Like many others in our industry, Rob's approach to drinking was to go at it like a kamikaze exercise rather than a relaxing or gastronomic experience. However, with the passage of a little time and a good calm working environment he has developed into a great all-round chef and, having married and settled down, has matured into the sort of committed individual anyone would want to have on their team.

Rob and I had sat down one evening after Simon had announced that he was leaving to see if he felt able to run the place with my help. He very wisely replied that he would love to take on the job eventually, but didn't feel that he was quite ready and would benefit from working a little longer under an experienced head chef. So we made the decision to bring in someone from outside, which was always going to be a challenge given that, up until then, I had always promoted from within.

Talk to any chef/proprietor who has had the responsibility of having to deal with the employment of high-end staff and they will start to spit nails whenever chef agencies are mentioned – rather as football chairmen and managers do when talking about their dealings with players' agents. Apart from anything else, it is an extremely difficult and laborious process, complicated if you are in a hurry by the fact that any decent chef is going to be working somewhere else and will have to give between three and six months' notice.

Of the first five replacements we tried, four very soon turned out to be unsuitable for various reasons. The exception was Lee Pattie, a young Scot from Inverness who had been working within the Roux brothers empire and who was recommended to us by Albert Roux himself. Albert is a member of the card school that Brian Turner and I belong to and which meets a couple of times a year to play poker until the early hours of the morning, lengthy sessions during which more than a shilling or two has been known to change hands. Most, but not all of us, are chefs and we are supposed to take it in turn to host the meetings at our respective homes, first preparing a meal for everybody. However, all the sessions that I have attended have been at Albert's house, although he hasn't always done the cooking. Whoever is in the kitchen, the meals tend to be fairly special, as you might imagine. The one that stands out in my memory featured a goat dish prepared by Albert's wife, accompanied by wines that almost tempted me to start drinking again. Also memorable was a pasta dish with wild mushrooms produced by Antonio Carluccio. Sadly, the last time I saw Carluccio, shortly before his death in 2017, was at one of those get-togethers at Albert's house.

Albert spoke highly of Lee and it seemed, when he arrived, that he was just what we were after. He liked us and we liked him very much, but, quite understandably, his wife found the move from Inverness to Faversham with their young family too much to cope with and so he decided, very regretfully, that he couldn't stay with us and returned to Scotland. Of the four agency candidates, a couple turned out to be no more than glorified Chefs de Partie, but we didn't find that out until they were a few weeks into the job and the £6000 agency fee had been paid and lost forever. As for the other two, they were simply not right for Read's. It is not always about the ability to cook or manage people that rules people out; one of these guys had waxed lyrical about his ability to maintain a 70% gross profit without any difficulty and then proceeded to buy £45 worth of buffalo mozzarella simply to put on top of the pizzas he cooked for the regular early evening meal provided for our ten kitchen and front-of-house staff.

At the time of writing, we are still trying to find the perfect head chef – even half perfect would do! It is frustrating because we are absolutely convinced that for the right person it is a golden opportunity, given that everything else is set up here for someone to make a name for himself. Or herself, come to that. Don't ask me why there are so few female chefs about. In these days of equality, that remains a bit of mystery. I guess it must have something to do with the unavoidable fact that, traditionally, commercial kitchens have always tended to be rather macho male preserves, the long and often exhausting hours and the high pressure nature of the work often creating an extremely volatile atmosphere, with plenty of bad language and a lot of fairly lewd banter. It has to be said that it is not a very female-friendly environment.

Earlier in the book, I mentioned Brian Turner. Although Brian and I have never worked together, we have been great friends for many years. My first contact with him was when I was a member of that Dorchester football team that played in Hyde Park, next to Rotten Row, back in the sixties. He used to play for the Claridge's team and I'm afraid that whenever our two teams played we were always trying to kick each other up in the air.

I only got to know him properly some sixteen years later, after I won Chef of the Year in 1986 and Michel Bourdin, the legendry Chef de Cuisine at the world-famous Connaught Hotel, asked me to join the Royal Academy of Culinary Arts, which Bourdin had founded in 1980 as the British branch of Académie Culinaire de France. Brian was already a member by then and when he became chairman, with Richard Shepherd as president, he asked if I would become his vice chairman, which I was obviously delighted to do. The vice-chairmanship is usually seen as a stepping stone on the way to becoming chairman, but I have never seen myself in such a capacity, being better suited to a supporting role. So when Brian took over as president from Richard, who had moved up to become honorary president, I was more than happy to continue as vice-chairman, while Brian's place as chairman was taken by John Williams, the Michelin-starred Chef de Cuisine of the Ritz Hotel in London.

The Michelin organisation does not always get everything right by any means and John Williams was for many years a glaring omission from their list of starred chefs. He is one of the truly great hotel chefs and we in the industry were delighted when he was belatedly awarded his star. In fact, his absence from the list was beginning to make Michelin look very foolish indeed. Brian and I share a lifelong love of horse racing and John, too, has become a keen follower in recent years. We all meet up regularly at various race meetings all over the country and are always at Cheltenham in March for the National Hunt Festival.

Academy plenary meetings are invariably held on a Monday, and as Read's is always closed on Mondays this means that I don't have to rush back after the meetings. In the early days, Brian and I would often retire to a pub, or more usually a wine bar, to discuss the issues arising from the meeting. One thing would then lead to another – and eventually to Langan's, where Richard would be waiting for us. The three of us would then move on to one of the many casinos that we each belonged to, not because we were necessarily big gamblers, but because these were the places that would stay open the longest at a time when the licensing laws were not quite as liberal as they are now.

This was back in my drinking days and we would emerge at 3.00am or thereabouts and I would set about trying to find my way home, the last trains from Victoria having long departed. I would stand in Berkeley Square holding a £50 note aloft and ask the first taxi to stop if they would take me to Faversham. I would usually explain that I had lost all my money in one of the casinos and the £50 note was all that I had left. The taxi drivers were usually very good and would phone around to see if any colleagues were going home that way.

The going rate for the fare to Faversham in those days was well in excess of £100, but I never had to wait longer than ten minutes to secure a ride home for £50. I resorted to that first £50 note ruse out of necessity, but I am rather ashamed to admit that I did it again many times in the future, even when the visit to the casino had been very profitable. It's strange – I wouldn't dream of doing anything like that stone cold sober, and these days the thought of standing in Berkeley Square at three in the morning waving a £50 note in the air fills me with horror.

In 1999 an occasional-regular (if that makes sense) called David came in to the restaurant one Mother's Day lunchtime and we got talking about boxing. It transpired that he owned an agency that could supply tickets for pretty much any event you cared to mention. I have used him many times over the years, when it proved impossible to get tickets anywhere else, mostly to take my mother to Wimbledon, which she loved.

The first time I got tickets for her also happened to be the only time in the history of Wimbledon that there has been no play for the whole of the day. Mum and I sat in the rain and had some strawberries and a half bottle of champagne that someone proceeded to knock over and spill all over the floor, without offering even a word of apology. We spent most of the afternoon in the Wimbledon museum, which was actually quite interesting, and to cap it all it then took us four-and-a-half hours to drive the eighty miles home, but Mum insisted that she still enjoyed it.

David also managed to get me three ringside tickets for the Evander Holyfield v. Lennox Lewis world title fight that took place at the Thomas and Mack centre in Las Vegas. Youngest son Alex was living in America at the time, having enrolled at Washington and Jefferson University near Pittsburg, Pennsylvania, and he flew over from there to Las Vegas to join Brian Turner and me for the fight. Brian was creating all the in-flight menus for British Airways at the time and we got upgraded, which helped to make a good flight great. Holyfield and

Lewis had fought each other the previous year and although Lewis was generally considered to have won, he didn't get the verdict on that occasion and it was declared a 'home-soil' draw. The re-match was eagerly awaited.

There are some very good restaurants in Las Vegas and the three of us spent the whole four days eating and drinking, with a spot of gambling both before and after each meal. I've been to many boxing matches, but this was the first time that I had ever watched a heavyweight world title fight close-up. It was pretty brutal and this time Lennox got the verdict, and deservedly so.

There was a great atmosphere throughout the evening, but especially after the result was announced and the huge British contingent were giving it plenty of "You're not singing anymore" to the Americans. It was also fun rubbing shoulders with genuine world superstars like Jack Nicholson and Sugar Ray Leonard, who were also ringside.

The night before the big fight, England were playing Scotland in the European Championships at Wembley and we heard that a bar in downtown Las Vegas would be showing the match live. While Brian was having a nap, trying to catch up on jetlag, I decided to nip out and establish where the venue was in order to save time messing about trying to find it in the early hours of the morning, local time, when the match was due to be screened. In the taxi, on the way over, the driver asked me what it was I was going there to see and I explained that it was a soccer match between England and Scotland, who were traditionally fierce rivals. He then surprised me by asking: "Weren't England the World Champions back in the mid-sixties?"

I made the fatal mistake of explaining that it was the World Cup we had won in 1966 and that this was the European Championships. He said that he understood that, but what was the difference? I then further explained that one was for teams only from Europe and the other was for teams from all over the world. At that point he started to get rather angry and repeated that he understood that, but what was the difference? I suppose that trying to explain that to someone from a nation that holds a World Series for a sport that no other country in the world plays was a little ambitious, to say the least. I should have known better.

As it turned out, it was a memorable night, with about two thousand Brits, most of whom were over for the fight, crammed into the biggest bar you have ever seen to witness England beat Scotland 2 – 0. Brian was probably at the height of his fame at that time and all I did for the whole evening was take snaps of him with various fans on their own cameras or phones, this being before the time of the 'selfie'.

Brian and I have had many memorable jaunts around the world over the years, none more enjoyable than when he was asked to do some cookery demonstrations on board a luxury cruise liner on a tour of the Caribbean Islands. We flew out to Barbados, where we joined the *Crystal Symphony*, a ship of 51,000 tons. There was a crew of about 540 looking after a full complement of about 1000 passengers, which gives you a rough idea of the level of service involved.

Brian jokingly asked me if I would commis for him while he was on board and, of course, I bit his hand off. I think the most strenuous thing that I was required to do for him during the whole trip was to get him a glass of water when he had a tickly cough in the middle of a demonstration to an audience of about two hundred people, mostly Americans.

Something that happened during that demonstration still makes me chuckle, Brian had asked for a volunteer to help him, something that people usually jump at, but this time, for some reason, no-one came forward. On television, Brian is conscious of not saying anything too risqué, but when he is off camera he sometimes has a bit of fun, often at his audience's expense. Generally, they don't even realise that they are having the Mickey taken out of them, which was just as well on this occasion. The demo involved preparing a white chocolate and raspberry trifle and, in an effort to encourage some sort of audience participation he suggested that in the absence of an individual volunteer perhaps a couple should come up and join in. As two huge American ladies waddled up, Brian asked: "So what happened to Cinderella? Did you leave her at home today"? I winced, but luckily they just didn't get it – and so he got away with it.

We spent ten days island-hopping, the only disappointment among those we visited being Curacao, of which I had very romantic notions in my mind's eye. As we sailed into the harbour the reality that confronted me was more like an oil refinery. My favourite part of the trip, by a long way, was going through the Panama Canal, more of which later. Apart from that, the most memorable island for me was Aruba, mainly because of one tiny little incident that took place there

At that time in my life I was beginning to regret the lost opportunities of my youth at school and was making an attempt to educate myself (I still am!). The book that I was reading when we arrived in Aruba was *The Catcher in the Rye* by J. D. Salinger. Brian simply wanted to sit on the beach, sunbathe, nap and relax – understandable, as he was the one doing all the work. So I decided to leave him alone and took a long walk on what was a beautiful, virtually deserted beach.

After about a mile or so I came across a very attractive girl, who was reading and sun-bathing topless, and, being a gentleman – at least, I like to think I am – I made a point of keeping as far distant from her as the depth of the beach would allow, while looking steadfastly ahead, not wishing to make her feel uncomfortable, as she and I were the only two people for literally miles around. I have to confess that as I passed I did sneak a glance in her direction and noticed from its very distinctive cover that, by a strange coincidence, the book she was reading was *The Catcher in the Rye*.

I was about half way through the book at the time and, to be honest, I was having difficulty understanding why it was considered to be such a great piece of literature. I just didn't get it. Had this girl not been topless I would definitely have stopped and talked to her about the book. Is it just me, or do all men find themselves embarrassed in such situations? How strange it was that there we were, to all intents and purposes completely alone on the planet and each reading a book that had been published at least fifty years earlier, and yet I chose not to engage her in conversation about it.

About three quarters of an hour later, when I walked back along the beach in the opposite direction to discover that she had packed up and gone, I immediately regretted that I had missed the opportunity to strike up what might have been a fascinating conversation. For some reason, I couldn't get her out of my mind for some days afterwards and often found myself wondering how the encounter would have gone had I stopped to talk. Though my thoughts were not in any way sexual, I continued to be niggled by the experience. I am sure that there must have been a polite and delicate way that I could have introduced myself, considering the circumstances.

After leaving Aruba the next day, we crossed paths at one point with *Crystal Harmony*, the sister ship of *Crystal Symphony*, which was on its way down to Australia for the Olympics. It was the first time that the two liners had met in the open ocean and, apparently, tradition dictated that we had to circle each other, with sirens blaring out and each ship sporting huge posters that read 'Surrender Harmony' or 'Surrender Symphony', while everybody on board partied and drank champagne. It was great fun.

The next highlight of the voyage came when we steamed through the Panama Canal – something that will always rank among the top ten most amazing experiences of my life. It is no surprise to me that the canal is considered one of the seven wonders of the modern world. We arrived at our starting point in the Caribbean Sea very late on the Thursday night and Brian and I were up at 4.00am the next morning, like a couple of excited schoolchildren, ready to witness our departure an hour later.

The whole principle of the Canal is that the huge artificially constructed Gatun Lake, created by building a dam across the Chagres River, allows the six locks to be filled as often as required. We travelled though the three upward locks before completing the three downward locks on the Pacific side. The upward cycle through the three locks uses about twenty-two million gallons of water for each vessel to get up to the Gatun Lake before using the same amount on the way down to the Pacific Ocean. Sometimes, however, when two ships are coming in opposite directions, the same water can be used twice, as the locks are twinned. The tolls are calculated by using a complicated system involving the size and tonnage of the vessel and, in the case of freighters, the number of containers on board. Cruise liners are charged according to passenger berths, and I seem to recall that *Crystal Symphony* was charged just over $75,000.

The most expensive toll ever charged was in 2010, when the massive cruise-ship Norwegian Pearl paid $375,600 to go through, although this information may well be out of date by now. The cheapest crossing ever was when an American, Richard Halliburton, swam the length of the canal for charity and was charged the princely sum of 37 cents, calculated on his body's water displacement.

Going through the canal is one of the few occasions when the captain of a vessel relinquishes responsibility for his ship in favour of a pilot, who takes over the whole journey through the six locks, although a select few captains have been made honorary pilots due to the fact that they have been through the canal so many times.

As you will have gathered by now, I can be something of a bore on the subject of the Panama Canal. The final staggering fact I learned is that some 29,000 people died during its construction, including 22,000 who perished during the initial excavation under French jurisdiction, most of them succumbing to disease rather than accidents or explosions. The Americans took over the unfinished project in 1904 and another 6,000 workers died before the 77-mile canal was finally completed in 1914.

Sadly, our arrival at the Pacific Ocean signalled the end of Brian's duties on board and the two of us disembarked in Costa Rica. Our onward journey to San José Airport was by car. This proved to be a memorably hazardous journey because many of the roads had been washed away by a hurricane the previous week. Some of the detours we had to make around massive craters, where the road had completely disappeared into the valley or the ocean below, were genuinely scary and we were both relieved to reach the airport. It's funny the sort of things that sometimes lodge in one's memory on such occasions; one recollection that stands out from that final stage of the trip is that I had the best cup of coffee I've ever had in my entire life at that airport in San José. But I suppose that is not really that surprising – we were in Costa Rica, after all.

Talking about Brian reminds me of another story that I hesitate to tell, and if this manuscript ever gets finished I will have to tear this page out in case my grandchildren, who have been led to believe that Granddad never swears, should get to read it. When we were chairman and vice-chairman of the Royal Academy, respectively, Brian was always calling me about various matters, but being a true professional, never at what he knew would be a busy time at the restaurant. One day, during a particularly frantic lunchtime service, Vanessa, our No.1 one girl front-of-house at the time, came into the kitchen whilst clearing a table and called out: "BT on the phone for you, David." Assuming she meant Brian Turner – we often referred to him by his initials – I picked up the receiver and in what Donald Trump would call "locker room talk" said casually: "Only a complete c*** would call a chef at 1.15pm". There was a prolonged silence at the other end of the line, after which a young female voice explained that she was Helen from British Telecom and wondered if I would like to renew my Yellow Pages subscription for another year!

I was, of course, mortified and apologised profusely, taking a few extra moments to try and explain myself and why it was that I had unintentionally been so disgustingly rude. I have to say that she was absolutely brilliant about the whole episode, insisting that she couldn't wait to get off the line so she could tell her colleagues about it. We both ended up having a laugh before saying goodbye. Thanks for being so understanding, Helen.

14 : Sins of the Father

Like many people of my generation, I have a love-hate relationship with modern technology. Mobile phones, fax machines, personal computers, laptops, iPhones, high speed broadband, smart TVs, wireless printers and so on – they're all wonderful when they're working, but a total nightmare when, for no apparent reason, they go wrong and you find yourself on a bad line to a call centre in Mumbai, talking to somebody who speaks in technological terms that only your twelve-year-old son or daughter can understand. Although normally the most placid of people, in those situations I very soon find myself enveloped in a red mist of anger and frustration, to the extent that I once literally hacked a fax machine to death with a meat cleaver!

The crime was committed in the early hours of one morning, and the fact that the victim was a fax machine shows how long ago that must have been. After a long hard day in the kitchen, I had sorted out my food orders for the following day and had gone into the office to fax them through to the suppliers, a regular procedure that would normally have taken about two minutes. However, on this occasion the machine had run out of paper and when I re-loaded the hopper it would not let me fax my orders through until the nine incoming faxes that were stored in its memory had been printed out. So, I had to sit and watch the machine devour reams of paper as it churned out page after page, mostly from wine suppliers sending me their latest lists. Unsolicited and mostly unwanted, these lists would come through up to twenty times a week, and would often run to thirty pages or more, incidentally costing me a fortune in fax paper and ink!

It was now about 1.30am and the machine continued to chunter on until, halfway through the seventh of the nine incoming faxes, the ink cartridge ran dry. Fortunately, I did have a spare to hand, but I had to exercise the patience of Job in order to carry out the rather fiddly task of fitting it into place. By now my blood was beginning to boil. Eventually, the confounded machine finished spewing out the seemingly endless pages of bumpf and allowed me to send my food orders. Having completed the task, I was about to go to bed when the machine burst into life again. I should have ignored it, of course, instead of which I made the mistake of waiting to see what the new message was, only to discover that, unbelievably, it was from some organisation called the Society for the Prevention of Unwanted Faxes, inviting me to sign up! At that point I suppose that I should have seen the funny side, but I didn't. I completely lost it! I marched back to the kitchen, grabbed a meat cleaver and returned to the office, where I set about the wretched machine like the mad axeman – or, to be truthful, more like Basil Fawlty famously thrashing his broken down Austin 1100. I left it smashed to smithereens, bits of it lying all over the office. I have to say that this release of pent-up frustration gave me an enormous amount of satisfaction and I actually lay in bed with a little smile on my face before drifting off to sleep.

Rona was first up in the morning and upon observing the scene of devastation in the office she understandably wanted to know what on earth had been going on. She certainly didn't share my sense of satisfaction when I told her the story. She also explained that I had not unplugged the offending fax machine from the wall socket before making my alterations to its design, which could have been quite dangerous, I suppose.

There is a serious point to this story in that the incident took place during my drinking days and my rather over-the-top rage against the machine was undoubtedly fuelled to a certain extent by alcohol, as I'd usually have a nightcap or two after finishing work in the kitchen. During the ramblings down Memory Lane recorded here I have referred on several occasions to the fact that I no longer drink alcohol at all, and it was because of episodes such as the one described above, not to mention several other slightly more embarrassing misadventures while under the influence, that I decided to become teetotal.

I don't really know if it is actually possible to inherit an addictive or compulsive gene, but I do wonder whether it might be in my DNA, passed on to me by my father. He, sadly, spent most of his life pushing the self-destruct button as a result of his addiction to alcohol and, but for Rona, I fear I might well have ended up doing the same.

Joseph Robert Heal Pitchford was born on May 12th, 1926 at Selly-oak, Birmingham. His father was a very strong-minded and successful engineer, while his mother was artistic, with a sensitive nature. It seems that Joe was more like her. He had an older sister, Marjorie, whom he adored. Indeed, she appears to have taken the place of Joe's mother after she died when Joe was only thirteen years old. I suspect that this was the one major unsettling episode in his life, although I don't offer that as an excuse for his later behaviour.

I don't know a great deal about his childhood and early life, but I do know that in many ways he had a privileged upbringing. He was sent to a good school and money certainly wasn't in short supply. I don't know if he came from a loving family, and it would be unfair to my grandparents on his side to speculate that he may not have done. In short, it would be guesswork, so I'm not going to go there, but I do know that because of his excessive drinking from an early age he managed to wreck whatever potentially good opportunities came his way. He spent much of the middle part of his life in and out of prison, mostly for minor and often stupid offences committed whilst under the influence of alcohol. He had been in line to inherit a large amount of money from his family's considerable estate when he reached the age of twenty-one, but his father realised his inability to control his drinking and instead set up a trust for him in the hope that he would one day be able to take more control of his life.

Joe continued to take a modest income from the trust until he died in 2005, when the remainder was shared between his three offspring. I say three because after divorcing my mother he married for a second time – a lady whom I met only a handful of times. Her name was Rose, and from her I have a half-sister called Tracey. They are good people and although they loved and worked hard to put my dad on the straight and narrow, just as my mother had tried to do, he proceeded to cause havoc in their lives as well.

As already stated, he walked out on our family when I was about two and a half years old, presenting my mother with all sorts of difficulties that she never shirked or failed to overcome. My first real recollection of anything to do with him is from a couple of years later, when we were living with the Maw family at Wood Green and he came to the house, waving a handgun and threatening to shoot Mum! Not that I realised this at the time, of course. And I didn't actually see him on this occasion. I vaguely remember being aware of some sort of commotion going on at the front door and of Bernard Maw suddenly rushing through the room where his son, John, and I were playing together and then running back with his 12-bore shotgun in his hands, just as two shots rang out in the garden. They were followed a few moments later by two blasts from the shotgun.

Being only four, I didn't understand what was going on. However, the events of the day were discussed many times later in my life and I now know that my father was very drunk and the two shots we'd heard had been fired into the air. I don't believe that he ever really intended to harm my mother – he just wanted to scare her, which he unquestionably did. This must have been about the time that Mum was trying to extricate herself from the relationship and goes part way to explaining his irrational behaviour. By the time that Bernard got back to the front door with his shotgun, Joe was already legging it down the driveway, but Bernard let each barrel go, one after the other and also in to the air, just to help him on his way.

Bernard later said that he had followed Joe a little way down the drive and saw him launch the handgun into the adjoining orchard. Apparently, we all searched for it later that same afternoon, but found nothing. I have seen John Maw a few times recently and he explained that some thirty years after the event, he found the gun one day whilst rotovating the piece of land that, by then, was an orchard no more. Apparently, the rusty weapon had become lodged in the blades of the machine and although badly corroded, was still easily recognisable as a gun.

Altogether, I only ever saw my father on five separate occasions after he left home to seek pastures new. The first time was about two years after the shooting incident, when Mum allowed him to collect me for a whole day, only for him to then make a sort of half-hearted attempt to kidnap me, having tried and failed to get official custody. He took me off to what can only be described as a gypsy-type caravan site, where I remember sitting around a fire with some of his friends. I now know that this was where he was living at the time, just outside Wellington, about twelve miles from Shrewsbury.

My recollections of that day are again sketchy, to say the least. But I do remember being awoken some time after nightfall by two police officers, one male and one female, who asked me if I was OK. After a heated exchange with my father, they took me from him and returned me to my frantic mother at the house in Moston Road where we were living at the time, at what she told me much later was about 3 o'clock in the morning.

Our next encounter came when I was about sixteen years old and a student chef in Wolverhampton. I had met his second wife Rose, who lived just outside Wolverhampton, and had actually baby-sat my half-sister Tracey, then an infant. My father wasn't living with Rose at the time, but I asked her if she would arrange for me to see him, which she did. The meeting took place at a pub (surprise, surprise!), opposite the bed-sit where he was living by then. We had a couple of pints of beer and he proudly introduced me as his son to several of his friends – or, at least, to several people who happened to be present in the bar at the time.

We then went over the road to the cramped bed-sit where we ate a meal that he had partially prepared before coming to meet me. The only recollection I have of the place is that it was lit by single bare light bulb, and that I sat on the only chair whilst he perched on the bed in the dimly lit room, with a small table between us. During the final preparation of the meal he took particular delight in showing me how to crush a clove of garlic between two spoons, the one and only time, sadly, that my father ever showed me how to do anything. Rather surprisingly, given that I was a full three months into my City & Guilds course and already conceitedly considered myself an expert in every aspect of gastronomy, I remember thinking to myself that the meal he had produced wasn't half bad, even though I am ashamed to say that I can't now recall exactly what it was that we ate.

The evening then took a slightly odd turn when he suddenly decided to entertain me by reciting four pieces poetry that were nearly all a total mystery to me at the time. The first was a poem by Byron that I now know was called *The Tear* and was about twelve verses long; the second was *The Ancient Mariner* by Samuel Taylor Coleridge, which went on for what seemed like eternity; the third was *The Owl and the Pussycat* by Edward Lear; and the fourth was *The Shooting of Dan Magrew* by Robert W. Service. Each one was delivered in what seemed to be word-perfect fashion, although I had no way of knowing whether this was actually the case. But he certainly gave the impression that it was.

The third time I saw him was at the wake following the funeral in

1989 of my aunt, Marjorie – his sister, whom he adored. This took place at 'The Owlets', the house in which she had been living when she died. My father was very drunk and everyone present was terrified of what he might do. Mum had attended the funeral with me and she stiffened like a board whenever he came anywhere near her. As it turned out, there were thankfully no really awkward or embarrassing moments. At the end of the proceedings, I learned that I had inherited a cheque for £10,000 from Auntie Marje, while my brother had inherited the remainder of her estate, which was worth a considerable amount of money..

Everyone assumed that I must have been unhappy about this apparent imbalance, but I genuinely wasn't and never have been. Joe had always had the thin end of the wedge in every aspect of our lives and I honestly didn't begrudge him a single penny. As well as sorting out Marjorie's complicated estate, he had also assumed the responsibility of managing my father's trust, and that was to cause him headaches for some years to come, there being many times when the old man turned up on his doorstep at unearthly times of the night, demanding money and adopting a threatening attitude if none was forthcoming.

Marjorie had left her brother nothing in her will except a piece of Royal Worcester porcelain, something that he knew she had loved. I suspect that it was her way of saying: "I love you and I am going to leave you my favourite thing in the whole world, but I am not going to leave you any money because I know what you will do with it". As far as I know, my father never sold that piece of porcelain, even though it was quite valuable. Yet he sold virtually everything else!

The fourth time I saw him was once again at my instigation. I was, by then, well into my fifties and wanted to make my peace with him. I discovered that he was living in a care home just outside Wolverhampton and telephoned to speak to someone about whether it would be possible to make an appointment to visit. Kam, the nurse who happened to take my call, turned out to be the one who cared for him on a regular basis and had got to know him well. She was excited by my call and promised to get back to me within a day or so. As it was, she didn't call for well over a week. And when she did eventually contact me, it was with an obviously heavy heart that she had to tell me that he had asked her to pass on the message that he had no wish to see me, complaining bitterly: "Where has he been all this time?" Where had I been! He did add, however, that I had his permission to go to his funeral, whenever that might be.

Kam urged me not to give up hope, promising to work on him over the next few days. A week or so passed before she called again to say that he had now had a change of heart and that he would be pleased to see me. I travelled up to Wolverhampton on the appointed day and was met by Kam at the front door. She was definitely the most excited of the three of us. She showed me around the ground floor of the home, where quite a number of people were sitting around playing cards or chess and generally chatting among themselves. This was where I was expecting to see him, but Kam explained sadly that he never took part in any of the social activities.

She led me upstairs along a small corridor and knocked on a door. "Bugger off" came the response from within, but Kam just laughed and opened the door anyway. I was quite shocked to see how small and frail Joe had become since the last time I had seen him. Kam asked if she could bring us something to drink, to which my father replied: "A bottle of whisky for me and whatever he's having," pointing at me. Kam smiled sweetly and replied that she would return with a pot of tea and some biscuits.

Left alone, the conversation between us flowed very easily and there were none of the awkward silences that I had anticipated there might be. At one point he got me to feel the bone in his hip, which I did rather tentatively, and he then explained that what I could feel was the bolt that was holding him together, as he put it. He then went on to reveal that some months previously he had organised a "jail-break" with a fellow inmate – an 80-year-old woman, as I later discovered. The two of them had gone to a local pub and had proceeded to get drunk together before the landlord eventually phoned the care home to let them know of the runaways' whereabouts. On the way back to the home he had then fallen and broken his hip. What followed, he said, was a seriously painful few months – but it was worth it, he assured me, for those few hours of freedom from the care home routine.

The tea and biscuits arrived and Kam was very anxious to know if everything was alright. Joe continued to talk very articulately and interestingly and I remember thinking what an educated man he actually was. He referred several times to making a total mess of his life, but stopped short of apologising for any of his misdemeanours. After about two hours' conversation he asked me if I wanted anything to eat, but having just eaten a load of biscuits I told him I wasn't hungry. He clearly was, because he took a small tin of baked beans out of his bedside table drawer and set about opening it with one of those red Swiss army penknives with all the attachments, before eating the contents, cold and straight from the tin, with one of the teaspoons that had come with the tea and biscuits.

There was a small TV in the room as well as a VHS recorder, with a pile of tapes nearby. He said that he was an avid film watcher (as I, too, have been all my adult life) but I was rather surprised to discover that his favourite movie was *The Blair Witch Project*. We spoke for another hour or so, making about three in total, and not once was the conversation in any way difficult. We shook hands before I left and kissed each other on the cheek. He gave me a mischievous grin and said: "Here's looking at you, kid". I replied: "No hard feelings" and he repeated: "No hard feelings". And on that note I departed, with tears rolling down my cheeks, which was strange, because I had never up to that point felt any sort of emotion for my father. I later regretted not looking back to see if there were any tears in his eyes.

I say that I only saw him five times in my life after he had walked out on us, but that is not strictly true. Because the fifth and final time that I was in his presence was at his funeral, and whilst I am pretty sure that he was there, I didn't actually see him. It was two years after that tearful goodbye at the care home that he died. He had gone into hospital to be treated for bronchitis, but had then contracted MRSA, and that was what did for him. When I asked why it did not say MRSA on the death certificate I was told that MRSA is never put on a death certificate for political reasons, even though it was often the cause of death.

When I returned home after visiting him in the care home, my mother had wanted to hear about every minute detail of the three hours that we had spent together. For much of her short relationship with my father she had actually been terrified of him, as he had often been violent towards her during his drunken rages. This fear had again manifested itself all those years later at Marjorie's funeral, so when she announced that she would like to come with me the next time I visited him I was quite shocked and dumfounded, as this was the very last thing that I had expected her to suggest.

As it was, that meeting was sadly destined never to happen, because even though we did try on more than one occasion to arrange for the three of us to get together, the rapidly deteriorating state of my father's health meant that it wasn't possible. And then it was too late. I often find myself wishing that I could have arranged that last 'date' for Mum. Even after all that she had been through with him, there was obviously a major part of her that still loved him. Once, when she, too, was in a care home, she and I were chatting and she mentioned a boyfriend she'd had after her relationship with my father had ended. She was a good-looking woman and I do remember one or two male companions. I had rather cheekily asked her who was the love of her life and there was absolutely no doubt in her mind that it was the father of her children. And, in the end, I think she yearned to make her peace with him, as I had done.

Some months after he died, a will was read, which rather surprised me as it had seemed to me when I last saw him that he had very few possessions of any note. I opened the small parcel I received, to find that it contained the red Swiss Army knife that he had used to open his tin of beans when we spent that final afternoon together. I am not a great one for reading too much into any given situation, but I like to think that his gesture in leaving it to me confirmed the way he must have felt when we made our peace.

I still have a couple of letters that he wrote late in his life, one to me and one to Mum. Although his typing style was rather erratic, the letters convey so much about him, revealing another side to his character. As previously mentioned, he was an intelligent, educated and surprisingly talented man. At various times he had written poems and stories, some of which had been published, including a short story entitled *The House That Cried* that was aired on BBC radio one Christmas, although I am not sure exactly which year. I still have a copy of the tape. If it hadn't been for the booze, who knows what might have achieved!

All this may help to explain why I decided to become teetotal. My father was an alcoholic in the true sense of the word and although I know that many people who drink a lot are in denial, I honestly don't believe that I ever got to the point of being an alcoholic, or anywhere near it for that matter. But I do accept that I could be greedy and stupid where booze was concerned, and I was genuinely worried about that addictive nature. Many is the time that I have woken up face down in the nettles, so to speak, wondering why I couldn't just drink moderately, as so many other people manage to do. But I couldn't, despite trying many times. And yet the mental strength required on a daily basis to stop drinking altogether is immense, so why couldn't I have successfully applied that strength to drinking moderately?

It was the same with smoking. I had been a smoker since I was about thirteen years of age and by the age of 27, when I finally gave it up, I was on 60-a-day, plus the odd cigar. I am immensely proud of having had the willpower and mental strength to kick the habit without the help of nicotine patches, vapes or hypnotism. And again, I wonder why I couldn't simply have enjoyed five or even ten cigarettes-a-day, as some other smokers appear to be able to do? But I knew I couldn't, so I accepted the fact and gave up altogether.

With gambling, however, it is different and I have managed to control what I am sure is just another addiction. From that very first moment when, as a 14-year-old boy, I placed my entire pocket money of two shillings on Arkle at odds of 2 to 1 on, in order to win a shilling, it seemed to me an entirely reasonable thing to do. When I lost all my council education grant money in Wolverhampton only a couple of years after that, I experienced the same 'face down in the nettles' feeling of helplessness that I was to feel much later in life on those occasions when I drank far too much. And yet with gambling I learned my lesson from that one bad experience and from then on only ever gambled responsibly and within my means, even in those days at the Dorchester when all we kitchen boys would bet on anything, up to an including flies crawling up the wall or raindrops sliding down a window. If only I could have applied the same discipline to my smoking and drinking! When it comes to my gambling, I very quickly learned when to cut my losses and to quit when still ahead. And I never worry that it will get out of control.

I was concerned at one point, however, about the possibility that I might be guilty of setting a bad example to my sons and, in Alex's case, decided to give him an object lesson in the dangers of heavy gambling. With this in mind, I took him on his 18th birthday to the Clermont Club in Berkeley Square – once a favourite haunt of the notorious Lord Lucan, among other high rollers – with the express intention of deliberately losing a couple of hundred quid in double quick time on the roulette wheel by betting on single numbers. This rather silly plan (I was only able to put it into action because Rona was away on holiday in India with our friend Anna Zeville at the time) then backfired spectacularly when I very quickly proceeded to win £6,800! So, far from being put off, Ali has been a serious gambler ever since, although I have to say that, like me, he has got it completely under control and only bets 'responsibly', as Ray Winstone makes a point of advising in the TV adverts.

Those people who know me well, and there are not many who actually do, would tell you that I try very hard not to be one of those holier-than-thou types now that I don't drink at all. You know the ones I mean; the sort who keep telling you how well they feel all the time since they gave stopped drinking, saying: "You should try it, too, because you will be a much better person".

It's not easy being a non-drinker, as people tend to pester you, always trying to find out why you're on the wagon. Are you ill? Have you been diagnosed with something dreadful? It actually becomes more of an interrogation than a sympathetic inquiry. In any social gatherings where I am not known, rather than ask for a glass of mineral water or orange juice I will sometimes accept a glass of wine and just stand there with it in my hand, simply in order to prevent the mind-numbingly boring inquisition.

It is also a well-documented fact that at any dinner party or other boozy get-together us non-imbibers have to suffer the slow but inevitable deterioration in the quality of the conversation as virtually everyone around you gets more and more pissed. I say "slow" deterioration, but as a stone cold sober observer I find it is actually quite amazing what a dramatic effect just two or three drinks can have on some people. Most people I know drink very sensibly and I honestly believe that, in moderation, alcohol is quite good for you in terms of the pleasure and relaxation it can provide. It's just that after many years I have finally and rather belatedly realised that I am not one of those who can always drink sensibly. I wish I were.

Strangely, I do not actually miss the physical effects of drinking at all, but I do miss the gastronomic association. My entire working life has revolved around food and wine and I genuinely love both. The only other times that I regret not being able to enjoy a drink are those moments when we are celebrating a major event in our wonderful family – perhaps a baby being born, a christening or a wedding – and we open a bottle of something special, maybe a bottle of Dom Perignon or Crystal Champagne. As I sit or stand there sipping my fizzy water, I do experience a touch of sadness, aware that I am missing out ever so slightly on the pleasure of the occasion.

Over the years, I have become quite adept at avoiding, or at least sidestepping the very direct question as to why I don't drink. I generally trot out the same old rubbish, depending on who it is that I am talking to; I might explain that I started by regularly stopping for a month every year, which is actually true. I didn't always succeed for the whole month, but generally I did. I go on to explain that a month became six weeks, then two months and, before I knew where I was, it was up to six months and I found I was actually enjoying the abstention, so just decided to carry on with it.

The real reason, which strangely I find easier to write about than to talk about, is that back in my drinking days I had once or twice been guilty of embarrassing my family and on several occasions had severely embarrassed my wife, and I simply did not want to do that ever again. Rona's idea of a real binge is having maybe two small glasses of wine or champagne, and my penance for all those years of behaving stupidly is that I now always drive her home after we have been anywhere together. Every now and again she will compliment me on my continuing abstinence and that is genuinely all the reward that I ever need.

Just as my father had done, my mother ended her days in a care home. She had begun to develop dementia and when she was no longer really able to look after herself we arranged for her to move into the home. During the next three years I visited her regularly, at least four times a week, and had to endure the agonising and heartbreaking experience of witnessing the gradual but relentless deterioration of her health. Sitting there together in her room, we had many long conversations, during which she would often reminisce about her early life in Guernsey, and although there were occasions when she was lucid and precise, this was not always the case. Driving the short distance from Read's to the home I sometimes wondered anxiously what on earth I was going to talk to her about during the visit, but, as time went on, I really didn't need to worry about that. The dreadful fact was that it didn't really matter if I had nothing new to say because, like any advanced dementia sufferer, she would usually have had no recollection of previous conversations, however recent, so you could just talk about the same things over and over again.

She died in 2014 and for the first few months after she passed away, the image that I had in mind whenever I found myself thinking about her was that of the old lady in the care home. But as time goes by, I find myself thinking of her more as she was when she was a younger woman – elegant, sophisticated and nearly always in control, or so it seemed to me at the time. And always so very caring.

One conversation we had in those final years that really sticks in my mind was when, on my 63rd birthday, in May 2012, I happened to ask her if she could remember exactly what time of the day I was born. By this time, her short-term memory had almost completely gone, but, strangely, she could still clearly recall certain episodes from her more distant past. She was able to tell me that I had been born at around two o'clock in the morning, and that then started her off remembering other things that had happened that day. She waxed lyrical for quite a few minutes and then suddenly stopped talking and I sat there watching her expression as she lapsed into her own private reverie, with a little smile on her face. After about thirty seconds she seemed to snap out of it, looked back at me and said simply: "Best day of my life, that was." That still brings a tear to my eye every time I think about it.

I have another very touching recollection from those days towards the end of her life. I had arrived at the home to find her in a very depressed mood, and in order to cheer her up a bit I said that I would organise to take her to what had been her regular hairdressing salon in Faversham the following week. There was a hairdresser who came to the home every week but I knew that to go back to the salon she'd used for years would be a treat that would really raise her spirits. I phoned the salon and spoke to the young woman who had always done her hair in the past to make the booking and she seemed genuinely delighted that she was going to be seeing Mum again. When we arrived for the appointment she came running out of the salon to greet us and when she saw how frail Mum had become she burst into tears and gave her a big hug, out there on the pavement.

When I returned an hour later to collect Mum she had been transformed and looked happier than I'd seen her for some time. I led her out to the car and then went back to pay, only to find the woman who'd been doing her hair again in tears, being consoled by other members of the staff. When she'd composed herself, she explained that my mother had once, as she put it, "saved my life". She then went on to reveal that she was a single mother of two young boys and that a few years earlier she had suddenly found herself in severe financial difficulties, struggling to make ends meet. On hearing this, Mum had gone back in the following day and handed her an envelope containing £200 to help tide her over. The grateful recipient promised that she would pay the money back as soon as she could, but Mum told her that she was not expecting to be repaid, that the money was a gift, not a loan, adding that she was delighted to help because someone had been similarly kind to her many years before when she had been in difficulties and that, as a result, she was only too happy to be able to do someone else a good turn. It touched me because the gesture was so typical of Mum, always caring for others before herself, as she had done with my brother and me after our father walked out and left her in the lurch, making many personal sacrifices and always doing the best she could in the circumstances.

Rona had lost her own mother twenty years earlier. Eva had suffered for years with severe rheumatoid arthritis but, in characteristic fashion, had refused to let it restrict her activities too much, still playing her golf and generally pushing on regardless. She had always been such a go-getter and such a powerhouse in the family. A few years after Bert died she had moved out of Painters Forstal to a bungalow of her own in Faversham that we bought for her, delighted to be able to return the huge investment that she and Bert had made when they sold their home and moved in with us in order to help us get started at Read's.

She had been living there happily for about nine years when she suddenly had a couple of unexplained falls. This was so out of character that we insisted on having her checked out, only to be confronted then with the devastating news that she was suffering from motor neurone disease. Worse still, it was a particularly aggressive form of this progressive neurological muscle wasting condition that had started developing from the head downwards, meaning that she very soon began losing the ability to eat or swallow properly and also the power of speech, so that before long she could only communicate by writing notes. She eventually became bedridden, with Rona and her brother

Alan taking turns to look after her at home, until, towards the end, the doctors suggested that she should be admitted to the local cottage hospital. But after three days there she begged to be moved back to her own home. The matron was very reluctant to let her go and got Alan and Rona to sign a formal declaration acknowledging full responsibility before allowing them to wrap Eva in a blanket and take her back to the bungalow. She died there two weeks later, eighteen months after being diagnosed. She was just 73.

For Rona, who had always been very close to both her parents, it was a grievous loss. But then, at the same time as I was regularly making visits several times a week to see my mother in the care home and sadly witnessing her gradual decline, Rona had to go through the even more distressing anguish of having to watch her much-loved brother Alan also fighting a losing battle against terminal illness.

After leaving school, Alan had joined the family electrical contracting business out of a sense of duty, even though everyone knew that it was not the career he would have chosen for himself – something that could be seen as having tragically ironic consequences given the way things turned out. He was made a director of the company at the tender age of eighteen and in 1977, shortly after Read's opened up in Painters Forstal and as his father's health started to deteriorate, he assumed total control of the business. By then he had married Heather and they went on to have four children – Benjamin, Simon and twins Charlotte and Hannah – before eventually divorcing. Alan then went on to marry his second wife, Thelma. He was always very interested in politics and local government and had he not inherited the family business, which took all of his time, he might well have stood as an MP. As it was, any political ambition he might have had went no further than becoming Mayor of Swale in 1980.

It was in his early days with the family business that he had been involved with contract work in the Chatham dockyards and elsewhere that had brought him into close contact with the asbestos lagging of pipework that ran alongside the electrical wiring. This was in the days before the potentially lethal effect of inhaling asbestos fibres had been fully recognised. In his mid-sixties Alan developed a repetitive cough and severe breathlessness that gradually became more and more persistent and in 2012 he was finally diagnosed with Mesothelioma, more commonly known as Asbestosis, for which there is no known cure. He died just over a year later in November 2013.

The insurance companies, who are notoriously difficult to deal with when it comes to compensation claims with asbestos-related diseases, were insistent that as a director of A. S. North Ltd he should have been responsible for his own insurance in respect of health and safety related issues at work. To cut a very long and distressing story short, Rona devoted two years of her life to fighting for and eventually achieving compensation for Alan's family. Our dear friend Eddie McIntyre, who by this time had retired as Principal of University College Birmingham, where he had become very experienced at dealing with complicated legal issues as well as awkward insurance companies, was an enormous help to Rona in finally bringing the matter to a reasonably fair and just conclusion.

All this came at a time when Rona and I, having reached our sixties, were starting to look ahead to a future without Read's. As Sam and Alex both had their own successful careers and weren't interested in taking over the restaurant, there was no prospect of leaving it to them as a going concern, so it had always been our long-term intention to sell up at some point. Meanwhile, although we were still just about okay with the total commitment of working there throughout the day and the evening, being permanently on call during the night as well had become too much for us and so, as part of winding down a bit, we had already moved out of the Coach House to a new home back in Painters Forstal, just two miles down the road, meaning that for the first time since we had originally opened up there all those years earlier, in 1977, we were no longer living above the shop, as it were.

It was in 2005 that Rona first became aware that the beautifully proportioned Georgian house on the outskirts of the village that she had always loved had come up for sale, following the death of the local solicitor who had lived there for many years. The property was rather like a smaller version of Macknade Manor, having been built in 1784, just six years after Macknade. At one stage in its history it had been used to accommodate disadvantaged members of the parish, who were put to work there in what became known as The Old Poor House.

I was a bit anxious about taking on another substantial property, especially one that was badly in need of extensive renovation, when we already owned not only Read's and the Coach House, but also a staff house in Faversham. However, Rona argued that although not quite what we had initially had in mind, it would be the perfect house for us to retire to eventually. And whilst it was in a very poor state of repair and required an awful lot of work doing to it, this was reflected in the price – and after renovating Macknade, we certainly had all the experience and expertise we needed to be able to do the job. Rona also insisted that if we didn't strike while the iron was hot, then we might end up always regretting a missed opportunity. So, having successfully applied for planning permission to demolish an ugly Victorian extension and the garages that had been added at various times, and to replace them with an extension at the back that was more in keeping with the original Georgian architecture, we went ahead with the purchase.

The first floor of the original part of the property was made up of two bathrooms and ten tiny bedrooms, all about 10ft × 6ft in size, which reflected its earlier use as a poor house. Everything there had to be recorded on videotape by the listed building people, who then allowed us to convert the upstairs to four bedrooms and three bathrooms.

Altogether, it took nearly five years to do all the work, which was finally completed in 2011, coinciding very conveniently with the arrival at Read's of Brad Gent to fill the newly created role of restaurant manager. Brad, a key appointment about whom I shall have a lot more to say in the next chapter, lived in local accommodation until we were able to move into The Old Poor House a few months after he appeared on the scene. He, in turn, then moved into The Coach House, relieving Rona and me of our night duties.

Looking back, this was when we really began the process of gradually letting go.

15 : Come On, You Shrews!

My love of football and my support for Shrewsbury Town F.C. have together served to keep me very much in touch with my roots, even though I left home for good more than half a century ago and have lived and worked on the opposite side of the country for most of the time since then. And now that I am a director of the club, it has brought my life full circle in many ways.

I was seven years old when, in 1956, I first stood on the terraces at Gay Meadow, Shrewsbury's original and memorably named home ground. My lifetime loyalty to the club was then sealed on the occasion mentioned earlier when the great Arthur Rowley acknowledged me in front of all my mates with a cheery "Thanks, Pitchy" as I tossed the ball back to him for a throw-in after it had been booted into touch, landing at my feet. At that time and in that place this was akin to being name-checked by David Beckham.

Like Beckham, Arthur, started his career at Manchester United, playing in a wartime league game against Liverpool in 1941 as a 15-year-old amateur before going on to play professionally for WBA, Fulham, Leicester and Shrewsbury. Nicknamed 'The Gunner' on account of the explosive left foot shots that were his trademark, he set a record that will stand forever as the most prolific scorer in the history of the old Football League, with an astonishing career total of 434 goals in 619 matches. Of those 434, 152 came during his six seasons as player-manager at Shrewsbury, including 38 in just 43 games in the 1958 season, club scoring records that still stand and are unlikely ever to be surpassed. He had got to know me through coaching my school soccer team and to be recognised and greeted by him in such a matey way in front of my friends gave me a kudos that made it one of the highlights of my young life.

From then on I was a regular at all the home games and even when

I left Shrewsbury and started working in London I remained an active supporter, returning to Gay Meadow whenever there was an opportunity and going to watch the Shrews when they were playing away games at London area clubs, such as Millwall, Luton, QPR, Charlton, Brentford, Leyton Orient and Reading. I even used to sell fund-raising bingo tickets on Shrewsbury's behalf to the four hundred staff at the Dorchester, sending the money I collected back to Ivor Hookway in the club offices back at Gay Meadow.

Later, when Rona and I were working flat out at Read's and under constant pressure, I would use visits back to Shrewsbury for home games as a way of relieving the pressure whenever things got on top of me. I'd drive up, watch the game and maybe stay overnight, and suddenly everything would be all right again. Rona must have wondered whether I had a mistress up there, but she need never have worried about that. I just needed to get out of the kitchen and have a bit of space to myself every now and again – and she understood that.

It was after we had moved to Macknade, that my involvement with the club developed to a much higher level. In 2002-3 the Shrews had an extraordinarily up-and-down season during which they performed a legendary giant-killing act in knocking Premiership side Everton out of the FA Cup, before losing to Chelsea in the next round, and yet at the same time ended up bottom of what was then still the Third Division of the Football League, meaning that they were relegated out of the League altogether for the first time since being admitted fifty-three years earlier.

In the non-league Vauxhall Conference they had fixtures against two local Kent clubs – Gravesend & Northfleet and Margate – and because of the long distance involved they had to travel down the evening before the game and stay locally overnight. Knowing this, I wrote to the club, thanking them for a lifetime of memories and offering to provide an evening meal, accommodation and breakfast at Read's for the directors when they came down to play those away games, plus a pre-match meal for the entire team and the management staff, an offer that was gratefully accepted. It happened that a great friend of mine was the official chef for the England team at the time and used to travel abroad with them wherever they went so, through him, I knew all about players' dietary requirements.

First up was the match against Gravesend & Northfleet, and the memorable thing about that game was that it marked the debut of future England goalkeeper Joe Hart, a local Shrewsbury lad, born and bred, who had been with the club since he was eleven years old and who had actually attended my old school, Meole Brace Secondary Modern. Playing on what was the day after his 17th birthday, he kept a clean sheet and we won 3-0. We also beat Margate 2-0 on the way to ending the season in third place, going on to win the play-off final against Aldershot at Stoke City's Britannia Stadium to clinch our return to the Football League at the first attempt, re-joining what had by then become League 2. Joe Hart stayed with us for another three seasons, before eventually being sold to Manchester City for £600,000, plus another £600,000 if he ever played for England. Taking into account various other add-ons, the deal ended up being worth around £2 million altogether, more than a small fortune at the time for a club like Shrewsbury.

Meanwhile, I had got to know everybody at the club as a result of those two Read's visits and shortly afterwards chairman Roland Wycherley invited me to join the board of directors, an invitation that I accepted with an enormous sense of pride and satisfaction.

One of the best players back in the late fifties, when I first started going to Gay Meadow, was an inside forward named Malcolm Starkey. Having started his career at Blackpool, where he played for five years alongside the legendary Stanley Matthews, Mal became Arthur Rowley's first signing after taking over as player/manager, joining the club in 1959 and proving to be even more of a shrewd acquisition than Arthur himself could possibly have imagined.

Known for his prodigious work rate on the pitch, Mal was initially given two simple instructions by Arthur – first, win the ball from the opposition and then just give it to me! (Alf Ramsey told Alan Ball to provide the same service for Bobby Charlton in England's World Cup-winning team a few years later in 1966) Apart from a short spell during which he left to play for Chester, Mal has spent virtually his entire working life with Shrewsbury and is now our president. Over the years he has occupied virtually every position within the club, having been player, manager, secretary and even stand-in groundsman during one critical period.

When I became a director, albeit a comparatively lowly one in the boardroom hierarchy, I was a little apprehensive about meeting Mal, but need not have been, as he is very easy-going and one of the loveliest people you could hope to meet. I sit next to him whenever I can and thoroughly enjoy talking about those old days when football was a very different game indeed. Even though he is now in his eighties, the insight he brings to any football discussion is remarkable. Sometimes, when we are watching a match together, he will suddenly make a statement, or point out something about positional play that will not be obvious to me until some moments later when the tactical change he has spotted will work out exactly as he predicted, showing that his professional football brain is very much intact.

I have been especially fortunate that my time as a director has coincided with one of the most exciting periods in the club's history, during which we moved from Gay Meadow to a brand new state-of-the-art, 10,000-capacity stadium in 2007 and have played at Wembley five times – three times in play-offs and twice more in the final of the Checkatrade Trophy, the knock-out cup competition for League 1 and 2 clubs plus sixteen Premiership and Championship 'B' teams. Sadly, we have lost out on all five occasions – most recently twice within a month at the end of the 2017/18 season, first being beaten 1-0 by Lincoln City in the Checkatrade Trophy final and then going down 1-2, after extra time to Rotherham in the League 1 play-off final. We had finished the season in third place, eight points ahead of Rotherham in 4th position, and had we won the play-off we would have been back in the second tier of English football for the first time in forty years. As the newspaper headlines said, it was a truly heartbreaking end to what had promised to be the greatest season in our history.

It's great being a director when things are going well on the pitch – we are treated like heroes, even occasionally being applauded off the team bus by our travelling fans when we arrive for away games. But things can soon turn sour if you have a bad season, such as we had in 2013/14, when we ended up being relegated back to League 2. At times like that you are more likely to find yourself being greeted by abuse for not putting your hands in your pockets and coming up with the cash to buy a new striker! Happily, we got promoted straight back into League 1 the following season.

Even at the best of times, being a director of a lower division club like Shrewsbury can involve wildly contrasting experiences at the different extremes of the football spectrum during the course of a season.

This is especially true if you happen to enjoy a decent Cup run and find yourself drawn against a top Premiership club or end up in a play-off at Wembley, while at the same time visiting the more remote outposts at the lower end of the Football League

For instance, in the third round of the League Cup in 2011 we were drawn against Arsenal at the Emirates. We directors arrived to be greeted by our Arsenal counterparts, who gave us a personal one-to-one guided tour of the stadium and changing rooms before we all retired to the directors' lounge to sample a glass of Laurent Perrier champagne. We were then led through to the dining room, where a sumptuous buffet was laid out. Among the starters on offer was an array of oysters, to which I am very partial, and things then got even better when the member of staff who served me asked whether I would prefer Whitstable Natives, Colchester Rock or the French Belon variety, all of which were available. I opted for two of each.

Arsenal were the most gracious hosts among all the premiership clubs we have visited over the years, hospitality that we repaid by then frightening the life out of them by taking a 16th minute lead, before finally losing 3-1. At the other end of the Premiership scale, Southampton didn't consider it necessary to open up the boardroom hospitality for the visit of such a lowly little club as Shrewsbury Town and merely offered us a cup of tea and a bag of crisps – cheese and onion, to be precise.

A million miles away from the glamour of the Premiership are wonderfully friendly clubs like Accrington Stanley, which proudly bills itself as 'The Club That Wouldn't Die', having gone out of business completely at one stage in 1966 only to be revived a few years later and restored to League status. The chairman greeted us as we arrived at the corrugated iron shack that doubled as their boardroom at the time with the words: "Fancy a brew?" Our chairman, Roland Wycherley, politely inquired whether a glass of wine might be a possibility, whereupon our host explained apologetically: "We don't usually drink before a game." "But we do," countered Roland jovially. There ensued some scurrying around behind the scenes, followed by the presentation of a bottle of claret that had obviously been intended for consumption after the game and which featured a label identifying it as 'Chateau Accrington'.

Having supported Shrewsbury for more than sixty years through thick and thin, the success we have recently enjoyed has been hugely gratifying. It has had a lot to do with our chairman, who has done so much to put the club on a solid financial footing. Roland is very strong personality and some would say he can be a bit cantankerous at times, but, with apologies to other hard-working and committed chairmen from the past, there is absolutely no doubt in my mind that he is the greatest the club has ever had. He took over in 1996, at a time when we were heavily in debt and playing in front of crowds of less than 2,500 in a dilapidated stadium that was one of the worst in the league in terms of facilities. With his business acumen and encyclopedic knowledge of lower league football, Roland has totally transformed the club's fortunes and we now regularly play in front of crowds of three times the size of those that he inherited, and when it comes to really big games we can accommodate a full-house of 10,000 plus.

A great deal of the credit for our success on the pitch in the 2016-17 and 2017-18 seasons has to go to our manager, Paul Hurst, and his assistant, Chris Doig. Paul took over in 2016 when we were rock bottom of League 1. On arrival, he completely re-organised the team, bringing in thirteen new players, mostly on free transfers, while also developing two that he inherited – midfield dynamo Abu Agogo and central defender Aristote Nsiala – turning them into key members of the title-challenging squad that transformed the club's fortunes.

Talented young managers such as Paul are like gold dust to a club like ours. He was obviously destined for much greater things and no sooner had he made his mark than a queue of much bigger clubs started lining up, all wanting to take him away from us. We had been hoping that if we won promotion to the Championship at the end of the 2017/18 season he might stay on, but it turned out that he had already decided to leave and join Championship and former Premiership club Ipswich Town, along with Chris Doig, even before the Wembley play-off final was played. That is the predatory nature of football at our level, with talented players and managers being poached as soon as they get noticed. He was quickly replaced by John Askey, who had just succeeded in taking non-League Macclesfield Town back into League 2.

Going back to Roland and Mal for a moment, there is a lot of playful banter between the two men that masks a great friendship and deep underlying respect for each other, formed over many years of shared, passionate devotion to the club. I remember overhearing a conversation between the two of them in the boardroom one day when they were reminiscing about Mal's debut for Shrewsbury in 1959, a match in which he netted the first of the 33 goals he scored for us. Mal's recollection of events was that winger Colin Whittaker beat two defenders on the way to the by-line before sending over a perfect cross that Mal, who had raced fifty yards from the centre circle, met with a flying header past the keeper and into the top corner of the net. The chairman's recollection tallied with Mal's version up until the point where the winger's corner came across. According to Roland, Mal was looking the other way at that moment and didn't actually see the ball, which struck him on the back of the head and bounced over the line.

Although I would have unquestionably been at that same game all those years ago, I can't remember what actually happened. I'm a bit of a romantic as far as my association with the club is concerned and find myself wondering where Roland Wycherley would have been standing on the day in question and where I would have been. Could we possibly have been standing next to each other before meeting again fifty years later at Read's? It could well be. Anyway, I just hope that he gets the credit he deserves for all he's done for his beloved Shrewsbury Town FC when he finally decides to pass the chairmanship to someone else. He will be a tough act to follow.

I go to just about every home game, even though it involves an average four-hour drive each way, and I also travel to as many of the away games as I can manage. That I am able to take the time to do so is down to two things – Rona's understanding and the fact that for the last few years the two of us have been able to delegate much of the day-to-day running of Read's to our brilliant restaurant manager Brad Gent.

As already mentioned, Brad joined us in 2011. He had originally trained as a restaurant manager at the Birmingham College of Food, where my great friend Eddie McIntyre was the Principal and Rona was a governor, but first came to my attention when, in my capacity as vice chairman of the Royal Academy of Culinary Arts, I was on the panel of judges before whom he competed successfully to qualify as a Master of Culinary Arts 'Achiever'. This coveted accolade is open to people who have been in the industry for at least ten years, working either front-of-house or as a chef.

As part of their prize, he and that year's other five 'Achievers' accompanied the judges and one or two other Academy members on a gastronomic tour of the top wineries in Italy, during which we enjoyed a number of combined wine tastings and meals, a memorable experience for all of us. I had been very impressed with Brad's performance in front of the panel and from conversations we had during the Italy trip it became apparent that he was looking to move on from his position at the top Birmingham restaurant Opus, so having first cleared it with the Academy, I offered him the job of restaurant manager at Read's.

We had never before employed anyone like him front-of-house – we had always simply taken on youngsters whom Rona then trained up to help her out. But we were both reaching a point in our lives at which we wanted to step back a little more, both in the kitchen and front-of-house, and felt that we needed someone with a bit more authority to act as maitre d'. And as it turned out, Brad was so accomplished and had such great all-round ability that far from just helping Rona out, he soon showed that he was more than capable of taking over! And before long, he had made such an impression that customers ringing up to book would ask for Brad rather than Rona or me, which was a bit disconcerting at first, although we are now more than happy to leave things to him. In this and many other respects, he has given us and Read's a new lease of life, taking a lot of the pressure off us and allowing us to contemplate keeping the restaurant going further into the future than we might otherwise have done.

For that to happen, what we desperately need now is another Brad to run the kitchen – a new head chef who will take over full control of all the cooking and kitchen management, leaving me free to assume more of a back seat role as executive chef, or 'chef ambassadeur', to use the posh title. But, as already mentioned in a previous chapter, that's easier said than done and in the run-up to publication we are still searching for the right person – although, as it happens, we are cautiously optimistic about a new candidate who came to us just a few weeks ago and seems to be shaping up very well. It's still early days, but we're keeping our fingers crossed that he will stay the course.

Why has it been proving so hard to fill the vacancy? Finding someone with the combination of personal and professional qualifications that will tick all the boxes when it comes to employing a head chef has always been notoriously difficult in the restaurant business, more so now that now there is a shortage of adequately trained staff, and especially in the case of a place like Read's that is not only long-established, but is also very unusual in having been operated by the same husband-and-wife team for forty-one years. Whoever gets the job will be expected gradually to introduce new things, keeping us up to date without losing sight of our history – not an easy task for aspiring young chefs who, in the age of the celebrity chef, are mostly intent on becoming trend setters, while at the same time slavishly following the modern food fashions and styles of presentation, decorating their dishes with an artistic flourish of swipes, dots, foams and dribbles.

Essentially, we need someone who is able to understand the difference between working in a trendy restaurant in the West End or elsewhere and working in a more traditional country restaurant, even one like Read's that still retains much of its old Michelin-starred reputation. In the former, the modern approach seems to involve serving a tiny piece of fish or meat with just a 'dolly mixture' garnish, without any starch in the form of potatoes, rice or pasta, and with no extra vegetables. Maybe it's because the more fashionable establishments attract the kind of people who tend to eat out all the time and don't really want more substantial meals, whereas out in the sticks there's a slightly different attitude; when people go out to eat there they mostly want a proper meal, with three courses or more. They certainly don't want to feel like stopping off for a Big Mac on the way home!

It follows that a big part of the challenge for our head chef is going to be his ability to compromise and meet our customers halfway – and sometimes, where the faddists are concerned, more than halfway. There are particular dishes that a lot of our regulars expect to see on the menu when they come to Read's and we wouldn't want to disappoint them. But while we would expect our chef to conform up to a point, we also want him to develop his own style. We're never going to be Heston Blumenthal, or into molecular cookery, but at the same time we want to be modern and innovative to a degree. And aside from that, on a purely commercial level, our head chef also has to be a 'money-maker', consistently maintaining that 70% profit level that I mentioned earlier.

If those are some of the challenges that he will face, the big challenge for me will be learning to let go even more. That's something I will struggle to do after being in sole charge in the kitchen for over forty years – and I do have a lot of deeply ingrained ideas about how things should be done. But I have gradually been loosening my hold and I've got great confidence in the young team we've been putting in place; all we have to do now is find the right person to lead them.

The great bonus of all this for Rona and me is, as already mentioned, that it means we have a little bit more time for ourselves – at least in theory – after all those years of regularly slaving away for sixteen hours-a-day and often longer, in what, as I've repeatedly made clear, can be a very demanding and stressful occupation. While I now have more opportunity to watch Shrewsbury home and away, Rona has enjoyed spending time creating and maintaining the large garden that surrounds the house at Painters Forstal, but best of all for both of us is being able to devote more attention to the family and, particularly, the grandchildren

Sam and his partner, Mel, live locally, so we get to see a good deal of them and their daughters Lola and Evie. Alex, his wife Sarah and their children, Wilfred, Millie and Margot, are a bit further away in Barnes, but that's hardly the other side of the world, so we also get together with them on a very regular basis. I absolutely adore the grandchildren – aged between eleven and two months at the time of writing in 2018 – and we have great times together.

From childhood, Sam was always car-mad and having run a BMW dealership in Ashford for many years he is, at the time of writing, in the process of setting up his own business. Alex came a little nearer to following in our footsteps. A very keen low handicap golfer, he started off working for the sports management agency IMG, before then changing tack and moving to a public relations agency that looked after Gordon Ramsay, progressing from there to work for Gordon himself for eight years. He decided to leave following the bitter business bust-up between Gordon and his father-in-law Chris Hutcheson, the former CEO of Gordon Ramsay Holdings, and moved to become the new business manager with Chris Corbin and Jeremy King's Rex Restaurants, which include The Wolseley, The Delaunay and the Brasserie Zédel. After eight years with them he was then headhunted by Selfridge's to develop their hotel and restaurant side, but that didn't suit him so he returned to Corbin and King in a senior position, while also taking on private consultancy work based on the vast experience he has gained through operating with top employers.

Looking back over my own career, I have very few regrets. I have managed to fulfill most of my professional ambitions – training in one of the country's, not to say the world's most renowned hotel kitchens, going on with Rona to open our own restaurant, turning it into a Michelin-starred success against considerable odds and hopefully earning the respect of at least some of my peers in the industry.

Most importantly, I was smart enough to marry Rona, a fantastic wife, mother and business partner without whose ideas, front-of-house skills, organisational abilities, hard work, total commitment and endless, unwavering support, little, if anything, of what we have been able to achieve together at Read's, would have been possible. I was delighted when, in 2015, she was inducted into the UK Restaurateurs Hall of Fame by the Academy of Food and Wine Service. Even so, it still bothers me that she never really gets the full credit she deserves for our joint success. It has always been 'David Pitchford, the Michelin-starred chef', never, as it should be, 'Rona and David Pitchford of Michelin-starred Read's restaurant'. And yet her contribution to the experience of dining there is every bit as vital in so many different ways as anything I and the rest of my team do in the kitchen. It was the same when I won Chef of the Year. Her input was massive and without the back-up and support she provided I doubt whether I would have come out on top. Let's face it, if it hadn't been for her absolute insistence I would never even have got round to submitting the entry form in the first place.

As well as enjoying a long and happy marriage, Rona and I have also maintained a highly effective and long-lasting forty-year business partnership that I think I can say is almost unique in our industry, our respective skills in the kitchen and front-of-house complementing each other perfectly, with one or other – and usually both of us together – actually present in the restaurant virtually every single day since we first opened our doors in 1977. To end with one final pun, that combined and committed personal and business relationship has proved to be an unbeatable recipe for success.

Postscript

As I stated in my introduction, the reason for setting out to write this book was to record my life story, along with that of Rona and of Read's, mainly for the benefit of my grandchildren and any future generations of the family. In that respect, it has given me great satisfaction to know that it is all there for posterity. But even before publication, the book also brought another totally unexpected and enormously welcome benefit – helping me to re-establish contact with the brother I had not seen or heard from for a great many years.

Exactly why Joe and I lost touch has always been a bit of a mystery. We remained quite close until the early seventies, when we actually shared the flat in Forest Hill where I was living at the time I met Rona. After Rona and I then married and moved out, Joe too went on to marry and start a family, ending up with three children; and while our kids were small we still continued to see quite a lot of each other. However, his marriage eventually broke up and that was when we started to drift apart. He went to live in Norfolk and gradually became more and more distant, eventually cutting himself off completely from both me and our mother. In her final years, almost by way of consolation, Mum accounted for his total absence from the scene and the complete lack of communication by persuading herself that he had actually died.

I continued to see his eldest daughter Jenny from time to time and she kept me vaguely up-to-date with what he was doing. However, she was never able to throw any light on why he had apparently turned his back on me and Mum. There was no great feud and never a serious argument or bitter falling out over any particular issue as far as I was aware. As I mentioned earlier, I had always felt a little ashamed of the way in which John Maw and I tended to gang up against Joe when we were kids together, but there was certainly no obvious sign of any lingering resentment or bitter sibling rivalry on his side when we were in our twenties and thirties and still quite close.

One way and another, it had got to the point where I had almost given up any hope of ever seeing him again, a prospect that saddened me greatly. So it was the most pleasant of surprises when, having contacted his daughter Jenny in an effort to track down some old photos of our father that I thought might have ended up with his side of the family, I received an email from him, completely out of the blue, that started: " 'ello R Kyd – long time no speak." It was our first communication in nearly twenty-five years.

Joe went on in very friendly tones to say what great news it was about the book, confirmed that he did indeed have the pictures I was looking for, offered to scan them and send them on to me and signed off with the hope that the book would be "a blockbuster".

I replied immediately, saying how delighted I was to hear from him and we then exchanged a series of emails, reminiscing about childhood days and bringing each other up-to-date with family events. The only direct reference to the years of estrangement was when he commented in one of his messages: "Ah well, I was always a bit of a funny bugger – you did nothing wrong. I do sometimes look back and wonder how the situation all came about."

And then, when I voiced my nagging worry that I had perhaps not shown quite as much brotherly love and support as I should have done when we were kids together, he put my mind at rest by writing back to say: "You will recall that we used to cycle to Meole Brace and that I, probably suffering from untreated diabetes for quite a time, used to get clapped out, hardly being able to cope with all the pedalling. On the route, a little way before Brooklands Roundabout, there was a steep railway bridge that seemed to draw the last reserves of my energy, occasionally resulting in my having to stop completely. Well, quite often you used to tow me up that hill, with our fingers hooked together. So that's my main Big Brother memory and the one that I would have you put on your CV as being representative."

Having that bit of reassurance really meant such a huge amount to me. And I'm just so very happy that we're back in touch. All this only happened very shortly before the completed manuscript of the book was due to be sent off to the printer and so, at the time of adding this hurried postscript, we have yet to get round to organising a proper family re-union. That's something to look forward to – a perfect opportunity to celebrate the publication of the book that has so unexpectedly made it all possible.

DP October 2018